Helion & Company Limited
Unit 8 Amherst Business Centre
Budbrooke Road
Warwick
CV34 5WE
England
Tel. 01926 499 619
Email: info@helion.co.uk
Website: www.helion.co.uk
Twitter: @helionbooks
Visit our blog http://blog.helion.co.uk/

Designed & typeset by Farr out Publications,
    Wokingham, Berkshire
Cover design by Paul Hewitt, Battlefield
    Design (www.battlefield-design.co.uk)

Cover art: *Desembarco de Alhucemas*
(Landing in Alhucemas of 1925), under
the command of General Miguel Primo de
Rivera: the first classic amphibious landing
involving air and naval assets. (José Moreno
Carbonero, Prado Museum, Madrid)

ISBN 978-1-804512-04-3

British Library Cataloguing-in-Publication
    Data
A catalogue record for this book is available
    from the British Library

We always welcome receiving book
proposals from prospective authors.

CONTENTS

Note: In order to simplify the use of this book, all names, locations and geographic
designations are as provided in *The Times World Atlas*, or other traditionally accepted
major sources of reference, as of the time of described events.

Dedication

I would like to dedicate this work to my wife, Carolina Martínez Zamora, for her support and patience to complete this manuscript during the holidays in Puerto de Mazarrón, Murcia, in August 2021, and to my fathers in law, to Chitina Zamora as she kindly let us work in her nice house on the beach, and Juan de la Cruz Martínez Manuel, whose father fought as a captain and was severely wounded in the Rif War's Larache sector. Also, I would like to thank to my friend Javier Martín for the old 1922 detailed military map of the Ceuta-Larache zone that he gave me as a present, that was vital to locate some remote and forgotten places of this war.

1

1921: The Reconquista

In the previous volume of this work, we left the Melilla District annihilated after the Disaster of Annual. In a rosary of 144 posts abandoned to their fate the bodies of 8,000 Spaniards laid under the sun. Another 500 were in captivity, including the second in command of the Melilla District, General Navarro, after General Silvestre collapsed and shot himself. Also, about 100 pieces of captured Spanish artillery went on to swell the inventories of Abd el-Krim. To top it off, some 4,000 soldiers of Moroccan origin were also missing from the lists: most had gone to the Riffians with all their equipment. With them and the artillery Abd el-Krim had the basic elements to form a modern army, the germ of a state. In addition, the kabyles (tribes, or tribal areas) of the central and eastern Rif had been joined by virtually all the warriors of the Guelaya. Melilla, the only position in Spanish hands in this district, seemed ready to be taken, ending 450 years of Spanish presence in the city. The western area, around Ceuta and Larache, organised in two districts, on the other hand, seemed to be quiet. The Spanish troops had conquered all the Yebala and the Luccus and had penetrated the Gomara to take the holy city of Xauén, religious capital of the Riffians, which no Christian had previously trodden. To the north-west, the only rebel that remained was El Raisuni, in the eagle's nest of Tazarut, in the kabyle of Beni Arós. On 21 July, as the Spaniards were going to launch the final assault on this fortress with several concentric columns, came the news of the Disaster of Annual, and the High Commissioner of the Protectorate, General of Division Dámaso Berenguer, gave the order to stop the operations and urgently send the new 1st and 2nd Banderas of the Legión to the area of Melilla.[1]

Creating an Army from Zero

During the night of 23 July, General Berenguer arrived in Melilla from Ceuta. He had only 1,800 soldiers and two 75mm cannons to defend the city. The panic was such that the civilian population tried to board the ships in the port to flee to the Iberian Peninsula. General Berenguer ordered the band to play military music in the streets of Melilla to calm the population. The next day the Corona Battalion disembarked, followed by General of Brigade Sanjurjo and Lieutenant Colonel Millán Astray with two Legión Banderas, the 1st and 2nd, one of them under Commandant Franco, the future dictator. Then came two Tabors of the 3rd Group of Regulares of Ceuta under Lieutenant Colonel Santiago González Tablas and his second in command, Lieutenant Colonel Emilio Mola Vidal.[2]

The Regulares were distrusted due to, allegedly, the native soldiers of Melilla having changed sides and killed their Spanish officers in the Annual Disaster and then moved to the side of the Riffians.

The truth, it seems, was that these soldiers were not the ones that rebelled, but their comrades of the Policía Indígena (Indigenous Police), and so this corps was dissolved, or, being more precise, their monetary allocation was cut until they disappeared. What happened with the Regulares of Melilla is that, in a tremendous mistake, on the night of 23 July General Navarro – having just arrived at the Spanish column escaping from Annual, and that was still fighting for its survival – as a result of the bad experience suffered with the Policía Indígena decided to disarm all the Regulares of Melilla that were accompanying the Annual column and to send them forward with the wounded to Uestia, and then to Nador. Once there, the Regulares were given a few hours of license to rest, but they never returned. So, of the 1,800 Regulares in the Melilla District during the Annual Disaster, only some 400 were still on the payrolls after the disaster. A company from a cavalry tabor did defect to the enemy in Zeluán, killing their officers. What is not clear is what happened to the Regulares that were still on the frontline: were they forced to surrender their weapons in the isolated posts or columns and then marched home in the middle of the enemy territory? For sure, the answer is no, so they fought with their Spanish comrades until the end, or a few of them may have defected to the enemy.

Additionally, during the following hours, the Borbón, Extremadura and Granada Regiments arrived from Spain. The Legión was sent to the foothills of Mount Gurugú, south-west of Melilla, in the Mazuza and Beni Bu Ifrur kabyles; the Regulares were deployed at Beni Sicar, in the north-west, where the only kabyle loyal to Spain was located under Abd el-Kader (although some sources cite him as present at the massacre of Monte Arruit). The Legión wanted to advance to aid Nador, Zeluán (Zelouan) and Monte Arruit, which were still holding out, but General Berenguer forbade it. On 31 July General Cavalcanti, the same general who had defeated the Riffians at Taxdirt with three prodigious charges in 1909, arrived in Melilla to take over the command. With two hussar regiments (Pavía and Princesa) reduced by half, he formed a cavalry brigade. Throughout August reinforcements continued to arrive, so that by mid-August or the end of that month, depending on the source, Cavalcanti had 25 infantry battalions, two Legión Banderas, two or three Tabors of Regulares, five cavalry regiments, 22 engineer and quartermaster companies, and 22 artillery batteries, adding 35,693 troops, almost double what Silvestre had a month earlier. Melilla had been saved definitively.[3]

A Chaotic Crowd

The question arises whether some of these troops could have been sent to the relief of Monte Arruit or Nador that fell between 2–9 of August, as in Melilla at that time there were 26,312 men. So, the fate of Melilla, dramatically depicted a few lines above, was less dramatic in reality, not to say that the probability of being assaulted and taken by the Riffians was near nil. Another point was the morale and the offensive capabilities of these troops. In fact, the first offensive move by the Spanish army was made on only on 15 August, when two columns under Colonel Riquelme and General Sanjurjo (3,000 men) moved to the foot of Mount Gurugú to build a blockhouse near Sidi Amarán, having to retreat after suffering some 29 losses. With this poor performance, the answer to this question lays in the fact that except for the Legión and Regulares, and some elements of the Burgos, Corona and Granada Regiments, all the other units were totally disorganised, untrained, and unprepared for war. All of August was needed to make ready these forces.

For example, in one artillery regiment some 50 individuals were asked about the purpose and management of the cannons' iron sights and nobody was able to answer. In the cavalry regiments, the barrels of the carbines were badly worn, and some riders had never mounted before. In some units the Colt machine guns only arrived at the same time as the men were landing in Melilla. Also, the cavalry lacked some 1,000 horses that were not available from the remount units in Spain, so they had to be bought from as far afield as the United States.

Finally, the Spanish War Secretary, the Viscount of Eza had the genial idea of sending troopers that had just begun their military service instead of ones who were near the end, to avoid revolts such as the Tragic Week in Barcelona during 1909 (see Volume 1). So, the soldiers sent were recent recruits and not veterans. In fact, the troopers of the Sicilia Regiment went directly to the front after training consisting of 10 shots per soldier, and the men of the Wad Ras Regiment after a mere five. There were lawyers handling the trains of mules to transport the artillery, having not the least notion about how to do it. The government also chartered a ship, the *Conde de Churruca*, to transport 6,000 tons of potable water to Melilla, but when the ship arrived it was discovered that the port was not deep enough for the vessel, and there were neither hoses, nor tanks to store the water, so the ship was kept loaded until October, and all the water went bad.[4]

There was also a huge scandal when it was known that the same Viscount of Eza had rejected and then delayed acquiring 390 81mm Stokes mortars from the British Army, remnants of the First World War, and at a very low price. These weapons had been destined to defend the 144 posts that finally fell into the hands of the Riffians. With these mortars, the fate of these posts may have been quite different.

Finally, when the command of the troops was offered to the Head of the Central Major Staff, General Valeriano Weyler,[5] he stated that he would accept the post only in the event of receiving the real and sole supreme command. He added that:

I wish to put on record that I have nothing to do with the affairs of Morocco. I have not intervened, nor do I intervene, nor will I intervene. All glory belongs to the Lord Minister of War (Eza). The General Staff that I preside over does not intervene at all in these matters.

So, Weyler suddenly revealed to the public that none of the Moroccan campaigns had been planned by the General Staff, but by the politicians, who were addressing the instructions directly to the commanders in Africa.[6]

On the positive side, when the news of the disaster reached the Spanish population, as the first mortal remains of the soldiers appeared, some of them horribly tortured and mutilated, the reaction was, paradoxically, mostly anger and wrath, but also generosity: they

Soldiers of the Legión's 13th Company 'Del Hierro' (note the flag), celebrate with their guitars. (Carrasco & de Mesa)

Heavy artillery positions in Zoco el Hach, defending Melilla in August–September 1921. (via Pando)

would avenge the honour of Spain and the fallen troopers. Boxes of tobacco were placed in banks, hotels, and casinos to be given to the soldiers. Religious parades with massive monetary donations and headed by the Queen of Spain, Victoria Eugenia, were arranged. In the bullfighting corridas the toreros threw their capes into the mud for the public to throw coins for the injured in Melilla, and in general, citizens of all social classes donated rings, money, and every kind of item to equip the army. Several DH.4 aircraft were purchased by Spanish cities, and the ones from Zaragoza or Granada received the coat of arms of those cities on their fuselages. Also, volunteers for the front appeared all across Spain. As the journalist and Generation of '98 writer Ramiro de Maeztu stated in the newspaper *El Sol* (*The Sun*): 'This is the first Spanish War in which the children of the rich are fighting like soldiers alongside the children of the poor.'

The reaction was not only in Spain, but also in Argentina, Cuba, the United States and Great Britain: on 18 August a large queue of 2,500 British ex-combatants was formed in Chelsea, at the Spanish Embassy, to sign up for the Spanish Legión. Some 200 volunteered in New York, and several hundred in Latin America (466 Spaniards, 225 Cubans, 287 Argentinians). The British volunteers were finally rejected as the Spanish authorities thought that they were excellent fighters but problematic in that they demanded good equipment, payment, and food, and all of this on time, as they had received in the British Army, something that for the moment could not be assured in the Spanish Army.[7]

The army was growing day by day. When the conservative Maura took power in Madrid on 13 August, some 10 additional battalions, 800 soldiers each, were sought for Melilla.[8] Also, another 15 battalions were sent to Ceuta, and nine more to Larache. If in the moment of the Annual Disaster, in July, there were 21,000 men each in Ceuta and Melilla, 8,000 in Larache, and 3,000 in Tetuán-Xauén, on 18 August there were 37,000 men in Melilla, 30,000 in Larache, and 50,894 in Ceuta-Tetuán. By the end of August, the Spanish troops in Melilla were 47,000 strong, overcrowded in the little city, sleeping on the floor, even in the streets. Only in November would Melilla receive enough tents for double this number of soldiers.

When this improvised and chaotic army was somewhat organised, General Cavalcanti sent a third of these troops, about 10 battalions, to the fixed positions, and with the rest he formed four columns of operations: those of General of Brigade Miguel Cabanellas,[9] formed by three battalions and three cavalry regiments, three companies of engineers and two batteries, totalling 6,300 soldiers, who would operate to the east, in the Restinga, next to the Mar Chica. The column of General Sanjurjo,[10] the most powerful group, formed by the Legión, the Regulares of Ceuta, the reconstituted cavalry of the Alcántara Regiment, and four battalions, five companies of engineers, and six batteries, totalling 8,300 soldiers. Federico Berenguer's column, with five battalions and a cavalry regiment, three companies of engineers and seven batteries, totalled 6,200 men. The reserve belonging to Tuero, the weakest column, had three battalions, and two batteries, for a total of 2,800 soldiers. However, as most of these mobile troops were finally added to the defensive positions, in the end there were only 12 battalions left for manoeuvre, about 10,000 men. As happened several times in the past, of the total troops available, barely a third were operational for offensive action.[11]

Table 1: Known forces in the Melilla sector under General Cavalcanti, August–October 1921[12]
1st, 2nd and 4th Banderas of the Legión
Two or three Tabors, 3rd Group of Regulares of Ceuta
71st Corona Regiment (one or three battalions)
11th Borbón Regiment (one or three battalions)
36th Burgos Regiment (one or three battalions)
15th Extremadura Regiment (one or three battalions)
34th Granada Regiment (one or three battalions)
23rd Valencia Regiment (one battalion)
68th África Regiment (reconstituted, three battalions)
59th Melilla (reconstituted, three battalions)
Cazadores de Alcántara (reconstituted), and Almansa; Hussars of Princesa, and Pavía; and Lancers of Farnesio cavalry regiments
Melilla Artillery Regiment
Melilla Coast Artillery Command
Engineer Command
Brigada Disciplinaria (Disciplinary Brigade)
Policía Indígena (Indigenous Police)(Replaced by friendly harkas in October)
Harka Abd el-Kader of Beni Sicar
Harka Aomar Abellán of Frajana
Harka Arauchi of Beni Sidel
Harka 'El Yaich' of Beni Sicar
Total: 25 Battalions, two Banderas, two–three Tabors, two Cavalry Regiments (mid-August 1921), with 12 units for manoeuvre; 15 manoeuvre battalions and five cavalry regiments in September; and 21 manoeuvre battalions and five cavalry regiments in October. All under General Cavalcanti, grouped in four columns (Cabanellas, Sanjurjo, Berenguer and Tuero)

The Siege of Melilla

Abd el-Krim's troops had reoccupied the hornet's nest of Gurugú, and they began to bombard Melilla. He had some 15,000 warriors according to some estimations, with three cannons moved to the top of the ridges by 150 Spanish prisoners (some of them dying in the effort). These cannons were also crewed by Spanish captives, such as corporals Rillo and Porres Martínez that were firing them, one by one, in turns, changing their location after every shot to avoid being detected. In any case, only two or three shells exploded out of every 10, as perhaps the Spanish corporals were not very interested in killing other Spaniards. One of these unexploded bombs fell into a room where two little children were sleeping, and as they survived without any major injury, the statue of the Virgin that hung on the wall was turned into a holy icon of the city of Melilla. In the end, the bombardment of Melilla was one of a very low intensity.[13]

What were not of such a low intensity were the nocturnal attacks made by the Riffians against the positions protecting the outskirts of Melilla. These posts, west to east, followed the line Tizza–Casabona–Zoco el Had–Sidi Musa–Sidi Ahmet el Hach–Atalayón. In the advanced post of the Extremadura Regiment, half of the garrison would be killed by a night attack made on 21 August, but Corporal Julio Ara Izquierdo survived surrounded by the dead and wounded bodies of his comrades, and held the post, winning the Laureate. In Taguilmanín, also known as the Death Blockhouse,

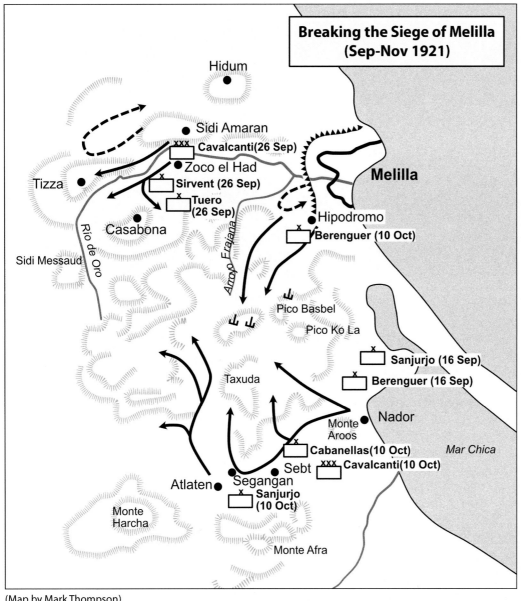

Breaking the Siege of Melilla (Sep–Nov 1921)

Hidum

Sidi Amaran

XXX Cavalcanti(26 Sep)

Zoco el Had

x Sirvent (26 Sep)

x Tuero (26 Sep)

Melilla

Tizza

Casabona

Río de Oro

Sidi Messaud

Arroyo Frajana

Hipodromo

x Berenguer (10 Oct)

Pico Basbel

Pico Ko La

x Sanjurjo (16 Sep)

x Berenguer (16 Sep)

Taxuda

Monte Aroos

Nador

Mar Chica

x Cabanellas(10 Oct)

XXX Cavalcanti(10 Oct)

Sebt

Atlaten

Segangan

x Sanjurjo (10 Oct)

Monte Harcha

Monte Afra

(Map by Mark Thompson)

all the defenders – from the Almansa Cavalry Regiment – were killed or wounded after another night attack on 30 August. When General Sanjurjo arrived with his relief column in the morning he found the post destroyed. His commander, ensign Maffioli-Rodés, who had abandoned the post, committed suicide.[14]

On 3–4 September the Riffians attacked the Mezquita blockhouse, defended by the Legión. That same day, a convoy protected by an armoured car supplying the positions of Casabona, Tizza and Corona, was also attacked: the Riffians dug a ditch that overturned the vehicle, and the escort had to repel the attack at close range, suffering 117 casualties. With these garrisons isolated, on 8 September General Neila left with the columns of Colonel Riquelme (new commander of the Policía Indígena, after the mighty Morales had died at Annual) and Sirvent, formed by the Legión and the Regulares. With the use of the bayonet they cleared the trenches that threatened Casabona and Corona, only to discover that there was a second line that in turn dominated those trenches.

Soldiers of the Legión defending an improvised position near Melilla in 1921. (Carrasco & de Mesa)

A wounded officer of the Regulares, being attended by two of his soldiers near Melilla in 1921. (Carrasco & de Mesa)

General José Cavalcanti de Alburquerque y Padierna, the hero of the Taxdirt cavalry charge that led the reconquest of the Melilla sector. This time he liberated Tizza with another charge against the odds, this time as a General but again personally leading it with only 25 riders. (Gárate Córdoba)

General Sanjurjo then sent them reinforcements and they managed to take the second line and were able to supply Casabona, at the cost of 134 casualties. At some points the trenches of both sides were separated by as little as four metres. The Riffian losses were estimated at 250 men.[15]

Finally, on 15–16 September, the Dat Hamet post, called 'El Malo' (the 'Bad Post'), near Atalayón, in the east, defended by 20 troopers of the Disciplinary Brigade was destroyed in another night attack. Instructions were sent to not assist the post, but Corporal Suceso Terrero and 14 volunteers from the Legión departed from Atalayón anyway. When they entered in the post, the Riffian cannons bombarded it at point blank range (200 metres), collapsing the roof of the post and burying the defenders alive. There were only two survivors.[16]

To the Gates of Hell and the Reconquest of Gurugú

On 12 September the Spanish counteroffensive began when Cabanellas' column of some 6,300 men landed at La Restinga in the Mar Chica, south-east of Melilla, and advanced south to Punta Quiviana and Zoco el Arbaá, in Quebdana. At the same time, another 12 battalions, as well as the Regulares and the Legión, totalling some 14,000 men and 50 cannons, descended from Melilla south to Nador and Tahuima (Mazuza) in two columns under Generals Sanjurjo and Federico Berenguer (brother of the High Commissioner). There Abd el-Krim had stationed 3,000 warriors from his kabyle, together with 3,000–7,000 more from the Guelaya, all well entrenched. With artillery support from the Atalayón and Sidi Hamet, to the north, gunboats from the Mar Chica to the east, and the fleet further east on the open sea, the Spaniards bombarded the Riffian artillery located in the Tetas de Nador. At the same time, the air force flew over the Riffian positions and attacked the slopes of the hills where the artillery could not reach. Abd el-Krim had made the mistake of abandoning his guerrilla tactics to offer battle, and so his lines were destroyed. Then came the assault, taking Nador at the cost of 117–146 casualties, including Lieutenant Colonel Millán Astray himself; shot in the chest, this the first of four combat wounds during his career. Millán was then replaced by Colonel Castro Girona in command of the Legión. After the victory, the kabyles of Quebdana, Bu Areg, and Ulad Setut, to the south-east, in the Riffian rear, were subdued.

Nevertheless, when the troops entered Nador on 16 September, the spectacle was unsettling to the extreme: the village had a foul smell of death. In the house named *Casa del Matadero* (the Slaughter House) there was, in Pando's words:

> blood in every corner and wall, bodies shattered, tortured, mutilated, quartered..., on the wall a chill in 49 words: 'If anyone were to enter this room, know that here we have been burned thirty men and two women. We have not eaten or drunk for five days, and they have made us a thousand dirty tricks. Spanish brothers, defend us and ask God for our souls. I, Juan, the *Botero* [wine leather worker] of Nador, born in Malaga.

Also, at the nauseating bottom of a cistern, full of mud and debris eight surviving soldiers of the Annual Disaster were found, little more than living skeletons. In total, up to 61 corpses of martyred Spanish settlers had to be buried in Nador. The Spanish Army were at the gates of hell. What would await them in Monte Arruit, with thousands of soldiers disappeared? On the 23rd the soldiers advanced towards Mount Arbós and Tahuima.[17]

The offensive, which was intended to continue towards Sebt and Segangangán, now was forced to turn north-west of Gurugú. There the Spaniards had to stop to deal with the attacks made by an enemy harka (a grouping of fighting men) on the Spanish positions of Zoco el Had in Beni Sicar, preventing the convoys from passing to Tizza. Tizza had been besieged for 49 days and so was on the brink of collapse. After concentrating troops to escort a large convoy, two columns finally departed, some 6,000 soldiers under Tuero's reserve, and part of Sanjurjo's column under Colonel Sirvent (4,000 men), with 13 batteries (some 40–45 cannons) to supply Tizza. Some 9,000 entrenched Riffians held back Tuero's advance and, in the middle of a plain, Tuero could neither advance nor retreat, offering a perfect target for the Riffian bullets. Three days later, General Cavalcanti tried again with 16,000 men, throwing even his last reserve to the front, the Valencia Battalion, which were also stopped. Then Cavalcanti said to Moreno Aranguren Landero, the Quartermaster Captain who led the convoy of 300 mules: 'I am going to Tizza, and you come behind me with the convoy [...] because you have the face of being one of those who arrive alive', then, in a fit of fury, and

Officers and soldiers with a captured enemy cannon that had been used to bombard Melilla in October 1921. (Lázaro, via Pando)

Troops of the Legión after taking Atlaten in October 1921. (Carrasco & de Mesa)

enveloping it continued with the capture on 5 October of Atlaten (Beni Sidel), opposite Nador, to the west, surrounding Gurugú to the south, after an assault by the 1st and 2nd Legión Banderas – the 1st under Franco – at the bayonet, in which they lost eight men. After this victory, Beni Bu Ifrur was dominated, and Abd el-Krim's kabyles retreated behind the river Kert, to the west, and most of the Moors of the Guelaya surrendered. On the 10th, the brigades of Sanjurjo (formed by the Legión, and Riquelme's column of Regulares, Policía Indígena, and the friendly harka of Abd el-Kader of Beni Sicar), Cabanellas, Berenguer and Fresneda, adding 21 battalions and five cavalry regiments, began the ascent to Gurugú. Cabanellas used his horsemen to block the attacks coming from the Sebt massif, while Berenguer and Fresneda climbed it on the Melilla side, and Sanjurjo left Segangan to attack the Taxuda Plateau and thus prevent the Riffians from occupying it and at the same time to force the Riffians to retreat from Gurugú. With air support, Berenguer's forces reached the top of the mountain without problems for a cost of 50 casualties and took the two Schneider 75mms cannons that were bombing Melilla. Nevertheless, Sanjurjo had a really hard time, as when he was rallying his forces, he was enveloped by the returning kabyles in Tlat, suffering 374 casualties. However, the Spaniards had managed to clear the Gurugú massif in 15 days, contrasting with the hard and long campaign to take it in 1909.[19]

On 14 October the advance continued southwards, taking Zeluán (Zelouan, Beni Bu Ifrur) almost without a fight, but discovering the unburied bodies of some 500 comrades. General of Brigade Cabanellas, leading one of the columns, was horrified and sent an incendiary letter to the Juntas de Defensa (a kind of trade union authorised by King Alfonso XIII that governed the military institutions) and blamed it for the horrors of the Annual Disaster. Cabanellas was deposed some weeks later and sued before the courts. Probably this was the reason why the General, despite being of the political right, became a strong supporter of the Republic, until he joined with the Nationalists in the 1936 revolt.[20]

remembering the charge at Taxdirt (see Volume 1), Cavalcanti – mounted on horseback – with his assistants, a company of engineers and even the medics, and charged like a madman for a kilometre under enemy fire coming from three directions. Despite this, he managed to enter Tizza with 25 engineers. With the Riffian fire focused on General Cavalcanti, the convoy was able to enter the position and relieve the garrison after suffering 69 casualties. The attacks in total had cost 464 casualties. Once again, Cavalcanti had changed the course of a battle, thanks to a burst of personal courage, into a victory rather than to a 'glorious' defeat, of which the Spanish arms seemed so fond lately.[18]

Once the northern front was cleared, General Cavalcanti turned again to the south-east and organised the attack on Sebt and Ulad Dau on 2 October, to dominate Gurugú: the columns of Cabanellas, Berenguer and Sanjurjo, about 20,000 soldiers, managed to advance in a coordinated manner and crush the Riffian resistance after suffering 447 casualties. The advance to control the massif by

General of Brigade Federico Berenguer, brother of High Commissioner Dámaso Berenguer, who retook Mount Gurugú with Sanjurjo. Behind is General Navarro, captured in Monte Arruit, then released to lead the Ceuta forces. (via Marín Ferrer)

Soldiers of the Legión in the recently captured Bugen Zein, Gurugú, on 14 October. Note the commander of the 2nd Bandera, Rodríguez Fontanés, the third on the left with binoculars, and the standard bearer, the Duke of Montemar (whose ancestor conquered Naples in 1734), in the centre. (Carrasco & De Mesa)

Return to the Kert and the Death Valley

On 24 October, turning south-west from Zelouan, the Spanish columns of Generals Sanjurjo and Cabanellas returned to the tragic scene of Monte Arruit, at the beginning of Beni Bu Yahi, on the plain of the Garet. There, the Farnese Regiment found the unburied and mutilated bodies of 3,000 comrades. As Pando recalled 'at many points the cadavers were lined up, in formation, just as they were surprised by death. [...] Even the crows and vultures had left Arruit a few weeks ago. There were not even the worms under that righteous and cold sun.' In the infirmary, the bodies of 107 murdered soldiers were found; on the slope to the position, more than 1,000; in the water supply area another 200 mummified bodies; on one threshing floor other 200 corpses; and in the houses of Ben Che-Lal another 600. Commandant Marquerie 'appeared at the head of his own men,

all formed in a four deep file; Captain Sánchez Monje, who was missing a leg severed by a Rif grenade, was on the slope, still on his stretcher; at his side, [there were] the four soldiers who were carrying him.' The body of Colonel Fernando Primo de Rivera, the hero of the Alcántara Cavalry Regiment who was annihilated covering the retreat (see Volume 1), appeared unburied, with his left arm amputated: the Riffians were intrigued to know what the hero who had fought on horseback against them was like, and had even broken the taboo of touching the dead body of an infidel, to be able to see him and offer him one last tribute. During six days the Spanish recovered the bodies of 2,618 men.[21]

In any case, the offensive had to continue. General Sanjurjo's column was then reinforced by the harkas of Frajana of Aomar Abellán and Beni Sidel of Arauchi. The Policía Indígena was dissolved after its massive desertion in Annual, and was replaced by the Confederation of Guelaya and its friendly harkas of Abd el-Kader and that of Beni Sicar of 'El Yaich', which would watch over the region from 29 November. Returning to October, a new 4th Bandera of the Legión, recently created, together with the 2nd, took Mount Magán on 28 October. Around that time, Castro Girona was sent to the western front at Ceuta. On 2 November, the Legión took the Taxuda Plateau with many casualties, after expelling the Riffians from the rocks at Esponjas. On the 11th they also took Tifasor and Yazamen. Then, on the 17th they conquered Uixán after a daring night raid in which Franco ordered his Legiónnaires to cover their rifles so that the moonlight would not be reflected, and on the 20th they took Ras Medua, where the 155mm heavy artillery pieces were used for the first time. In December the Legión captured Zoco el Jemís (Beni Bu Ifrur) on the 2nd, Muley Rechid on the 5th, and Batel (Beni Bu Yahi) on the 21st. After this string of victories, General Cavalcanti was replaced as General Commander of Melilla by General Sanjurjo who was commanding his spearhead.[22]

On 22 December the Spaniards crossed the river Kert and took Tikermin, south of Beni Said, and in a great advance towards the west, following the bend that this river makes in that direction, the

Lieutenant Colonel Núñez de Prado, with his tarbuch (red Fez cap), looking to the left, and his Regulares, atop Gurugú. (Carrasco & de Mesa)

Soldiers of the Legión, Regulares and friendly harkas (below), from Sanjurjo's column, celebrating the taking of Gurugú. (Carrasco & de Mesa)

Friendly Moors with the flag of the harka of Melilla. (Carrasco & de Mesa)

Friendly harka flying the Spanish flag in 1921. (Carrasco & de Mesa)

Legión Corporal Justo Mejías is promoted to sergeant, in Melilla, 1921. Notable is the St Andrew's Cross on the flag, the symbol of Habsburg Spain, the Tercios, and the Spanish Legión (that at the beginning was known as the Tercio). (Carrasco & de Mesa)

A view of the ruined post at Monte Arruit, recovered by the Spaniards in October 1921, with the mutilated bodies of 3,000 comrades executed there. (Marín Ferrer)

negotiations with Spain. El-Krim reacted by sending some 4,000 troops to Beni Sidel and taking Kadur Namar as prisoner, but the Riffians in the zone continued leaving the war. A Spanish aviation raid on 22 January bombed the Zoco (market) of Bu Hermana, in a ravine of Mount Mauro, Beni Said, where 4,000 persons were gathering, killing or injuring some 260 of them.

Also, a column under Colonel Riquelme occupied all the left margin of the Muluya river to protect the area from the French interventions in Beni Bu Yahi, and Hasi Berkan and Reyen on 14 January and Zoco Arbaá de Haraig and Kans Siacha on the 20th. With this, all Ulad Setut kabyle, the most powerful tribe in the region, fell into Spanish hands. Finally, a concentration of some 3,000 Riffians under Abd el-Krim detected in Dar Quebdani was bombed and dispersed by Spanish aircraft.

troops of Federico Berenguer, brother of the High Commissioner, arrived at Dar Drius (M'talza) on 10 January 1922. There, General of Brigade Cabanellas pretended to camp and then pounced on Dar Drius by surprise. The Riffians ran, abandoning their meals, and the Spaniards recovered 14 trucks and seven cannons from the Annual Disaster, but they also found the bodies of mutilated Spaniards there. Then Riffians from Abada surrendered to Spain. A garrison of 2,500 soldiers was deployed there and the advance was halted for the time being. Also, with the fall of Dar Drius, Kadur Namar, leader of the Beni Said, lost the larger part of his followers that moved over to support Spain, and he even asked Abd el-Krim to begin peace

The Forge of a New Spanish Army

A new Spanish army was being forged, replacing the recruits from Spain with natives and volunteers that would act as shock troops. So, the four Banderas of the Tercio were increased to five in 1921, and then seven in 1925, each also receiving an additional company. Also, the four Groups of Regulares based at Tetuán, Melilla, Ceuta and Larache, were increased by another from Larache in 1922. The two

Soldiers of the Legión resting after taking Ras Medua. (Carrasco & de Mesa)

Soldiers of the Legión in Tauriat Hamed, near the river Kert. Note the canteen woman bearing the standard. (Carrasco & de Mesa)

The ruined post of Ras Medua, after being taken by the Legión. (Carrasco & de Mesa)

existing Mehalas, from Tetuán (in 1914) and Melilla (in 1909) were expanded by those of Larache and Rif in 1924. Also, the friendly harkas were divided into Tabors and Mías and began to be led by

prestigious Spanish officers such as Varela or Muñoz Grandes, and even some gum units began to appear, inspired by the French Army's Goums, being irregular units for mountain operations. A *gum* was similar to a company or *mía*, three gums formed a *tabor* or battalion, and three tabors formed a group. In any case, the Spanish conscript recruits were still the larger part of the army, being left in general as garrison troops, with the exception of the Cazadores de África, that were still acting as frontline troops, used to cover the flanks of the shock troops, or to protect freshly conquered positions. At the end of 1921, there were 63 Peninsular Expeditionary Battalions: some 60,000 men. Between 1921 to 1923 the conscript recruits were always, at least, some 50,000 men. Based on paper strength, there were 50,640 Spaniards, for 63,655 men in all.

So, now, a new Spanish army, led by more experienced and capable commanders, with the new Legión and the Regulares as their spearhead, and, it must be said, with twice as many troops as Silvestre, in a couple of months had reached the lines of 1912, and then in one push the lines of 1920. Would General Sanjurjo make the same mistake as Silvestre again, and overextend his lines?[23]

2
1922–24: Returning to Annual

The Conquest of Beni Said, Tafersit and Ulixek

In January a conference was held in Pizarra, Málaga, attended by the head of government, Antonio Maura, the Secretaries of War and the Navy, and High Commissioner Berenguer. It was agreed to remain on the defensive and to study the possibility of a landing in the Bay of Alhucemas to attack Abd el-Krim from behind. However, with the fall of Maura's government in March 1922, replaced by Sánchez Guerra, the project was cancelled, and the traditional offensive was resumed.

Between 7–14 March 1922, three columns, and one in reserve, resumed the offensive. On the 15th, the Spanish took Kandusi, and the Ras Tikermin Plateau, on the western side of the river Kert to protect the right flank of the main effort. The troops of Dar Drius, under General Fernando Berenguer, advanced across the plain of Sepsa and the Arkab plateau, turning north and establishing a camp at Ichitgen. The aim was to envelop Beni Said from the south, as Silvestre had done, but less ambitiously, making a more limited arc. On the 18th the offensive against this village began, using tanks for

the first time in the history of Spain: 11 Renault FT-17s, six Schneiders and eight armoured trucks. These vehicles moved in front of the 1st and 2nd Banderas of the Legión under commandants Franco and Fontanés to take Ambar, north of Ichitgen, in the direction of Tungutz. However, due to the Riffian fire, the infantry retreated, leaving the tanks isolated. Finally, two tanks were abandoned for lack of fuel and ammunition along with 16 dead, including Commandant Fontanés of the 2nd Bandera. Still, the Spanish forces took Tuguntz to the north with two columns totalling 20,000 troops on 29 March, suffering 417 casualties. This was made by two brigades converging from Dar Drius and other from Kandusi. From there, these same brigades turned north-east, taking Chamorra and Dar Quebdani on 8 April. When this last village was being fortified the Riffians launched a counterattack that was repulsed by the fire of the tanks and armoured trucks. These operations were supported by the aviation, using for the first time improvised airfields at Dar Drius and Batel to refuel and load bombs. Abd el-Krim's kabyles, to avoid being pushed against Mount Mauro and the Kert, retreated

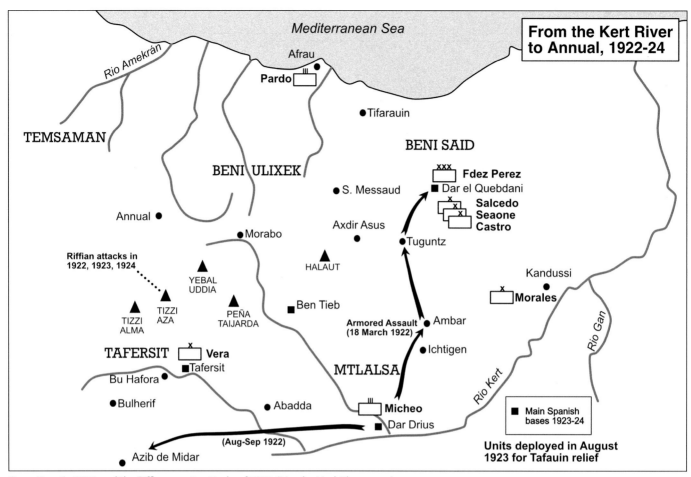

Operations in 1922, and the Riffian counterattacks of 1923. (Map by Mark Thompson)

A standard bearer of the Legión arriving for the operations in Tafersit. (Carrasco & de Mesa)

Burguete, the new High Commissioner appointed in July 1922, but dismissed on 2 January 1923 because he disagreed with the government's way of conducting operations. (Marín Ferrer)

east to Beni Ulixek, and then to Tafersit. Beni Said kabyle troops then surrendered, less a fraction that escaped to Afrau. On the left flank or south, the Spaniards took Chief on 17 April and the natives of Guerrauao (Beni Bu Yahi) surrendered when Afsó was taken on the 27th, to the south-east in the Spanish rear, connecting with the French zone on the level of Melilla.

With Beni Said almost entirely occupied, General Dámaso Berenguer (brother of Fernando) repatriated 12,000 troops to Spain on 10 May.[1] Also, since 12 April, General of Brigade Sanjurjo was moved to Larache, assuming the post the Division General Ardanarz y Crespo. At the same time, following instructions from the government, talks were entered into with Abd el-Krim. However, everything changed when on 15 July General Dámaso Berenguer was replaced by General Burguete as High Commissioner in the process of purging responsibilities for the Annual Disaster. Burguete imposed a more aggressive line as he thought that Abd el-Krim was only buying time instead of negotiating peace, so he resumed the offensive.[2]

A machine gun nest of the Legión, preparing to support the advance of a Renault FT-17 tank. (Carrasco & de Mesa)

After a long rest, on the 26th and 29 August the axis of march was changed and the line was extended to the south, advancing then towards the east, through the Tafersit kabyle, taking Azib de Midar, Azrú, Ichen Lasen and Tauriat Uchen, with their flanks covered by cavalry and tanks.

In September, the aviation near alone managed to conquer a position. The aircraft located an enemy harka of 1,200 men at Dar Hach Buzian, or the Red Alcazaba, and bombed it.

A company of Renault 17 tanks in Latil, ready to join the action of 17 March, this first tank action of the Spanish Army. (Lucas Molina via Marín Ferrer)

When that harka dispersed, a friendly harka followed by the Policía Indígena took the post. Then, for the first time in Morocco, gas projectiles were fired by the Instruction Group 155/13 Schneider of the Central Shooting School, over Sidi Mesaud and Tzayudait (or Tayuday) on 7 September. The Artillery Group was based at Dar Drius, and coincides with the claim launched by Abd el-Krim before the League of Nations.

Then, at the end of October, they advanced again with several converging columns in Beni Said, Beni Ulixek and Tafersit gathering 30,000 soldiers. The main two columns based in Dar Quebdani and Dar Drius marched in parallel. The one in the north, in Dar Quebdani, would take Ben Tieb, Sidi Mesaud, Afrau and Side Dris, and the one in the south, in Dar Drius, would take Tafersit, Tazyudait, Tizi Azza, Igueriban and Annual. On the 26th they occupied Ben Tieb, Axdir-Asus (Beni Said, west of Tuguntz), Mount Tzayudait (north of Tafersit), Bulherif, Buhafora or Bu Afora (west of Tafersit), Ichen Lasen, Nador de Beni Ulixek (north-east of Ben Tieb, entrance to the gorge of Annual) and Mount Halaut (between Tuguntz and Ben Tieb), in Beni Ulixek.

Now, the Spaniards were beginning to approach the fateful scene of the disaster of 1921. To distract the kabyles, the fleet simulated landings at Afrau and Sidi Dris, in Temsaman. On the 28th they advanced against the mountain range which, in a south-east to north-west direction, prevented access to Annual from the south, taking the crags of Peña Tahuarda, Tizi Alma and Tizi Azza to the north of Tafersit. The operation to capture Peña Tahuarda was

interesting, as the friendly harkas of Bacha and Tafersit took it by surprise, then lit several fires and the Dar Drius Brigade moved forward to consolidate the post. The taking of both the Tizis mentioned above was made by another brigade that marched by night with the friendly harka of Beni Tuzin and Tafersit. From there a road led after 15km to Tensaman, capital of the kabyle of the same name, enveloping and threatening Annual from the west. However, this time the Spaniards did not act like General Silvestre and did not enter the gorges but established a base for a future advance from there to Alhucemas Bay. Even so, the Spanish had advanced almost as far as Silvestre, choosing a parallel route further south than the one used previously at Annual. Tafersit town was surrounded by a third brigade, and then on the night of the 29th it was occupied by a vanguard of assault cars and a friendly harka. Then Yebel Uddia was taken, the highest crag in the mountain range north of Tafersit. On 6 November, on the right flank, to the north of the gorges of Annual, the Regulares advanced to Sidi Messaud, west of Dar Quebdani, to Izumar even further west, and then on the coast to the north, at Afrau on 7 November. Thus, the front was stabilised on the Midar line in the south, to Beni Tuzin to the north, and on the sea at Afrau. The line was between Tensaman and Beni Ulixek kabyles, with a salient in the centre in a mountainous area at Tizi Azza.

Meanwhile, new native forces were being organised. Throughout 1922, the Policía Indígena of the whole of Africa was disbanded and grouped into Mehalas, each made up of three infantry tabors and one cavalry unit. The first unit was the 1st Mehala of Tetuán, existing

Soldiers of the Legión advancing in Beni Said. (Carrasco & de Mesa)

Lieutenant Colonel Franco in Annual, showing the enemy positions to General Marzo, at the end of 1922. (Gárate Córdoba)

from 21 November. The friendly harkas were also reinforced, such as the one of Beni Said under Amar Uchen. In Afsó, the friendly harkas of Ulad Setut and Beni Bu Yahi were formed with 150 warriors. And finally, on 21 July 1922, the 5th Group of Regulares of Alhucemas was created.[3]

The Great Expansion of Aviation

The year 1922 was also the year of the great expansion of the Spanish air forces in Morocco. Using the first units of the new aircraft acquired by Prime Minister Maura, on 13 October 1921 a second DH.4 squadron was formed under Captain Moreno Abella in the Melilla area, and in November a third squadron arrived under Joaquín González Gallarza.[4] Then, the Rolls Group, or 2nd Morocco Group, was formed with these three units. They moved to the new Nador airfield in Melilla, which would be their base until the end of the war.

In the western zone, the 1st Group had been formed with the Tetuán and Larache squadrons with Breguet XIVs, and the Tetuán Squadron with Ansaldo A.300s under Captain Luis Riaño. The Ansaldos began to arrive in Morocco in October 1921, but after four

months they returned to Spain due to their poor performance. The African aviation was commanded by Colonel Jorge Soriano, and the commanders of the Groups were Aymat and Delgado Brackenbury.

Also, the first multiengine aircraft of the Spanish aviation had been present since 1919 in the form of three twin-engine Farman F.50 bombers. The first one arrived on 18 August 1919 at Tetuán, forming a flight with the two other examples between October 1919 to 1920, under Captain Sáenz de Buruaga. Buruaga and Martínez Baños also led the first air attack against El Raisuni's bands, then arranged several other attacks by night. An F.50 was destroyed in an accident in June 1920 during a trip from Morocco to Seville, only being replaced in 1923 when another F.50 was bought. These Farmans were used until 1924.[5]

Table 2: The Aviation in Africa (Autumn 1921–Spring 1922)
1st Group (Tetuán)
Breguet XIV Squadron (Tetuán)
Ansaldo A.300 Squadron (Tetuán), October 1921, replaced in February 1922 by another Breguet XIV squadron
Farman F.50 Flight (Tetuán): two examples (three in 1923, active until 1924)
Breguet XIV Squadron (Larache)
2nd 'Rolls' Group (Nador, Melilla)
Three DH.4 squadrons (Melilla)
Light Group (from March 1922, Melilla)
Two Bristol F.2B squadrons (Melilla)
One DH.9A squadron (Melilla)
S.16 Seaplane Flight (Atalayón, Melilla): three examples

In 1922 the 1st Group supported the conquest of Dra El Asef, in Tetuán-Larache. During February, in the face of the Riffian attacks on the Rock of Vélez, the Spaniards carried out a shuttle operation for the first time: 21 aircraft of the 2nd Group left Nador, Melilla, and heading west bombed the Riffian artillery in front of the Rock to continue then to Tetuán. There, they refuelled and took the same route back, bombing the enemy again. That same month, a second Breguet XIV squadron replaced the Ansaldos in Tetuán (the first Breguet squadron had arrived earlier), in the 1st Group.

At the end of March, the first DH.9As and Bristol F.2Bs began to arrive, which would equip a new three-squadron Light Group in Melilla, as well as three Savoia SIAI S.16 seaplanes for the Atalayón base, also in Melilla, under Captain Roberto White. The two Bristol squadrons were under Captains Vicente Roa and Felipe Díaz Sandino, with their first mission on 29 March attacking Tugunt on the river Kert. The campaign record of the Bristol was brilliant, with 64 being ordered through the war, plus six trainers. Of these, 28 were destroyed, 15 due to enemy fire.

In April, two squadrons were sent from Melilla to the 1st Group, to help in the attack on Tazarut, in the west. In the summer, the second Breguet squadron was equipped in Larache, and the Martinsyde fighters were deployed in Melilla. With these reinforcements there were now five air groups, which changed their names: the 1st Group, in Tetuán, under Captain Pastor Velasco, with two Breguet squadrons; the 2nd Group, in Larache, under Captain Matanza Vázques, also with two Breguet squadrons; the 3rd Group in Melilla, under González Gallarza, with three squadrons of DH.4s; the 4th Group, also in Melilla, under Captain Moreno Abella, with two squadrons of Bristols, one of DH.9As manufactured in Spain, and another of Martinsydes, under Captain Carmelo de las Morenas; and the Seaplane Group, in Atalayón, Melilla, of Captain Santiago White, with a squadron of SIAI S.16s.

Table 3: The Aviation in Africa (April 1922)
1st Group (Tetuán)
Two Breguet XIV squadrons (Tetuán)
Farman F.50 Flight (Tetuán): two examples (three in 1923, active until 1924)
2nd Group (Larache)
Two Breguet XIV squadrons
3rd 'Rolls' Group (Nador, Melilla)
Three DH.4 Squadrons (Nador, Melilla)
4th Group Light Group (Nador, Melilla)
Two Bristol F.2B squadrons (Nador, Melilla)
One DH.9A squadron (Nador, Melilla)
One Martinsyde squadron (Nador, Melilla)
Seaplane Group (Atalayón, Melilla)
S.16 Seaplane squadron (Atalayón, Melilla)
Naval Aeronautics (carrier Dédalo)
One mixed squadron (Macchi M.18, S.13 and S.16)

The Martinsyde fighters were acquired at the end of 1921 at a low price due to the bankruptcy of the manufacturing company, with the intention of suppressing any potential Riffian air force. The Martinsydes served in Morocco from May 1922 to September 1924. Some 16 of the S.16 seaplanes were acquired, plus another 16 built in Barcelona from February 1922. These were the first operational seaplanes of the Spanish aviation, beginning their actions with a bombing over enemy lines on 29 March, and saving Afrau from being taken by the Riffians.

The aviation cooperated in the conquest of Dar Drius in the eastern sector, in January 1922, and aircraft from both east and west sectors also cooperated against El Raisuni, in the Tetuán-Larache area, comprising a DH.4 squadron from Melilla together with aviation from Larache and Tetuán. In the operations against Beni Ulixek, southeast of Annual, the Riffians shot down a Bristol F.2B on 10 May, capturing its crewmen. The Bristol had been hit four times and so its engine was stopped dead and the aircraft had to make an emergency landing at Ben Tieb. To prevent the aircraft from falling into enemy hands, the Spanish air force bombed and destroyed it in what would be its first ground attack mission against an 'enemy' aircraft, and the first

A Bristol F.2B Fighter taking off behind a rider of the Regulares. (via Sánchez & Kindelán)

A detailed view of a DH.4 in the hands of commandant Soriano. This aircraft was bought by the citizens of Zaragoza, hence the city's coat of arms appears on its side. Notable is an unidentified personal insignia applied over the toned-down national roundel, and the rear fuselage painted in white. (Lázaro, via Pando)

A view of a Martinsyde F.4A. These formed the first fighter unit of the Spanish aviation, being used in ground-support role and active until 1936. ('Canario' Azaola file, via Permuy)

A Breguet XIV, serial number 106. (Sánchez & Kindelán)

Several Savoia SIAI S.16 seaplanes at their Atalayón base. (Sánchez & Kindelán)

one in Africa. Later, on 26 July, Lieutenant Observer Ramón Ciria López was mortally wounded in flight at Azib de Midar, river Kert, being the first Spanish aviator to be killed in combat. That same month Kindelán returned as commander of the Moroccan air force, replacing Colonel Soriano.

Finally, this year also saw the emergence of naval aeronautics. In April 1922 a British-built merchant ship flying the German flag, named *Neuenfels*, was transformed into the seaplane carrier *Dédalo*, setting sail for Ceuta on 3 August with Macchi M.18 training seaplanes, S.13 and S.16 combat seaplanes, and an SCA airship onboard. A bombing raid was carried out on Cebadilla

beach in Alhucemas with these airframes, and then the Naval Division returned to its base in November. The first two Macchis were received at the end of 1921, reaching up to 15 machines, and then 45 more being manufactured in Barcelona. Their first combat mission was conducted on 6 August 1922 under Navy Lieutenant Taviel de Andrade and Guillén, bombing Morronuevo and Azibfazar. One sample of the S.13 was acquired in 1921, and in September, seven more began to be delivered, manufactured in Barcelona, with another six from 1924. Only one squadron served aboard *Dédalo* up to 13 November 1925. Also, at the beginning of 1923 two new Do Wal seaplanes arrived at Mar Chica, Melilla, that

Soldiers of the Legión being transported to the Rock of Vélez to defend the island from the Riffian attacks in April 1922. (Carrasco & De Mesa)

would be used as bombers, as with several Farman Goliaths, that arrived in September. The first ones could carry 100kg of bombs, and the second ones up to 1,000kg of bombs, so the Spanish aviation bombing capability was hugely improved.[6]

Abd el-Krim's Counteroffensive at Tizi Azza

The increasing opposition to the war from the Socialists, Republicans and even Liberals, forced the new government of Sánchez Guerra to impose a halt to the operations, but Abd el-Krim, seeing the Spanish overextended, had already organised a counteroffensive. At the beginning, he focused on the Tizi Azza salient between Beni Ulixek and Tafersit, attacking the position during 1–2 November, causing 34 casualties among the escort protecting the fortification works, 100 losses in all. Meanwhile, Lieutenant Colonel Millán Astray was removed from the command of the Legión in November 1922, due to clashes with the commanders, and assigned to the St Cyr Academy and then as liaison in the French Protectorate, being replaced by Lieutenant Colonel Valenzuela.

Probing further north, Abd el-Krim then attacked the post of Afrau – between Beni Said and Tensaman, on the coast – on 23 November. This time the Regulares defending it did not defect. The Riffian then returned to the southern sector and attacked Tizi Azza again between 14 and 18 December, surrounding the position and repulsing a supply convoy on the 17th. Only a brilliant bayonet attack carried out by Franco with the Legión, flanking the Riffians, managed to lift the blockade. In January 1923, the 6th Bandera of the Spanish Legión arrived from Ceuta.

Meanwhile, there was a new change in the command, and in February 1923 Burguete was replaced for the first time in the Protectorate by a civilian: Luis Silvela. After new failed negotiations between the Riffians and the government, Abd el-Krim continued his offensive, attacking again in Tizi Azza in April and May. The Spanish finally reacted, and the new commander of Melilla, General Vives Vich, began works to improve the defensive positions. On 20 May, Colonel Coronel Cubría arranged the posts of Tifarauín and Izumar 2, but these posts began to be attacked on the 27th. Silvela then arranged a column from Tafersit, under Lieutenant Colonel Llano de la Encomienda (Mehala of the Rif, 4th Bandera of the Legión, two tabors of 2nd Group of Regulares of Melilla, a battalion from 5th Princesa Regiment, a squadron of Regulares, and three batteries) to rescue the posts. The problem was that Silvela, the High Commissioner, trapped in the middle of peace negotiations with the Riffians, ordered that there should be no fighting and to

withdraw if the rebels attacked the convoy. Also, the aviation should only explore the area but avoid any bombing of the enemy. As soon as the column departed they were heavily fired upon by the awaiting Riffians against the flank and rear. Then, Lieutenant Colonel Kindelán, commander of the Spanish aviation, disobeyed his orders and launched several flights of Bristol F.2B and DH.4s that dropped 673 bombs over the Riffians. Only the appearance of these aircraft and the reinforcements to protect the Spanish rear (the 1st Bandera of the Legión, a tabor and a squadron of the Alhucemas Group of Regulares and a battery) saved Llano de la Encomienda from being destroyed. The clash with the Riffians in Buhafora, about 5km west of Tafersit, caused 52 casualties. At the end the Spaniards were able to open the road for the convoy to Tizi Azza, but General Vives, in disagreement with Silvela's orders, was replaced by Echagüe Santoyo.

Nevertheless, the Riffians were still there, occupying the heights dominating Tafersit, Bu Hafora, and Tizi Azza, and were entrenching. General Echagüe then launched a massive offensive to clear the sector once and for all. On his left wing, he arranged three columns in Tafersit and one in Bufarcuf, that would make the main effort, under Colonel Fernández Pérez. The first one, under Colonel Coronel Cubría (from Bufarcuf) would move to protect the east of Peña Tahurda; the second, under Colonel Gómez Morato (and including Lieutenant Colonel Valenzuela's Legiónnaires), would move to Bu Hafora and then Tizi Azza to open the road for the convoy; the third, under Ruiz del Portal would protect the convoy; and the fourth, under Colonel Morales Reinoso would protect the extreme left or south of the line. There were two further columns under Colonel Salcedo Molinuovo to protect the right wing of the front in Dar Quebdani, and a reserve column under General Echagüe in Dar Drius. All these forces included six battalions of recruits, five tabors of Regulares, three Banderas of the Legión, six artillery batteries, tanks, 1,000 men from the Mehalas, and, allegedly, 6,000 Riffians from friendly harkas. For the air component, a squadron from Tetuán reinforced the aviation of Melilla that would support the attack. Also, a medical aircraft was used for the first time in Africa to evacuate the wounded. At the same time, the fleet would bombard the coast of Beni Urriagel.

On 5 June the offensive was launched, Coronel's column attracting the fire of the Riffians in the plain of Tzayudait. The other three columns to the left were able to pass the whole of Tafersit, but then, they began to suffer from Riffian attention. Gómez Morato's column had to fight with the rebels entrenched in the ravine of Benítez-Iguemiren, that dominated the route of the convoy, so Coronel's column (made up of recruits in one battalion of the 52nd Andalucía Regiment and two companies of the 50th Wad Ras Regiment) arrived there to help his colleague. In any case, the convoy was stopped, so the Regulares of Melilla had to assist in clearing the heights. In the end, the larger part of the Riffians was resisting in the lower part of the ravine, so now came the hour of the Legión. Lieutenant Colonel Valenzuela, in command of the 1st, 2nd and 4th Banderas of the Legión, launched a bayonet assault to clear the bottom of the ravines, personally leading it with a pistol. Valenzuela, who had come with two Banderas from Larache, sensing his death, the night before had asked to a priest to confess his sins. The brave officer died from a shot to the head and another in the chest. So, Commander Franco progressed again in his career: with Lieutenant Colonel Valenzuela dead, Franco assumed the command of the several Banderas, a group the size of a small regiment, being soon promoted to lieutenant colonel and commander of the Spanish Legión. The fighting was fierce, with 146 dead and 466 casualties in all, but Tizi Azza had been saved again. Also, this combat was

Colonel Valenzuela, commander of a Group made of the 1st, 2nd and 4th Banderas of the Legión sensed his death and confessed his sins the night before of the assault to Tizi Azza. With his death, Commandant Franco assumed command for the first time of the Group of Banderas of the Legión. (Marín Ferrer)

Commandant Franco, in the Legión uniform, was promoted soon after the death of Valenzuela. Note the typical Legión barracks tassel cap, and the Mills belt, with a semi-automatic pistol instead of a revolver. (Carrasco & de Mesa)

Soldiers of the Legión with an enemy cannon captured in November 1922. (Carrasco & de Mesa)

Several 155mm heavy guns in the Zaio River area, in the winter of 1922. (Lucas Molina, via Marín Ferrer)

An enemy artillery piece captured by the Regulares of Alhucemas under Lieutenant Colonel Rafael Valenzuela in October 1922. (Carrasco & de Mesa)

the end chapter of the commander of Melilla, Echagüe Santoyo, who was replaced by Division General Martínez Anido on 6 June. Finally, this combat also saw the experimental use by the artillery of a new gas, mustard gas or yperite, instead of the previously used phosgene and chloropicrin. The new gas was far more efficient than the other ones.

At the same time, new native troops were organised throughout 1923: the 2nd Mehala of Melilla, and the harka of Melilla of 1,443 warriors under Abd el-Malek. This unit was destroyed in a clash at Hidar, losing 500 men and its own leader, so it went on to Tetuán to be replenished under Commandant Valdés. In addition, on 1 June several Mehalas were created, including the 5th Mehala of Tafersit, formed by the harka of the Rif, that of Sidi Idris, and the Goum of Melilla.[7]

Flying the 'Spanish Way'

During these operations over Tizi Azza there were several aircraft incidents due to the Spanish pilots' habit of flying devilishly low in their attempts to locate the Riffians, who, excellent marksmen, would shoot them. The French pilots who observed this practice, and who had Great War experience, said it was a suicide, and called it 'flying the Spanish way'. According to Miguel Sanchís:

Flying too high and showing a photograph taken of the comrade from below was almost a dishonour… flying too low, an almost necessary suicide; there were observers who in low flight at 10 metres above the enemy could not see anything at all, and instead the pilot was injured and the aircraft was hit by numerous impacts, shots which even often came from a higher altitude than the aircraft.

Thus, on 28 May, Captain Mariano Barberán, commander of the 1st Bristol Squadron, carried out a reconnaissance and was only saved from the massive enemy fire thanks to the timely intervention of the squadrons from Tetuán (although at the cost of losing several aircraft, luckily without suffering personnel casualties, and recovering all the airframes). To support the supply operations in Tizi Azza, two air groups from Melilla – reinforced by a squadron from Tetuán – moved to a provisional airfield in Dar Drius, closer to Tafersit.

In one of these 'Spanish way' missions, Lieutenant Colonel Kindelán himself, head of the aviation, flying as an observer for Captain Llorente, head of the 2nd Squadron, was seriously wounded on 5 June, when trying to protect the above-mentioned major effort and the convoys to save Tiza Azza. Kindelán, recently promoted to lieutenant colonel by seniority, upon returning from a mission on the Tafersit and Tizi Azza fronts, learned that Captain Rafael Llorente Solá was ready to depart. As the scheduled bomb aimer – Captain Baeza – did not appear at Nador aerodrome, Kindelán quickly removed his combat flag (which distinguished him as head of the aviation), and the flag was now installed on the left pillar of the Bristol in the hands of Captain Llorente. Kindelán would act now as the bomb aimer. The bombing mission was without incident, but at the end of the mission, on the last pass, as Llorente had not felt the release of the bombs being dropped, he turned to tell Kindelán to drop them, realising, at that moment, that his boss had received a bullet between the neck and the left shoulder causing a great haemorrhage and paralysis. Without wasting time, he landed as best he could near the Legión troops, where Kindelán was treated by medics and transferred to the Military Hospital in Melilla and was later evacuated to Madrid. It took practically a year to be discharged as fit for service and Kindelán would not return to Africa until September of 1925.

These missions were repeated continuously, stopping only to refuel, rearm, and to take off again, and all of the airframes would be full of holes by night. For these actions, Captains Carrillo, Moreno Abella, Sáenz de Buruaga, Llorente and Barberán were awarded the Individual Military Medal on 22 July.

A less heroic and rather sad first was the use of gas by the Spanish aviation, occasionally as an experiment. During the Great War, gas projectiles were used by the artillery but never dropped from the air. The Commissioner, Silvela, a civilian, in trying to avoid the scandal of a massive number of coffins filled with the bodies of recruits being returned to Spain was enthusiastic for the use of aviation to smash the Riffian rebellion. He advocated using poison gas against the Riffians, as the British had done in Iraq or Afghanistan, but, on top of using artillery he proposed to use the aircraft. So, during 13th or 14th, and 26th and 28 July, the Bristol F.2Bs of the 4th Group, sadly, executed the first gas bombing by air over the village of Amesauro in Tensaman, and then again during August. On the 13th, two gas bombs were dropped, on the 26th the Kebir River was bombed with 90 explosive bombs and one gas bomb, and then another village on the 28th with 42 projectiles and one gas bomb. During August further bombings were made in the Kebir, Amesauro, Nekor and Guis Rivers on the 1st, 5th and 10th of the month, dropping eight gas bombs each day. Silvela also planned the first aerial carpet bombing in history against the kabyles of Beni Urriagel and Tensamen, 'without leaving a single metre without a bomb', but the cost was excessive, so finally this was not done.[8]

Abd El-Krim Turns to the North, to Tifarauín

Abd el-Krim suffered severe punishment on the southern front (perhaps 600 deaths and many more wounded) and moved his forces to try his luck to the north, to the position of Tifarauín in Beni Said, between Afrau and Dar Quebdani. Also, he took advantage of Silvela's instructions to suspend all attacks for the duration of the peace talks with the Riffians. Tifarauín was surrounded on 17 August, and the rebel attacks were repulsed by the 1st Bandera of the Legión, but the column sent the next day from Dar Quebdani to break the siege was in turn repulsed with some 100 dead and hundreds of wounded. This latter column consisted of a battalion of 35th Toledo Regiment, the 2nd Bandera, a mía of the 2nd Mehala of Melilla and a mounted battery under Lieutenant Colonel Pintado Cabrera.

A second attempt was made by three columns coordinated by Colonel Salcedo: the one on the left, under Lieutenant Colonel Pintado with 1st and 2nd Banderas of the Legión, two battalions of the 35th Toledo and 11th San Fernando Regiments that would move forward over the ridge that began on Sidi Mesaud and ended in Tifisuin; the column of the centre, under Colonel Pérez Seoane with 1st and 2nd Tabors of the 2nd Group of Regulares of Melilla, and two battalions of the 19th Galicia and 55th Asia Regiments that would escort the convoy to Tifarauín; and the column on the right, under Lieutenant Colonel Olmos Fernández with the 3rd Tabor of the 2nd Group of Regulares of Melilla and a battalion of the 23rd Valencia Regiment, that would march from Dar Quebdani to Izumar, take the hill to the left of Ibuseganen, and then moving to Timayst, to cover the flank of Seaone's column. As a reserve, in the Kadía plain were held the battalions of the 50th Wad Ras, 42nd Ceriñola and 29th Isabel la Católica Regiments, and, with a 155mm battery that would bombard the enemy lines, to support the moving columns. Nevertheless, again the Spaniards were forced back after suffering 343 losses. This was alarmingly similar to the events of Abarrán and Igueriben, that preceded the 1921 Annual Disaster.

Then, on 19 August, the Tifarauín garrison advised that they had only food, ammunition and water for three more days, so Silvela authorised a massive relief operation. General Sanjurjo planned an offensive along the entire front between Tizi Azza in the south and Afrau on the coast, with air and naval support and nine columns, calculated at 30,000 men by French sources. The actions in the south would be mere feints to distract the enemy, but the real thrust would be in the north, in front of the Riffian main lines, and also in their rear. Lieutenant Colonel Franco arrived at Melilla from Tetuán on the 20th, where he jumped into an aircraft to make an air reconnaissance and then landed in Dar Quebdani to discuss the manoeuvre with the other commanders and the High Commissioner. An indication of the popularity of Franco amongst

Table 4: The Tifaraiun Operation (August 1923)		
Commander	**Composition**	**Location/ objectives**
General Fernández Pérez	Four Columns (see below)	Relief of Tifarauín
Colonel Pardo	Harkas of Amar Uchen and Guelaya; a tabor of the 5th Mehala of the Rif; two machine gun companies; a battalion of the 52nd Melilla Regiment	Landing at Afrau
Colonel Salcedo	2nd Group of Regulares of Melilla; Lieutenant Colonel Franco's Legión; two Battalions of the 11th Borbón and 17th Guipúzcoa Regiments	Dar Quebdani, to march in the centre through Farha
Colonel Seoane	5th Group of Regulares of Alhucemas, and one battalion each of the 55th, 19th and 45th Regiments of Asia, Galicia and Garellano, and two mountain artillery batteries	Dar Quebdani, to march in the left through Sidi Mesaud
Lieutenant Colonel Castro Vázquez	A battery of 155mm howitzers, and a battalion each of the 42nd Ceriñola, 29th Isabel la Católica, 23rd Valencia and 50th Wad Ras Regiments	Reserve at Dar Quebdani
Colonel Morales	A battalion each of the 22nd Gerona, 52nd Melilla and 7th San Marcial Regiments; a squadron and machine gun section of the 12th Cavalry Regiment; a Group of 14th Light Artillery Regiment	Kandussi, to march towards Ben Tieb and then north of Peña (Rock) Tahuarda
Colonel Vera Valdés	Six Schneider K-1 tanks; two and a half companies of the 5th Group of Alhucemas; a battalion each of the 22nd, 26th and 53rd Álava, Albuera and 68th África regiments	Tafersit, march to Tizi Azza Norte (North)
Colonel Micheo y Díaz	65th Battalion of Cazadores of Valladolid; three squadrons of the 10th Alcántara Cavalry Regiment; two batteries on horseback; two batteries 9th Light Artillery Regiment; a Group of 14th Light Artillery Regiment	Dar Drius, as a reserve
	Cavalry	Dar Drius to Batel
	Cavalry	Tistutin to Monte Arruit

Cavalry of the Mehala de Tetuán in the Melilla sector, October 1922. (Carrasco & de Mesa)

the troops was that Captain Boy departed in an aircraft on the same day to provide supplies to the garrison, with a note to increase his morale that just said: 'Franco has just arrived from Tetuán'. Boy died during this mission.

General Fernández Pérez, with four columns, would coordinate the right flank as the main effort. His forces were made of the column that would land in Afrau, under Colonel Pardo with the harkas of Amar Uchen and Guelaya, a tabor of the 5th Mehala of the Rif, two machine gun companies and a battalion of the 52nd Melilla Regiment; then the column of Dar Quebdani, to the east, under Colonel Salcedo with the 2nd Group of Regulares of Melilla, Lieutenant Colonel Franco's Legión, two battalions of the 11th Borbón and 17th Guipúzcoa Regiments) that would march in the centre through Farha; another column based in Dar Quebdani under Colonel Seoane with the 5th Group of Regulares of Alhucemas, and one battalion of the 55th Asia, 19th Galicia and 45th Garellano

Regiments, and two mountain artillery batteries, that would march, on the left, through Sidi Mesaud; and a reserve under Lieutenant Colonel de Castro Vázquez with a battery of 155mm howitzers, and a battalion of the 42nd Ceriñola, 29th Isabel la Católica, 23rd Valencia and 50th Wad Ras Regiments.

The left flank, that would make the fake attacks, was made up of the column of Kandussi, far in the rear, under Colonel Morales with a battalion of the 22nd Gerona, 52nd Melilla and 7th San Marcial Regiments, a squadron and machine gun section of the 12th Cavalry Regiment, and a Group of the 14th Light Artillery Regiment that would march towards Ben Tieb and then north of Peña (Rock) Tahuarda; and the column of Tafersit, further to the south, under Colonel Vera Valdés preceded by six Schneider K-1 tanks, two and a half companies of the 5th Group of Alhucemas, a battalion of the 22nd Álava, 26th Albuera and 68th África regiments that would march to Tizi Azza Norte (North); a reserve column in

Lieutenant Ramón Topete with the survivors of his Policía Indígena, defenders of the Tifarauín post, that held all the Riffian attacks until being relieved in August 1923. (Carrasco & de Mesa)

Dar Drius, far in the rear, under Colonel de Micheo y Díaz with the 65th Battalion of Cazadores of Valladolid, three squadrons of the 10th Alcántara Cavalry Regiment, two batteries on horseback, and two others of the 9th Light Artillery Regiment, and a Group of 14th Light Artillery Regiment that would remain static, waiting for the results of the other columns. There were two further columns protecting their lines of communications with Melilla, one between Dar Drius to Batel, and the other, from Tistutin to Monte Arruit, both being made up of cavalry forces.

On 21 August, troops from the Mehala and the harka of Guelaya landed on Afrau beach, supported by the sixteen 305mm guns of the battleships *Alfonso XIII* and *España*, reinforced in the afternoon by the 400 warriors of the harka of Beni Said. There, they occupied defensive positions to protect the landing of the bulk of Colonel Pardo's column, 2,300 men in all. The latter advanced the next day to the south-east, against the back of the Riffian hills that dominated Tifaraouin to the north and north-west. The Riffians, with the largest concentration of troops to date (according to some sources, 9,000 warriors), blocking the direction of Dar Quebdani, were bombarded with phosgene gas by the columns marching from Dar Quebdani, enveloped on their flanks by the Dar Quebdani columns and the rear by the lading forces in Afrau, and abandoned their positions, leaving Tifarauín to be liberated by the Salcedo column. The operation, a very brilliant example of how to avoid an ambush attacking from an unexpected direction behind the enemy, would go on to be included in all Spanish military manuals. It was also the first case of a land, naval and air cooperation by the Spanish military. Even so, the Spaniards suffered 324 casualties, without counting those in the columns of Quebdani, Kandussi, and Tafersit, so perhaps reaching 437 losses in all. The Riffians also suffered heavy losses, as 200 bodies were taken from the field by the rebels, counting only those of Beni Urriagel. Also, 235 dead men (with 183 rifles) were recovered by the Spaniards around Tifarauín. If we add the wounded men, the amount could reach 1,000 losses, or even double that.[9]

During the air operations carried out to supply Tifarauín, the aircraft manned by Captain Boy (mentioned above) was shot down

on the 20th, and on the 22nd that of Lieutenant Salgado, both being killed along with their observers. The supply missions under enemy fire were a success and captains Ramón Franco (brother of the future dictator), Ortiz, Loriga and González Gallarza received the Individual Military Medal. The aircraft carrier *Dédalo* also participated with several Macchi M.18s, four S.16 bis, an airship and a tethered balloon, although they were more focused on the rescue of castaways.[10]

Destroying the Riffian Aviation

On top of these operations in the Melilla District, the Spanish aviation had to deal with a new threat: the new-born Riffian Republic was creating an armed aviation branch. Since the beginning of Abd el-Krim's tenure in 1921, he instructed his warriors to try to capture intact any Spanish aircraft obliged to land in his territory. The Spanish commanders consequently ordered the destruction of any of these aircraft to avoid them being captured, as they successfully achieved in Zeluán during the Annual Disaster (see Volume 1) and by bombing a Bristol F.2B in Beni Ulixek on 10 May 1922, as already noted. Nevertheless, one year later, on 13 August 1923, a DH.9A coming directly from Granada to Melilla under Captain César Herráiz made an emergency landing in Cape Quilates, to the east of Alhucemas. Herráiz was captured with his aircraft, but the Spanish, noticing the absence of their colleague, sent two squadrons to try to locate him. Despite being camouflaged with vegetation, the aircraft was detected, and so on 21 August a group of aircraft was sent to bomb it, managing to destroy it. The fuselage and engine were saved and hidden in a house in Alhucemas, to be captured by the Spanish a couple of years later.

Nevertheless, the Riffians tried again to form their aviation, so Abd el-Krim a message to his deputies Qaid Haddou and Azerkan in Algeria to buy three Dorand AR.2 aircraft from the bankrupted French company SRAT.[11] After testing some of them, the Riffian negotiators found one of them suitable to fly, probably No. 4, registration F-AFAC. So, on 24 December 1923 an a SRAT pilot called Perrier (also called Periel in some sources), flew it from

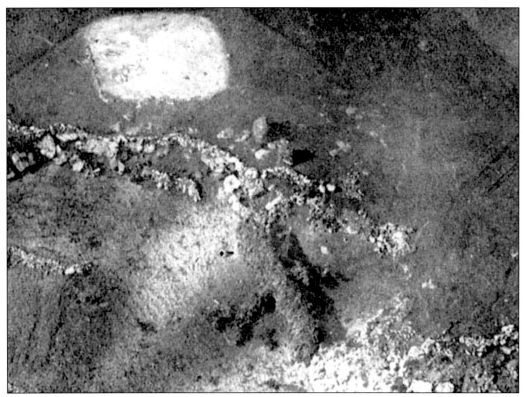

A picture of the DH.9A aircraft of Captain César Herráiz captured by the Riffians in August 1923, and camouflaged by branches and grass. The shape of the aircraft remained visible from the air. (IHCA, via Dr David Nicolle)

The Rif Republic was only able to buy a single Dorand AR.2 from SRAT, on 24 December 1923, like the one shown here, to create an air force. The Riffian example was probably SRAT No. 4, plate number F-AFAX. (Jarrige archive, via Dr David Nicolle)

contacts to recruit pilots, such as with Carlos Greco, an Italian-Argentinian aerobatic pilot. In the meantime, it seems that the Spanish aviation had lost track of the Riffian aircraft until a patrol of two Bristols from Melilla (No. 21, under lieutenants Manuel Martínez Merino and Armando Solís Flores; and No. 40 with Ensign Francisco Coterillo Llano and Commandant Luis Rueda Ledesma) spotted it in Tizzi-Moren, Alhucemas, in an excavation near an airstrip that was being completed and protected by a machine gun nest. The airmen thought that the aircraft was a Breguet.

Then, on 22–23 March, the Spaniards launched an attack by the DH.9s of the 3rd Group, and the Bristols of the 4th Group, dropping 540 bombs over the objective, and machine-gunning it. Several Spanish aircraft were damaged during this attack by enemy fire. The De Havilland No. 51, piloted by Lieutenant Juan Antonio Ansaldo, a future hero of the Nationalist aviation during the Civil War, bombed the enemy aircraft from a height of 50 metres, making eight passes. After destroying it, he was seriously wounded in the left leg. Even so, he warned the observer so that he could take control of the aircraft and, after bandaging himself, he continued his mission as far as the house of Abd el-Krim, in Beni Urriaguel, next to Axdir. Ansaldo then reduced the power and dropped the last two bombs. He then recovered the controls of the machine and returned with it intact. Ansaldo received the Laureate for this feat of arms.

On 24 March, the head of the DH.9s of 3rd Group, Commandant José Carrillo with observer Ángel López Orduña, flew a reconnaissance mission to Tizzi-Moren and observed that the wings of the Dorand were broken: the new-born Riffian aviation had been destroyed. Nevertheless, several days later, in the middle of April, again commandants Carrillo and Orduña, in a Bristol, detected that the airfield had been expanded with additional sheds. Perhaps the Riffian aviation had been reborn again? J. Abad, on 22 June had tried to recruit a new pilot, named Joly, from Latecoere airlines, and perhaps even kidnap him with his aircraft and thus Spain kept

Hussein-Dey in Algiers to Tlemcen, where he probably took Qaid Haddou as a passenger, and then continued to Toufits, north of Taza. As several witnesses spotted the Riffian emissaries and the departing of the aircraft, the French authorities were informed, interdicted the departure of further Dorands and informed the Spanish government. Perrier was killed soon after in an aircraft accident.

The Spanish aviation tried to locate the Riffian aircraft in the Rish and Nakor valleys, south of Alhucemas, and finally on 25 and 26 January 1924 they found it in Ait Kamara, where a precarious airfield was being built. Luckily, for the moment the Riffians had no pilots, but they were trying to solve this problem. A Spaniard named J. Abad was appointed as head of the aviation and began seeking

The Italo-Argentinian aerobatic pilot Carlos Greco was contracted to handle the first aircraft of the Riffian aviation. (José Vila Collection, via Dr David Nicole)

several fighter squadrons in North Africa to prevent any surprise and dramatic appearance of the Riffian aviation.[12]

The last chapter in these efforts to prevent the creation of a Riffian aviation arm was rather heroic. On 19 April 1925, Lieutenant Senén Ordales, when flying at ground level to bomb Had de Ben Buyari, in the Melilla sector, discovered the Bristol No. 25 that had just been shot down by the Riffians. He had the audacity to land there to recover the aircraft and the bodies of his comrades, defending himself with his gun until the arrival of ground troops, then taking off again, winning the Individual Military Medal. He would shortly receive the Laureate.[13]

Primo de Rivera's Dictatorship

Returning to 1923, despite these last victories in the Melilla District, Commissioner Silvela resigned over wanting to continue with the peace talks against the wishes of the military commanders. He was replaced by an old acquaintance, General Luis Aizpuru, who had been fighting since 1909 and had assumed the command of Ceuta in 1916. However, the pacifist party returned to power within days when General Miguel Primo de Rivera, another veteran of the African wars since 1909 and brother of Fernando, the hero of the Alcántara Cavalry Regiment at Annual, staged a coup d'état in September 1923 with the support of generals Cavalcanti, Federico Berenguer, Sanjurjo (returned to Spain in 1923), and of King Alfonso XIII.

Gerald Brenan gives a somewhat harsh, but very graphic description of the dictator:

As for his intelligence, it can be said that he was that of a man of natural gifts, but of little instruction. He had no preparation for statecraft. He despised intellectuals and technicians, hated politicians, and had an arsenal of superficial ideas on all subjects. [...] Primo de Rivera is really an anachronism in the Spain of his time. His simplicity, his informality, his disorderly customs belonged to the previous period, when the poor and the rich had not yet begun to feel separated. He had no air of 'gentleman', like so many of today's landowners. He wore clothes of the cheapest, dressed with a preference of plain clothes, and when he began to gain weight, instead of taking care of new suits, he had the old ones fixed for him....

His dictatorship arrived 'wrapped in a wave of optimism and good intentions. It reached its climax in 1926, three years into its existence, and soon began to decline. In 1928 it was already unpopular even among the army, and in January 1930 its end came.'

However, Brenan acknowledged that:

A public works plan was carried out that almost ended with unemployment. The roads built by the previous governments were tarred and left in a condition to serve for the circulation of cars. New ones were drawn up, and at the same time plans for power plants and irrigation were undertaken. An admirable network of Paradores [national hotels], built by the State, encouraged tourism in several provinces. Ancient monuments were restored. The exhibitions of Barcelona and Seville were inaugurated, of a luxury disproportionate to the resources of the country. Expenses that created a false sense of prosperity...

Brenan concludes by stating that 'Primo de Rivera

A picture taken on 21 March 1924 by Lieutenant Solís Flores in Bristol No. 21, locating the Riffian Dorand, that would be destroyed by the Spanish aviation on 23 March. (IHCA, via Dr David Nicolle)

rose to power in the most favourable circumstances and luck was propitious, and yet, after three years of fortunate management, the approach of his fall was only a matter of time [...] His last days of physical prostration and bitterness [April 1930] were spent between the cabaret and the church...'[14]

At heart General Primo de Rivera was a practical man, unsophisticated, but very competent and effective. We must not forget that among his achievements, apart from those mentioned, was the protection and relaunch of Spanish industry, the creation of the strategic companies Telefónica and CAMPSA (for the incipient development of telephone communications and oil exploration and exploitation, respectively), and the integration even of the Socialists in their cabinet, for the first time in the history of Spain, to form stable government and broad consensus, gives us a clue that he was a much more flexible and open minded man than is usually thought. And, of course, the improvement in the effectiveness of the army and the end of the Moroccan War, which ended with the subjugation of the Rif and the creation of the Spanish Protectorate, were also part of his merits, even despite his initial intention of abandoning Morocco to end the rosary of coffins arriving in Spain.

A Menu Made of Eggs

During the winter of 1923–24 the front lines were quiet, but the 3rd Bandera of the Legión was sent to Melilla in anticipation of further hostilities. General Primo de Rivera reorganised the front to leave it on the defensive, creating a vanguard zone in contact with the Riffians, some forward positions that would be supported by three or four large columns based in Dar Quebdani, to the north (Beni Said); in Ben Tieb, in the centre (Beni Ulixek) – where there was a combat group of the Legión that guarded the gorge of Annual – in Dar Drius, in the southern rear (M'talsa), and in Tafersit, also in the south, but further forward, near Tizi Azza. Behind them there would be the rear area, with supply depots and reserve troops in Tistutin (Beni Bu Yahi), Segangan (Beni Bu Ifrur) and Nador (Mazuza, south of Melilla).

The aviation was also being increased, with 137 aircraft deployed in all North Africa at the beginning of 1924, consisting of 72 reconnaissance and bombing aircraft, six fighters and eight seaplanes of them in the Melilla area; 30 reconnaissance and bombing aircraft, plus six fighters in Ceuta-Tetuán, and a reserve in Seville made of 16 reconnaissance aircraft, and three bombers. Also, on 16 June a squadron of 12 Potez aircraft was incorporated into the Melilla aviation. In any case, a large number of them were destined only for training purposes or were under repair. Also, these old airframes carried 11kg bombs, that were useful in open terrain, but not against houses or entrenchments.[15]

In March 1924, Abd el-Krim struck in the western area of Ceuta, and in the east. In the latter area, he again attacked Tizi Azza in the mountains of Tafersit-Beni Ulixek, in the southern sector. It was necessary to organise a large operation led by General Aizpuru himself on 2 March to supply Tizi Azza. On the 7th, Lieutenant Colonel Franco managed to break the siege by leading a convoy to the post. Then, Abd el-Krim moved north, and attacked Sidi Messaud, west of Dar Quedbani, encircling it in April. On 3 May the post was totally isolated, and the attacks made to relieve it on the 4th and 7th were repulsed. Then, the next day, General Sanjurjo arrived at Melilla to coordinate the offensive, stating that the objective of the Spanish attack would not be to save the post but to destroy the Riffian host deployed around the post. On 10 May the attack was launched with a vanguard of tanks, but the first of the vehicles fell into a hidden hole, covered with wood, in the middle of the road, so the other tanks were not able to follow as the road was now cut. In the end, the aviation saved the day, and on 11 May Franco's Legiónnaires lifted the siege of the position with a bayonet attack. The Legión was proving to be an elite corps, superior even to the Regulares. Finally, another major attack was made by the Riffians against Afrau on 14 August, that was saved by three columns supported by the aviation, that machine-gunned the rebel trenches.

During the rest of the year, due to the negotiations with Abd el-Krim, the only Spanish operations were air attacks. On 21 May, Abd el-Krim's house at Axdir was attacked with 14 bombs of phosgene, on 22 June, his headquarters in Ait Kemara was bombed with 22 C-1 yperite (mustard gas) bombs, and his home with another 20. In all, there were some 14 additional bombing attacks with gas between June and July. Despite the awful effects of the gas, the Spanish pilots were treated well, probably for the prizes granted by the Spanish authorities for any pilot helped to return to the Spanish lines: on 30 July, the engine of the aircraft in the hands of Lieutenant Rodríguez y Díaz de Lecea was stopped dead by enemy fire, but the pilot was able to make a forced landing in enemy territory. Then, a rider appeared with a white flag and told Rodríguez: 'Ride on the horse, me, friend'. The Riffian was Abd al Zab Mehal, who took the Spaniard to his lines, and then was appointed as the chief of his kabyle. Also, the operations of the seaplanes, very important for their larger bomb load, increased as the Spanish placed several vessels near the island of Alhucemas, loaded with bombs and fuel, to supply the seaplanes out at sea.

General Sanjurjo (nearest to the camera), the most capable commander of the Spanish forces, who led the Reconquista in 1921–22, and then in 1925–27, the winning of the war. He was with Primo de Rivera when Franco and his Legión, according to legend, offered to them a menu based on eggs, as an indication of his opposition to leaving Africa. (Fernández Riera)

Dictator from September 1923 to 1930, General Miguel Primo de Rivera, had the support of General Sanjurjo and Alfonso XIII. He tried to end the war in Africa with a partial withdrawal but was forced to continue due to the resistance of the *Africanistas*. Then, Primo de Rivera took advantage of the Riffian attack against French Morocco to forge an alliance with Paris that would gain the final victory. (Painting by José Ribera, via Desperta Ferro Magazine)

With all sectors of the Protectorate on the defensive, the dictator, Lieutenant General Primo de Rivera, began to develop his plans for

Spain leaving Morocco definitively, but to do so, he first had to check the opinion of the high-ranking officers there. Primo made a visit to the Legión camp of Ben Tieb in July 1924. There, he met very strong opposition to abandoning the positions recovered after the Disaster of Annual. Primo, accompanied by General Sanjurjo (his friend and main supporter amongst the militaries), proposed abandoning the lines and withdrawing to Abadda, on a plain halfway between Tafersit and Dar Drius, which would mean abandoning this village and that of Beni Ulixek. Then, some quite violent scenes occurred and, according to some chronicles, Sanjurjo had to reach for his gun to calm the spirits of the military. Franco led the opposition to this project, supported by the Legión and Regulares commanders and had a harsh discussion with the dictator.

How was it possible that a mere Lieutenant Colonel had such an open confrontation with the President of Spain? Several months before, in October 1923, Franco returned to Spain to marry Carmen Polo, and he met King Alfonso XIII. According to some debatable sources, King Alfonso was the best man in his wedding, so in any case, it seems that he had a close relationship with the monarch and perhaps Franco thought that Alfonso would support him in the event of being prosecuted for insubordination. Franco wrote in the *Colonial Troops Magazine* in April 1924 that he would disobey any orders to retreat from Africa, but there were no negative consequences for him. A legend says that even during these harsh meetings in Ben Tieb in July 1924, Franco had the audacity to entertain the dictator with a menu made of eggs or 'Huevos' (in Spanish, another way of referring to the testicles...).[16]

3
1921–24, Xauén, Another Annual?

If General Primo de Rivera's plans were partially abandoned in the eastern sector because of the resistance of his subordinates, in the west he was ready to carry them out. Then a general insurrection in the Ceuta region broke out in 1924, altering all his plans. However, we have to go back to 1921 to understand what was happening in this sector. When news of the Annual Disaster spread to the western part of the Protectorate, the rebellion roused there in August 1921. We left El Raisuni on the verge of being annihilated (see Volume 1) at Tazarut (Beni Arós) but saved by the suspension of operations due to the events of Annual. Now the rebellion broke out in Ajmás, to the east; Beni Issef, to the south; and Sumata, to the south-west; all places surrounding the area where El Raisuni was based in Tazarut. Thus, during the night of the 27th to the 28th the entire position of Akba el-Kola, 175 men, was annihilated. In addition, the revolt in the Garb spread to Gomara, to the east, under the leadership of M'hammed Abd el-Krim, brother of the Riffian leader, who entered the area with a harka and two cannons.

The government reinforced the garrisons of Ceuta, Tetuán and Larache, awaiting developments in these sectors. On 22 October, the Gomaris and Riffians attacked the coastal posts of Tiguisas, Magán and Kaseres or Keerkeses (in Beni Siat, east of Xauén, on the eastern side of the River Lau), using artillery captured from the Spaniards. Captain Capaz (a future hero at the end of the war, as we will see) was reinforced with half a bandera of the Legión and tried to save Magán

but was repulsed with 50 casualties. On the 24th, General Marzo, commander of Ceuta, managed to introduce a convoy escorted by 1,200 men with the 2nd and 4th Banderas of the Legión, but suffered 175 casualties. In the Gomara, only the village of Beni Seyel, south of Beni Ziat and north of Xauén (Ajmás) remained loyal to Spain. General Marzo reacted with a punitive expedition to the Gomara at Beni Ziat on 28 October, causing 500 Moorish casualties for 35 Spanish dead. Then, the Gomara again submitted, for the moment.[1]

Once Gomara was pacified, new units were formed in the western sector, in preparation for resuming the campaign against El Raisuni. In November, the 5th Bandera of the Legión was formed, and with the 3rd Bandera, both units as well as the Tetuán Section of the Policía Indígena were sent against Tazarut under Lieutenant Colonel Millán Astray himself. In December, High Commissioner General Berenguer ordered the resumption of operations against El Raisuni in Beni Arós. The Spaniards first would take the barracks of Hamido Succan, El Raisuni's second commander and leader of the Beni Ider and Beni Lait abyleks to the north and east. With the arrival of bad weather, operations were suspended until January 1922, when the encirclement of the kabyle was completed. Between April and May, the Spanish advanced against Tazarut itself, the eagle's nest where El Raisuni was sheltering. On 27 April, the Larache column, with 9,500 soldiers under the command of General of Brigade Sanjurjo (transferred from Melilla), would attack from

The body of Lieutenant Colonel Santiago González Tablas, commander of the Regulares of Tetuán, who died in May 1922 attacking Tazarut, El Raisuni's eagle's nest. (Villalobos)

Lieutenant Colonel Santiago González Tablas. (Marín Ferrer)

Abd el-Krim Attacks in the West

As we have already mentioned, General Primo de Rivera staged a coup d'état in 1923 and tried to implement a plan to gradually abandon Africa. As his policy was opposed by the militaries in the eastern zone, the General tried to apply it first in the western zone, ordering a stop to all operations. In the meantime, new native units were created on 1 June: the 3rd Mehala of Larache and the 4th of Tetuán, from the Policía Indígena of these areas. In any case, thanks to the alliance with El Raisuni, the Yebala and the Garb seemed to be calmed again. On 17 January 1923 the Army of Africa was reorganised, the command of the Army was divided directly in two Commands, one of Ceuta and the other of Melilla. The Command of Larache was dissolved and put under the control, as a sub-district, of the Ceuta Command.

Everything changed when Abd el-Krim, on the defensive in the eastern zone, tried to expand his territory in the western zone in 1924, taking advantage of the vacuum left among the rebels by the defection of El Raisuni. Thus, he sent a harka of Riffians under Ahmed Jeriro, formerly a collaborator of El Raisuni and now the second in command of Abd el-Krim. On 16 February, Jeriro attacked M'ter, the most advanced Spanish position on the Gomara coast, at the mouth of the River Lau, and besieged it for a month. The Spanish tried a new tactic, that of supplying the position from the air, with success.

In May, El Jeriro returned to the charge and attacked M'ter again, but he now infiltrated deeply behind the Spanish lines, through Beni Said (Beni Hosmar) until he reached the southern outskirts of Tetuán (El Haus), attacking Ben Karrich and Buharrax. Then, Jeriro destroyed the cavalry of the Mehala of Tetuán in Tafugal. The harkas of Haddi Ben Azus, the one of Abd el-Krim ben Siam, from Messuar, and the one of Al-luz Addu Ali, from Bocoya, coming from the Central Rif, also joined this offensive. M'hammed, brother of Abd el-Krim (who had studied in Madrid under a scholarship), concentrated his harka in Beni Malaa, near Tazza (Beni Zeyyel), in Lau. On 14 June, Mohammed Azerkan, 'El Pajarito' (Little Bird), Abd el-Krim's cousin, attacked Tiguisas or Taguesut, further south, on the same river. On 30 June, Tazza was attacked also, being rescued by a column of General Federico Grund, who commanded in the sector, including the 5th and 6th Banderas under Lieutenant Colonel Franco, a tabor of Regulares of Tetuán, and air support. Thus, the Spanish defensive positions along the River Lau that ran almost from the sea to Xauén, between Beni Said and Beni Ziat, were constantly attacked, and again and again the Spanish shock troops (Legión, Regulares and Mehalas) had to march to rescue them.[3]

the south, and the Ceuta column would attack from the north, under the command of General Marzo, with 9,000 soldiers. After heavy rains, the first column arrived together 7 May at Haddadim, killing Hamido Succan, and then taking Tazarut, though the head of the 1st Regulares Group of Tetuán, Lieutenant Colonel Santiago González Tablas, died in the assault. Even so, El Raisuni managed to escape again with a dozen followers, arriving at Mount Buhaxen, being strafed by the Spanish air force. At the same time, General Sanjurjo, to the south of Beni Arós, put an end to the last resistance in Ajmás kabyle. When all seemed lost again for El Raisuni, the new Protectorate Commissioner, General Burguete, reached an agreement with him on 25 September, whereby he was given back his properties in exchange for cooperating with Madrid to subdue the Yebala. Once again, El Raisuni had been saved at the last minute. Once the area was pacified, the new 6th Bandera of the Legión, formed in September, was sent to Melilla.[2]

Air and Land Forces Saving Kobba Darsa

The first action that endangered the whole defensive line was an apparently minor one, at Kobba Darsa or Cobba D'Arsaa (Beni Ziat).

Table 5: Forces in the Defence of Xauén
Probable initial forces
3rd Mehala of Larache
4th Mehala of Tetuán
3rd, 5th, and 6th Banderas of the Legión
1st Group of Regulares of Tetuán
2nd Group of Regulares of Larache
1st Group Regulares of Ceuta
69th Serrallo Regiment
60th Ceuta Regiment
49th Otumba Regiment
51st Vizcaya Regiment
76th Victoria Regiment
Battalion of the 77th Military Orders Regiment
Battalion of the 72nd Jaén Regiment
Battalion of the 63 Mahón Regiment
18th Talavera Cazadores Battalion
12th Segorbe Cazadores Battalion
9th Arapiles Cazadores Battalion
4th Barbastro Cazadores Battalion
6th Figueras Cazadores Battalion
Reinforcements
July 1924 (mainly from Melilla)
1st Bandera of the Legión
15th Ceriñola Cazadores Battalion[4]
Battalion of the 15th Extremadura Regiment
5th Regulares of Alhucemas Group (four tabors)
Reserve Brigade (from Almería)
1st Barcelona Cazadores Battalion
4th Estella Cazadores Battalion
3rd or 5th Alfonso XII Cazadores Battalion
6th Reus Cazadores Battalion
Reinforcements Middle August 1924:
Castro Girona Brigade
Expeditionary Battalion of 6th Saboya Regiment
Expeditionary Battalion of 31st Asturias Regiment
Expeditionary Battalion of 2nd La Reina Regiment
Expeditionary Battalion of 34th Granada Regiment
Reinforcements September 1924:
2nd and 4th Banderas of the Legión
Battalion of 41st Gravelines Regiment
Battalion of 46th España Regiment
Battalion of 5th Infante Regiment
Battalion of 37th Murcia Regiment
Expeditionary Battalion of 75th Segovia Regiment
Expeditionary Battalion of 16th Castilla Regiment
Expeditionary Battalion of 27th Cuenca 27 Regiment
2nd Mountain Artillery Regiment

M'hammed (left), brother of Abd el-Krim (centre), was an engineering graduate in Madrid, and the commander of Riffian forces in the west in 1924–25 that led the offensive against the French during this last year. (SHD, Courcelle et Marmié)

This was a position without water of its own, defended by a mere 42 soldiers of the Serrallo Regiment, 16km from the mouth of the River Lau. The post was surrounded on 26 June. On 30 June or 2 July (the sources disagree), an attempt was made to supply it by air, but the aircraft of Sergeant Julio Pina García and the observer Lieutenant Manuel Bonet Ullet was shot down by Riffian fire, killing both. On 1 July, a battalion from the Ceriñola Regiment landed at the mouth of the Lau (Beni Said) to rescue the position, but it was repulsed with 199 casualties. The 1st Bandera of the Legión, a battalion of the Extremadura Regiment, those of the Serrallo, Otumba, Ceriñola, and Vizcaya Regiments, and several Tabors, mainly from Melilla, were sent as reinforcements. Then, two relief columns were organised under Lieutenant Colonel Serrano Orive (whose usual command was the Ceuta Regiment) and General Grund with part of these forces.

On 2 July the advance began with strong air support from all available aircraft. These aircraft also had to supply the defenders. To get the necessary airframes, an expeditionary group of novice Breguet pilots from Melilla made their debut, landing in Tetuán. They took off for the sector of Kobba Darsa, on 1 July, just arrived from the eastern front and exhausted. In total, up to five aircraft were shot down trying to rescue the position, and at least one pilot was killed in these very dramatic operations to save the outpost. The Breguet XIX of the squadron commander, Captain Joaquín González Gallarza, was one of the aircraft shot down, although he was able to reach the Spanish lines. On the 3rd, four aircraft from Sania Ramel, Tetuán, managed to drop several parcels on the position, a remarkable achievement to hit a rectangle barely 15 metres long. The aircraft under captains Ruiz de Alda and Mariano Barberán suffered many hits but managed to land at Uad Lau. On the 5th another air mission was organised, and again the aircraft of captains González Gallarza and Ochando Chumillas was hit, now with both pilots wounded, although they were able to land with the machine more or less serviceable. On the other hand, the two

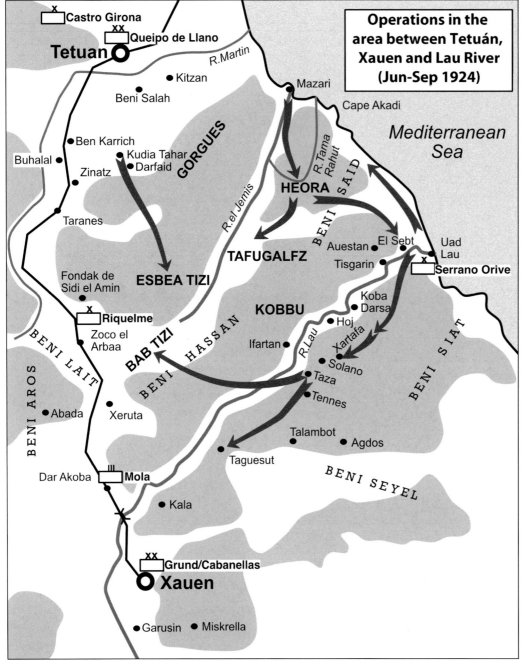

Operations in the area between Tetuán, Xauen and Lau River (Jun–Sep 1924)

(Map by Mark Thompson)

On the 4th, the new Commandant General of Ceuta District, General Luis Bermúdez de Castro, arrived in Uad Lau and went on to personally direct the operation. The column on the right, under García Fuentes with a cavalry squadron of the Mehala, two tabors of Regulares, a battalion from the Ceuta Regiment, another from the Serrallo, and two batteries, and the one on the left, under Lieutenant Colonel Enrique Nieto with the 1st Bandera of the Legión, 400 novice Legiónnaires of the Instruction Group, a squadron of Regulares from Ceuta, a battalion each from the Vizcaya, Otumba, and Ceriñola regiments, a howitzer group and two batteries, resumed the advance, both being coordinated by General Serrano Orive. The harka commanded by El Jeriro and M'hammed Abd el-Krim had concentrated in the area, answering with heavy fire. Covered by machine guns, the Legión rushed across the Lau with water up to their chests, taking a high mountain to the right of Cheruda after suffering 330 casualties, but they had not yet managed to liberate Kobba D'Arsaa. The columns of García Uría and General Grund (based at Adgós) also moved in conjunction with this attack. From the south, they advanced to Taza, also following the river.

aircraft piloted by Villalba and Díaz Trenchuelo, and by Esteve and Florencio were shot down, the latter in Tisgarín.

Lieutenant Colonel Franco pointing to an enemy position. (Gárate Córdoba)

Franco's 5th Bandera broke away from him and was sent by sea to the north, to Uad Lau. On the 6th, at 1400, General Serrano's whole column crossed the river again, and with Lieutenant Colonel Franco in the vanguard, a bayonet charge dispersed the Riffians and entered the post, saving it.[5]

The Lau Line, Perforated

In any case, seeing the intensity of the fighting, the 5th Alhucemas Group with four tabors under Cuban Colonel Temprano Domingo was sent from Melilla to Serrano Orive's column. Also, a Reserve Brigade with battalions of the Barcelona, Estella, Alfonso XIII and Reus Cazadores was being formed in Almería under General José Riquelme, who was also a personal friend of Abd el-Krim. In the meantime, on the lower River Lau was Serrano's column, and on the upper River Lau was Grund's column in Taguesut. At the same time, the area of Xauén, further to the south-west, was controlled by Colonel Virgilio Cabanellas (brother of the deposed General of Brigade Miguel Cabanellas). This sector consisted of a 50km line

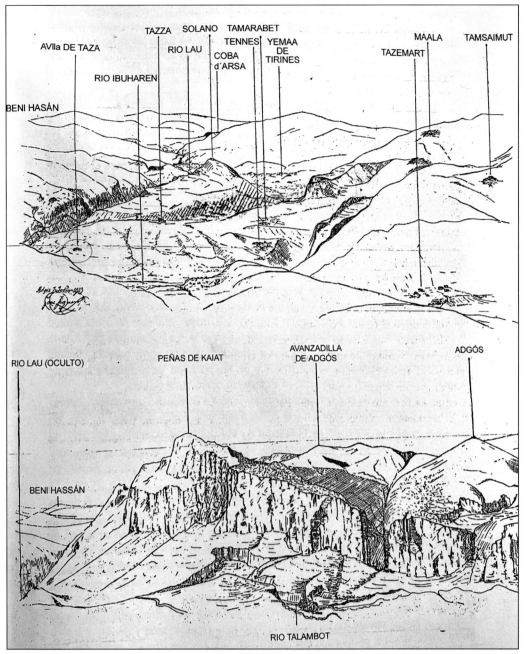

Sketches of the hills surrounding the posts of Adgós, Taza, Kobba d'Arsaa and the River Lau. (Fernández Riera)

from east to west between Agdós and Bad Haaman, and 40km from north to south between Miskrella and Fondadillo, adding some 10,000 soldiers including the 6th Bandera of the Legión, the 2nd Tetuán Tabor or the Talavera Battalion, amongst others. To the north, the just arrived 'Almería Column' or Reserve Brigade under General Riquelme was deployed in Zoco el Arbaá de Beni Hassan. Several units were deployed to defend the constantly attacked road: a tabor of Larache in Hámara, another one near Zoco, and a third one, a battalion of Military Orders in Ramla, at the middle of the road. [6]

In August, the Riffians of El Jeriro were already acting through Beni Hosmar and Beni Hassan, just south of Tetuán, in the rear of the River Lau line, a still active but useless line, with dozens of blockhouses and troops tied to protect it, like a hole-filled Gruyère cheese that was only able to supply Xauén from the sea. Also, the road that linked Tetuán and Xauén was still held by the Spanish, but the rest of the territory was controlled by the enemy. Beni Said and Sumata now defected to the rebels and in Beni Arós, Beni Gorfet, Beni Ider, and Wad Ras to the west of Xauén and Tetuán, a partial

Machine gun section of the Legión in Zoco el Arbaá of Beni Hassan. (Carrasco & de Mesa)

The post at Uad Lau, on the coast, that controlled all the River Lau line posts. (Fernández Riera)

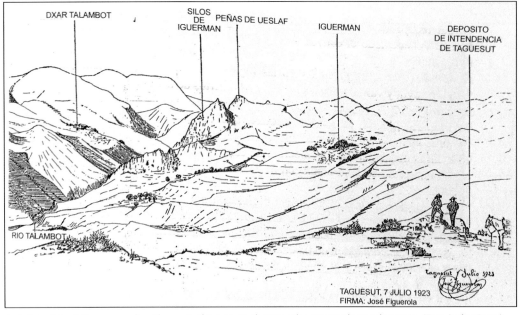
A sketch of the hills surrounding the post of Taguesut, showing the extremely rough terrain. (Fernández Riera)

from Spain. Meanwhile, an expedition was organised on the 17th to rid the village of Beni Hassan of rebels: from the north, General Riquelme with a tabor from Ceuta, Larache and Tetuán and the cavalry of the Victoria Regiment, later reinforced by battalions from Jaén and Ceuta, would fall on Bad Tizzi, east of Zoco el Arbaá. General Serrano Orive with the Arapiles and Barbastro battalions, a squadron of Regulares and a mehala, moved further north, landing at Cape Mazari (Beni Hosmar), east of Tetuán, and from there would go south to Emsa (Beni Said). Lieutenant Colonel Franco with the 1st and 5th Banderas of the Legión with 1,068 Legiónnaires, and two tabors of Alhucemas, would march north to Beni Said from the south at Uad Lau, on the mouth of the river, to join General Serrano Orive.

In the end the columns converged on Emsa, with the exception of General Riquelme's column, that with his recruits of the Almería/Reserve Brigade was repulsed and had to return. While this expedition failed to clear the

uprising took place. At the same time, Spanish positions began to be attacked: Chentafa was burned and abandoned by its defenders. Others, such as Xeruta (Beni Said) and Dar Akoba (El Ajmás), on the Tetuán-Xauén road, were continuously attacked and relieved at the cost of heavy casualties. The 25,000 Spaniards in Yebala and Gomara were tied to their lines and constantly attacked. Xauén was also surrounded from August.

The next significant Riffian attack was at Agdós, a rainy, misty eagle's nest, so inhospitable that not even the rats visited it, and which covered the post of Taguesut, further down the line of the Wadi, north-east of Xauén. In Agdós there were 700 soldiers from a tabor of the 2nd Larache Group and part of the Segorbe Battalion; and in Taguesut, were the forces of Lieutenant Colonel Permuy with the 6th Bandera of the Legión, the 1st Tabor of the Regulares of Ceuta and part of the Segorbe Battalion. General Serrano Orive continuously led convoys to supply the position, escorted by the Regulares of Alhucemas, as well as Grund's troops from Xauén, and Riquelme's soldiers, which marched to Dar Akobba. The post of Tazza, further north of Taguesut but on the same line, was supplied by convoys from the Serrallo Regiment and the Alhucemas Regulares.

When the Beni Said uprising took place on 11 August, the Riffians attacked Colonel Permuy's post at Taguesut. The Ifartan post was annihilated with its 50 Regulares. Seeing the expansion of the revolt, on the 12th General Castro Girona's Brigade of expeditionary battalions from Saboya, Asturias, La Reina and Granada departed

rear of Riffians, another Spanish position, Chentafa or Xartafa – held by 41 soldiers of the Vizcaya Regiment – on the River Lau (Beni Siat), fell. In the meantime, General Serrano Orive with Franco's 3rd and 5th Banderas, three Alhucemas tabors, and the Ceuta, Ceriñola and Mahón battalions, continued his clearing operation on the 20th, now covering the entire north bank of the River Lau from its mouth, being able to relieve Hoj (Beni Siat) after heavy fighting. Then, Serrano Orive was pinned down without being able to relieve the Taza post, further south, which fell.

The Solano outpost, defended by elements of the Vizcaya Regiment, closer to General Serrano Orive's forces, was also under attack. To save the outpost until help could arrive, on 21 August a squadron of Breguet XIVs under Captain Capaz took off to drop ice blocks to it. Capaz's rear aircraft, which was to protect him on his mission, was Breguet No. 114 under Corporal Gómez del Barco, with Ensign Iruretagoyena as observer. On reaching Solano, Gómez del Barco strafed the Riffian trenches, which responded to the fire. Not being deterred, del Barco descended and made a low pass to draw all the enemy fire to him, being hit several times, but then, with the Riffians distracted, Captain Capaz managed to drop the ice blocks. Del Barco was hit in the temple and through the shoulder, but he did not cease in his work until the mission was over, for which he won the Laureate. On the 26th, an aircraft under Díaz Sandino, future commander of Republican aviation in Barcelona during the Civil War, managed to drop some packages to them, but

Table 6: Groups of Columns defending Xauén and thr River Lau Line (June–15 September)			
Date	**Commanding officer**	**Location**	**Composition/notes**
June – 1 September	General Grund	Xauén–Taguesut–Upper Lau–Dar Akoba	10,000 men in August. Relieved by Colonel Cabanellas on 1 September
Mid-August	General Queipo de Llano	Tetuán	Commander Ceuta District. Relief column to Riquelme, 6 September: three Banderas of the Legión, two tabors of Regulares de Ceuta, Mehalas of Larache and Tetuán, squadron of Regulares, machine guns Infante and Murcia Battalions, Expeditionary Battalions of Segovia, Castilla, Cuenca, Saboya regiments (3,600 men)
August– mid-September	General Riquelme	Road Tetuán to Dar Akoba	Reserve Brigade from Almería: August: tabor from Ceuta, Larache and Tetuán Regulares, cavalry of the Victoria Eugenia Regiment, Jaén and Ceuta battalions 1 September (near destroyed): España, Ceuta and Military Orders battalions, squadron of Regulares
August	General Serrano Orive	Uad Lau: River Lau Line	Franco's 3rd and 5th Banderas, three Alhucemas Tabors, and the Ceuta, Ceriñola and Mahón battalions
Mid-August	General Castro Girona	Ceuta-Tetuán	Mid-August: Brigade (Saboya, Asturias, La Reina and Granada Expeditionary Battalions)
24 August	Lieutenant Colonel Mola	Dar Akoba	Under Grund, then Cabanellas: 1,062 soldiers (1st Tabor of Tetuán, 4th of Larache, Figueras Battalion, a battery)

the aircraft was riddled with bullets and it crashed on landing.[7] In the meantime, General Serrano Orive made another push to reach Solano, but the Riffian fire was tremendous: a company of the 1st Bandera was reduced from 83 to 36 soldiers in minutes. Unable to be rescued and despite all these efforts from land and air, the Solano position finally fell, though held to the last man. Alarmed by the situation, Aizpuru appointed General Queipo de Llano to command the Ceuta District.

A new column was then formed under Lieutenant Colonel Mola, which was to defend Dar Akoba (El Ajmás), on the southern stretch of the Tetuán road, near Xauén, with 1,062 soldiers from the 1st Tabor de Tetuán, 4th de Larache, the Figueras Battalion, and a battery from St Chamond, and relieve General Riquelme's troops that were there. From Dar Akoba Mola would also have to take care of the mountains surrounding Xauén, to the south, and the position of Abada, isolated to the north-west, in Beni Hassan, where there were a handful of men from the Madrid Battalion. On the upper River Lau, General Grund was relieved by Colonel Cabanellas, included Mola's forces at Xauén and Taguesut. Meanwhile the revolt spread through the Spanish rear, and on 1 September, Alalex (Wad Ras), west of Tetuán, fell, only one soldier from the Granada Battalion surviving.[8]

Destruction of Riquelme's Column and the DH.4 Rolls Group

In September, the withdrawal plan in the western area devised by General Primo de Rivera began to be executed. The idea was to reduce the front to free the needed battalions for other sectors. The line would be moved to more to the rear, abandoning Xauén but keeping Tetuán, with the new frontline being called the Estella Line. The line roughly followed the shape of the western coast of the Protectorate, several dozen kilometres in parallel to the shore in the interior, from Alcazarquivir, in the south-west, north to the Tangier International Zone, then turning west to reach Tetuán, and from there to the sea. Again, the Spaniards were planning another retreat while under the attacks of the Riffians, as happened to Silvestre in Annual. Xauén, the white and holy city of the Rif, never

trodden by any foreigner until the arrival of the Spaniards, was a village submerged in a cauldron surrounded by mountains, a mortal trap. Would another disaster befall in Xauén, as happened in the cauldron of Annual?

To facilitate the rally operation several battalions were sent from the Peninsula. Two brigades had already arrived, and the 2nd, 3rd and 4th Banderas of the Legión were also sent. Thanks to El Raisuni,

General Riquelme observing the enemy lines. He was on the brink of disaster in the Xauén campaign, having to jump into a truck through a window, but he later redeemed himself in the Larache sector. He was one of the few *Africanistas* who sided with the Republicans in the Civil War. (Fernández Riera)

The post of Ben Karrich, near Tetuán, protecting the city and used as a base to bomb the enemy or to launch offensives. (Fernández Riera)

Rio Martín camp, near Tetuán. (Fernández Riera)

Saboya Regiments, adding up to 3,600 men. A tractor-trailer was also used to carry seven armoured units to transport the supply convoy and evacuate the wounded. At 1400, Queipo de Llano's column arrived at Zinat, and General Riquelme began the withdrawal of his units. Casualties were heavy, and the Legión alone lost 153 men out of its 1,582 soldiers. Queipo then left two batteries of the 2nd Mountain Artillery Regiment at Ben Karrich to support the withdrawal, but Riquelme's soldiers disbanded, and Riquelme himself had to enter the tractor-trailer through a window. Queipo's sardonic description of Riquelme's actions undoubtedly drove a wedge between the two men, and it is not surprising that they ended up on opposite sides in the Civil War. Paradoxically, both would be dismissed for this campaign.[10]

On the brink of disaster, due to the delicate nature of these operations, Tetuán received as reinforcement the entire 3rd Rolls Group of DH.4s of Commandant Carrillo. This commander chose as the Group's motto 'Al toro!' (To the Bull!), later used by a rebel aviation group in 1936 and afterwards. Nevertheless, this air group was near destroyed in the operations launched to save Riquelme's forces and then to supply Xauén: on 4 September, Commandant Carrillo's own observer, Captain Orduña, was killed in flight, and in the following days Commandant García García, captains Altolaguirre and Luengo, and two NCO machine-gunners also fell in combat. On the 28th the leader of the Group himself, Commandant Carrillo, and his machine gunner, Sergeant Amat, were killed in action. In all these actions there was the surprising circumstance that the aircraft were hit from above, as the Riffians were higher up in the hills. This was more evidence and further examples of 'flying in the Spanish way'.[11]

the Beni Arós kabyles and part of Ajmás were open to collaborate with the withdrawal. In any case, on 1 September the rebels again attacked the positions on the outskirts of Tetuán, just south of the Martín River: at Beni Salah, the troopers from the Saboya Regiment were needed to rescue the post. On the 2nd, a convoy of 1,000 men of the La Reina Battalion and the 3rd Bandera of the Legión, which was to supply the positions of Gorgues (Beni Hosmar), south of Tetuán, was badly defeated with even the Legión's troopers panicking and losing 175 soldiers out of 352. The next day, another supply convoy of the Gravelinas Battalion departing from Ben Karrich, also south of Tetuán, was destroyed, losing 55 dead and two machine guns. In the opposite direction, General Riquelme with the España, Ceuta and Military Orders battalions, and a squadron of Regulares departed from Zoco el Arbaá of Benis Hassan and was attacked the same day, not being able to reach Ben Karrich. Riquelme's column had to shut up in Zinat, halfway on the road to Tetuán, to survive. Only the action of Commandant Beorlegui, managed to save the artillery.[9] However, General Riquelme was still surrounded, so General Queipo de Llano organised a rescue column on the 6th from Tetuán, made of three Banderas of the Legión, two tabors of Regulares of Ceuta, the Mehalas of Larache and Tetuán, a squadron of Regulares, the machine guns of the Infante and Murcia battalions, and the expeditionary battalions of the Segovia, Castilla, Cuenca and

4

1924: Leaving Xauén

The Beginning of the Withdrawal

The populations of the hostile kabyles were bombarded to dissuade them from attacking the Spaniards. Then, on 6 September, the River Lau line began to be dismantled. To evacuate the 700 men of Permuy's command in Agdós and Taguesut (Beni Zeyyel), two converging columns were moved, one under Colonel Cabanellas, from Xauén, to the south-east, and other under Lieutenant Colonel Mola, from Dar Akobba, in the south-west. At the same time, the forces of the eagles' nest of Agdós would leave the position at night, taking advantage of the fog, to join Taguesut's forces. Mola's forces, with the 4th Tabor of Larache and the Figueras Cazadores Battalion arrived in sight of the Taguesut post, and Permuy's troops abandoned it. The 6th Bandera of the Légion remained inside the fort covering them, and then it departed with Lieutenant Colonel Mola, in turn helped by the 1st of Regulares of Tetuán and the Queen Victoria Eugenia Cazadores cavalry squadron. The operation resulted in 200 casualties. However, distracted by this operation Lieutenant Colonel Mola was not able to rescue the position of Abada, isolated to the north-west of Dar Akkoba, defended by 22 soldiers of the Madrid Cazadores Battalion. Meanwhile Lieutenant Colonel Franco, to the north, was preparing a reserve force to cover further withdrawals at Ben Karrich, near Tetuán, with the 2nd, 3rd and 4th Banderas of the Légion. On 8 September the retreat continued with the evacuation by sea of 800 soldiers and six cannons from the post of M'ter, at the mouth of the River Lau.[1]

Clearing El Fondak (Wad Ras)

As we have already mentioned, the rebellion had spread deep into the Spanish rear, in Wad Ras, west of Tetuán. As we have already seen, El Fondak of Ain Jedida (see Volume 1) was a major crossroads linking Tánger (Tangier), Ceuta and Larache with Tetuán, so it was extremely important to clear and take El Fondak. Thus, Lieutenant General Primo de Rivera ordered a pause in the evacuation of Xauén and decided to attack now against Wad Ras. General Castro Girona's column with a Bandera, a tabor, Mehala and several battalions would lead the left wing, which was to occupy El Harcha and Mount Cónico, where a position had been held for more than 10 days by a sergeant of the Granada Battalion; and then, General Queipo de Llano's column with Franco's 2nd and 4th Banderas, four companies of Regulares of Ceuta, and the Saboya Battalion, on the right, which was to take El Fondak.

These two columns would leave from Laucién, in the north-western peaks of Tetuán. A third column under General Riquelme, with units of the Légion, would remain as a reserve. In the opposite direction, almost on the border with the Tangier Zone, a column under Lieutenant Colonel Irigoyen would depart from the west, at R'Gaia. General Castro Girona took Mount Cónico on 11 September and going further west buried the corpses from the razed position of Alalex. General Queipo advanced to the Harcha, and entered the gorge leading to El Fondak, contacting with Irigoyen's column on the 12th. Then, Queipo assaulted El Fondak on the 13th. However, Primo de Rivera reprimanded Queipo for the way he placed several posts, which increased the animosity between them. To make matters worse, Primo assigned General Riquelme to the post of Commandant General of the Larache District (with the 2nd Bandera of the Légion), a post Queipo de Llano aspired to.[2] During these days, on 21 September, according to Queipo the wily Franco tempted him with the proposition of a coup to bring about the fall the dictator Primo de Rivera.[3]

Mola in Dar Akkoba

Meanwhile, returning to the sector of the Tetuán-Xauén road, to the east, the situation was getting more and more serious. The forces of Xauén, Dar Akkoba and Zoco el Arbaá were cut off from each other by the Riffians who had intercepted the road. In Dar Akkoba, a little to the north-west of Xauén, Lieutenant Colonel Emilio Mola was trying to defend his position and at the same time to help the many positions that surrounded him: Kalaa Alto (Upper Kalaa) and Kalaa Bajo (Lower Kalaa), to the south-east. His situation was desperate, and Colonel Cabanellas left Xauén with a column, and then, reinforced, with three columns, to rescue both Kalaas on 8 September, and again on the 12th. During these operations, 'the brave Permuy', in Lieutenant Colonel Mola's words, died, and the columns failed due to the rough terrain. The Riffian attacks extended to Xeruta, on the road north of Dar Akkoba. Zoco el Arbaá's column hoped that Lieutenant Colonel Mola would also come to its aid, but that was too much. On the 13th even Mola's own position, in the area of Pilón de Azúcar, to the north, was attacked. The Riffian

El Fondak de Ain Yedida, a crossroads between Ceuta, Tánger (Tangier), Larache and Tetuán, and one of the main bases of El Raisuni that was conquered by General Queipo de Llano's Spaniards. (Fernández Riera)

Lieutenant Colonel Mola of the Regulares was one the finest soldiers during the Rif War. He stood in Dar Akobba until being relieved by Franco, and then commanded brilliantly some of the columns of the final campaigns in 1926 in Axdir, and 1927 in Ketama, Senhaja and Gomara. Deposed for being anti-Republican (he had to manufacture toys to survive, then was reinstated in 1934), he would organise the 1936 rebellion as the 'Director' (efficiently but, coldly, also defending a policy of terror to freeze his enemies) and would lead the Army of the North until he died in an aircraft accident when he was going to conquer Bilbao. (De la Cierva)

operations were probably directed by the engineer M'hammed, Abd el-Krim's brother, who managed to build a line of trenches as far as Dar Akkoba. These trenches left the 4th Tabor isolated from the rest of the position, after the tabor had made a sortie, and so, Mola had to make another sortie and assault the enemy trenches, to make an escape route for them.

Meanwhile, Colonel Cabanellas was still blocked without being able to rescue Kalaa Bajo, so he desperately sent NCO Baltasar Munar Munar with 16 Legiónnaires with backpacks full of water and hand bombs to infiltrate between the Riffian lines, and incredibly they succeeded. At the same time, the 6th Bandera of the Legión and the Regulares rose up 'like the flow of a spring' in the words of Colonel Cabanellas, and covered the remaining 200 or 300 metres, attracting enemy fire, which allowed the rest of the column to advance and save the position. Munar won the Laureate. Even so, the casualties were very high, many more than those of the rescued position (133 men fell from the Legión alone).[4]

Dar Akkoba and Xauén, however, were still isolated and surrounded by enemies. On the 15th Lieutenant Colonel Mola recovered the so-called Pilón de Azúcar (Sugar Pylon), north of Akkoba, assaulting it with the 2nd Tabor of Larache. From there, Mola would have to supply 'Loma Verde', even further north. Near running out of ammunition, with only enough for one day of combat, Mola luckily received a convoy from Xauén to the south on the 16th. In the meantime, the Pilón de Azúcar was recovered by the Moors.

Lieutenant Colonel Mola on the Verge of Suicide

Meanwhile, once again Kalaa Bajo was under attack and had to be rescued. To do so, Colonel Cabanellas would also count on Lieutenant Colonel Mola's column, which would descend towards the River Lau. This manoeuvre was very risky, as it implied weakening Dar Akobba at the moment when it was under heavy pressure. The fall of Dar Akobba would provoke the fall of Xauén,

as the road that supplied the holy city would be cut off. Lieutenant Colonel Mola, seeing that even his native troops were on the verge of insubordination, refused to obey, threatening to commit suicide, although he explained the reasons. Then Colonel Cabanellas, who was no fool, revoked the order. Thus, on the 17th Colonel Cabanellas marched alone, and his central force of the Regulares of Tetuán under Lieutenant Colonel Martínez Monje, managed to enter Kalaa Bajo after suffering 109 casualties. In any case, the troops of the Figueras Cazadores Battalion remained in the position, which had to be rescued again on the 29th.

Table 7: Forces in Xauén (September–December 1924)
3rd Mehala of Larache
4th Mehala of Tetuán
5th Regulares of Alhucemas Group
Mehala of Xauén
Harka of Xauén
Harka Muñoz Grandes of Melilla
1st, 2nd, 3rd, 4th, 5th and 6th Banderas of the Legión
1st Group of Regulares of Tetuán
4th Group of Regulares of Larache
3rd Group Regulares of Ceuta
69th Serrallo Regiment
60th Ceuta Regiment
49th Otumba Regiment
Battalion of the 77th Military Orders Regiment
Battalion of the 63rd Mahón Regiment
Battalion of the 68th Las Palmas de Gran Canaria Regiment
Battalion of the 73rd Badajoz Regiment
Battalion of the 55th Asia Regiment
Battalion of the 47th San Quintín Regiment
Battalion of the 10th Córdoba Regiment
Battalion of the 41st Gravelines Regiment
Battalion of the 74th Valladolid Regiment
Battalion of the 36th Burgos Regiment
Expeditionary Battalion of the 6th Saboya Regiment
Expeditionary Battalion of the 16th Castilla Regiment
Expeditionary Battalion of the 27th Cuenca Regiment
Expeditionary Battalion of the 34th Granada Regiment
Cavalry squadron of the Victoria Eugenia Cazadores
15th Ceriñola Cazadores Battalion
18th Talavera Cazadores Battalion
12th Segorbe Cazadores Battalion
3rd San Fernando Cazadores Battalion[5]
1st Cazadores Brigade
9th Arapiles Cazadores Battalion
4th Barbastro Cazadores Battalion
6th Figueras Cazadores Battalion
1st Madrid Cazadores Battalion
11th Llerena Cazadores Battalion

The Regulares of Tetuán remained protecting Xauén in Kalaa Alto and had to be supplied by climbing the slopes daily with 100 buckets of water. Meanwhile, the three batteries of Xauén had been reduced to just one, and of the 32 machine guns only 10 remained. The food rations were reduced to 100 grams of bread daily. The Spanish garrison of the holy city was formed by the 6th Bandera of the Legión, several tabors of the Tetuán and Larache Groups, the Mehala of Xauén, and the Cazadores battalions of Arapiles, Figueras, Talavera. The garrison also had the remains of the Gravelinas Battalion that had been defeated under Riquelme in the fighting at Ben Karrich, next to Tetuán, but had managed to reach Xauén.[6]

Although the situation at Xauén was desperate, it still had to take care of the small garrisons that surrounded it. The small garrisons of Magó, located to the south-east of Xauén, on the peaks that protected it, at 1,061 metres, were 'real eagles' nests, simple shelters placed among rocks with sheets and lights [...] wrapped in snow; to reach them was pure mountaineering', as stated Colonel Cabanellas. 'The loads [of supplies] had to be carried on shoulders, climbing a long way from the bottom of the ravine.' The Magó post fell on the 24th, and then that of Peñas Bajas del Magó, after the heads of the defenders of the previous post were thrown at them. Its garrison was able to escape by descending to Magó nº 1. Magó nº 2 was literally hanging on the middle of a cliff, and had also to be abandoned by its garrison of the Madrid Battalion. On the other hand, the blockhouse Magó nº 2 (despite its name, a different post from the previous one), defended by the Llerena Battalion, held until the final evacuation. These positions had to protect that at Miskrella, located in the plain. Halfway was Cudia el Gazoli, 860 metres away, which was rescued on the 26th by a column of Lieutenant Colonel Muñoz Barredo consisting of the Talavera Battalion, two tabors of Tetuán and the Mehala of Xauén, the friendly harka of Xauén, and two batteries, after a very fierce fight. Only the 6th Bandera of

the Legión was left in reserve. In Mura Tahar, Lieutenant Colonel Muñoz Barredo's column was attacked from the left, from the Magó posts. The Riffians were protected by a ravine parallel to the road. With the convoy stopped, in a desperate action Muñoz Barredo assaulted the gully with the 6th Bandera, throwing hand bombs, and managed to supply Mura Tahar and Miskrela nº 3. Nevertheless, after suffering 200 casualties he was not able to continue advancing. On the positive side, the Riffians also suffered much damage and they were silent for several days after.[7]

To the Rescue of Dar Akkoba and Xauén

Meanwhile, to clear the threat that loomed over the Tetuán-Xauén road from the east, on the 18th General Castro Girona began an operation to clear the Gorgues massif area, in Beni Hosmar, reopening the road and lifting the siege of Dar Akobba and Xauén. Five columns departed from Tetuán: four of them, under General Queipo de Llano himself, attacked Gorgues massif from the front, just south of the city, and the fifth column, under General Castro Girona, would envelop the massif from the west, to attack the Moors from behind. The rightmost column of the frontal attack was that of Lieutenant Colonel José Molina with the Mehala of Tetuán, a tabor from Larache and the Cuenca Battalion, that would ascend 858 metres to take the abandoned blockhouses of Izarduy and Hafa el Ma; next came the column of Lieutenant Colonel La Viña with two Tabors from Ceuta and a Peninsular battalion, that would penetrate on the right side of the Barranco (ravine) de Mers; the Legión column under Lieutenant Colonel Franco with 4th and 5th Banderas of the Legión and the Reina Battalion, would go on the left side of the Barranco de Mers; and the fourth column, under Lieutenant Colonel Benigno Fiscer Tornero with the Mehala of Xauén, tabor of Ceuta, Battalion of Military Orders, and a squadron of Regulares, which would go down the Barranco (ravine) de Beni Salah, dominated by the Borch

Table 8: Groups of Columns relieving Xauén and Dar Akoba (18 September – 18 November)

Date	Commanding officer	Location	Composition/notes
1 September	Colonel, (later General) Cabanellas	Xauén–Taguesut–Upper Lau–Dar Akoba	Besieged. Relieved by Castro Girona and Serrano Orive
24 August	Lieutenant Colonel Mola	Dar Akoba	Under Cabanellas: 1st Tabor of Tetuán, 4th of Larache, Figueras Battalion, a battery (1,062 men)
Mid-August	General Queipo de Llano	Tetuán	Commander Ceuta District. Commands the relieving force for Xauén (18 September): Five columns from Tetuán: Lieutenant Colonel José Molina with Mehala of Tetuán, a tabor from Larache and the Cuenca Battalion. Lieutenant Colonel La Viña with two Tabors from Ceuta and a Peninsular battalion. The Legión column under Lieutenant Colonel Franco with 4th and 5th Banderas of the Legión and the Reina Battalion. Lieutenant Colonel Benigno Fiscer Tornero with Mehala of Xauén, Tabor of Ceuta, a Battalion of Military Orders, and a squadron of Regulares General Castro Girona with 3rd Bandera, and a tabor of Regulares from Alhucemas (also see below)
18 September	General Castro Girona	Tetuán–Dar Akoba–Xauén (interior line)	Part of Queipo's column. Relieves Dar Akoba with Regulares of Alhucemas, 1st and 3rd Banderas under Franco (1,169 men), Battalions of Arapiles, San Fernando and others, two batteries
18 September – 18 November	General Serrano Orive (killed when covering the withdrawal from Xauén)	Tetuán–Dar Akoba–Xauén (road, exterior line)	Part of Queipo's column Relieves Xauén
24 September	General Federico Berenguer	Tetuán to Dar Akoba–Xauén	Part of Queipo's column: Legión column: supports Castro Girona and Serrano Orive

face stone. General Queipo was obliged to execute a plan drafted by Lieutenant General Primo de Rivera that he disliked, since he would only have attacked with two reinforced columns, one by the Barranco del Mers, and another by Ben Karrich. Some commanders insinuated Queipo should arrest Primo de Rivera and to take the command…

Franco's column achieved its objectives with some difficulty, thanks to artillery support and machine guns from Tetuán. On his left, Fiscer Tornero's column was stopped at Beni Salah, leaving the vanguard of the Regulares de Ceuta, that was ascending the Borch ridge alone under Commandant Juan Mendoza Iradier. Mendoza almost succeeded, but died in the assault, and the whole tabor was annihilated with only 18 men escaping alive. The corpses were thrown by the Moors from the top of the rock. Meanwhile, Lieutenant Colonel Franco, on the 19th, after fortifying his positions, continued advancing on the 20th, with the 4th Bandera coming out of the Barranco and turning to attack it from the rear while the 5th Bandera assaulted the last crest of the front. At the same time, Castro Girona's column (3rd Bandera, and a tabor of Regulares from Alhucemas), that was to surround the Gorgues from the west, made its appearance climbing the crests of the massif from the back and joining the attackers from the north. The mountain was cleared and almost all of Beni Hosmar dominated. Then, the Barbastro Battalion was left as a garrison, which relieved the 200 soldiers of the Badajoz Battalion that were there.[8]

A view of the mountain of Beni Hosmar or Hozmar, with the smoke of the Spanish bombs impacting on the Riffian cannon that had been deployed by the Riffians to bombard Tetuán. (Gárate Córdoba)

The forces of Serrano Orive's column liberating Xauén. (Fernández Riera)

Now the advance had to continue further south, through Beni Hassan, to liberate Zoco el Arbaá and Xeruta, on the Tetuán-Xauén road. First, General Castro Girona cleared the mountains south of Beni Hosmar, on the height of Taranés, but as he moved forward at the pass of Dar Raid the Riffians set fire to the weeds and panic appeared among the 3rd Tabor of Regulares of Alhucemas. A young captain, the only one unharmed, forced the soldiers to return at gunpoint. He was no other than Heli Rolando Tella, future assailant of Madrid in 1936, who won the Laureate. In the end the Spaniards had to retreat after suffering many casualties, 122 in just the Legión.

In any case, on the 24th the advance continued as far as Keri-Kera and the Najela River. On the right was General Serrano Orive's Column, protecting the supply convoy at Zinat. On the 25th the two columns continued advancing towards the south, through the Najela valley: General Castro Girona's column through the interior, and General Serrano's column along the side of the road. They would be supported by a Legión column, under General Federico Berenguer. On the 26th, after leaving Taranés they entered Beni Hassan. From there, they threatened to liberate the distant isolated position of Buharraz, so the kabyles moved towards there, but then both Spanish columns continued the march until they reached Zoco el Arbaá, saving the garrison, which had been isolated since the disaster of General Riquelme. From there, several isolated posts to the west, at Ben Lait, were relieved.[9]

Then the columns continued to Xeruta, defended by 87 soldiers under Captain Francisco Rosaleny of the battalions of Córdoba and Madrid, which had been surrounded for a long time. On the 24th, Rosaleny had reached his limit and affirmed in a heliogram that they would hold out until the 25th, blowing up the ammunition depot

The Alcazaba or fortress of Xauén. (Fernández Riera)

'and leaving the Chief of the position in the fort.' That day the air force managed to drop some ice blocks to him, which enabled him to hold out for a few more days. From Zoco el Arbaá, General Castro Girona's column with the Regulares de Alhucemas, two Banderas of the Legión, the battalions of Arapiles, San Fernando and others, and two batteries, continued its advance, with a vanguard of 1,169 Legiónnaires of the 1st and 3rd Banderas under Lieutenant Colonel Franco. The position was surrounded and finally the Regulares squadrons reached Xeruta on the 28th. The moment was very exciting, as from the south at the same time Lieutenant Colonel Mola was able to advance and also arrived at the same moment, so Franco, Mola and Rosaleny met in a hug.

The casualties for the whole march from Tetuán had been extremely high: the Alhucemas Group of Regulares was a shadow of itself, its battalions being reduced by half, merging the 1st with the 3rd, and the 2nd with the 4th, and later, the whole Group was reduced to a single tabor. Meantime, General Serrano Orive's Column with a squadron of Regulares from Ceuta and the 3rd Tabor from Larache, surrounded Xeruta and continued to Dar Akkoba. Lieutenant Colonel Mola moved ahead to make contact with Serrano: Dar Akkoba had been saved at last. Meanwhile, General Berenguer covered the rear at Zoco el Arbaá. Finally, without a fight, General Serrano Orive resumed the advance and reached Xauén, being met on the way by General Cabanellas' troops on the 29th. Xauén had also been saved, although not entirely, as the troops that arrived were without supplies, which followed days after in a large convoy. However, there was a great rivalry between generals Serrano Orive and Castro Girona, both fighting for the greatest prestige. Serrano Orive, a kind and straightforward man, but of great temper

due to an ulcer that made him vomit blood, would later pay for it with his life.[10]

Xauén, Still Surrounded

Although Dar Akobba and Xauén were now protected with enough troops, there was still no food or water for them, as the convoy was marching behind. Until its arrival, the Spaniards dedicated themselves to clearing the road of enemies for the convoy and to rescue the surrounding garrisons. General Felipe Navarro, a survivor of Annual and Monte Arruit, released after the Spanish government paid a ransom to Abd el-Krim in 1923 (although he was the last of the Spaniards to leave the prison), was appointed as the new Commandant General of Ceuta District. Navarro went to Tetuán, where he held talks with generals Primo de Rivera and Aizpuru, and then marched escorted by Ovilo's column to Xauén.

Meanwhile, on 30 September General Castro Girona began an operation with Lieutenant Colonel Mola's forces to liberate the Abada blockhouse, which was still holding north-west of Dar Akobba. The column of Mola was reinforced with the Arapiles and Figueras battalions. They would march north along the road to Xeruta, and from there they would rescue the position by marching west, while protecting the supply convoy. Lieutenant Colonel Miaja,[11] in command of the San Fernando Battalion, was left to defend the camp. Another column was also organised under Lieutenant Colonel Losada to protect the area of Xeruta, to close off access to the road for Riffians of Beni Hassan and the lower Lau, and also protecting access to Abadda from the east. However, unexpectedly for Lieutenant Colonel Mola, the Moors had already crossed the road. Mola's column first had to cross a tree-covered ravine between Loma Verda and Loma Negra, north of Dar Akobba. The 2nd Tabor penetrated, but when Mola descended he found himself under attack. Fortunately, Franco's tabor of Alhucemas and Legión closed the ravine at its ends and trapped the Riffians there, recovering 87 corpses, three of them of Qaids. In this action Franco himself was shot at point blank range by a Riffian, but el Mizzián, an officer from the Regulares of Alhucemas, saved his life.[12] Franco then continued with his column of 1st and 3rd Banderas, Alhucemas Regulares and two batteries, to rescue Abadda, which had not received help since 23 August, more than a month earlier. This time, however, Franco did not reach the position in time, which had been destroyed and its occupants killed, except for 22 prisoners, by M'hammed Abd el-Krim and El Jeriro. M'hammed was organising a veritable army in his barracks at Talambot, grouping his soldiers under the command of officers bearing ranks, such as lieutenant and captain, in the European style.[13]

On 1 October General Castro Girona moved the 1st and 4th Tabors from Larache, and the Arapiles Battalion from Lieutenant Colonel Mola's command, to Xeruta, to defend the road at this point. Finally, the long-awaited supply convoy arrived on 5 October. Xauén was saved, but now it was necessary to evacuate the position without being destroyed. During the entire siege of Xauén in the period between 4 September and 5 October, the garrison had suffered 792 casualties, without counting defectors. The native troops had acquitted themselves very well, including the Mehala of Tetuán and the Xauén squadron, but, despite this, the Mehala of Xauén was completely disbanded as its base, Xauén, was going to be abandoned. Lieutenant Colonel Mola was then sent to rest with his troops to the rear, at Zoco el Arbaá, and General Castro Girona was reinforced with the Órdenes Militares Battalion.

Meanwhile the relief operations continued: first Buharrax (Beni Ider), south-west of Tetuán, defended by three companies from

A friendly harka in Tetuán, making a war dance. (Fernández Riera)

Soldiers of the Mehala de Tetuán in parade dress. (Carrasco & de Mesa)

The Tetuán Xalifian Guard escorting the Xafila. (Carrasco & de Mesa)

A view of the walls of Tetuán, on the northern side, showing the Ceuta Gate. (Fernández Riera)

the Ceuta and Granada Regiments, besieged since 27 August. It was supplied several times from the air with milk and ice blocks, although on one such mission the aircraft of Lieutenant Luis Luengo Muñoz and NCO David Gil was shot down, though Gil was saved by a sortie from the garrison. Colonel Ovido's column with the Tabor de Ceuta, battalions of the Asia, Las Palmas and Serrallo Regiments, and the harka of Melilla under Muñoz Grandes (future commander of the Blue Division in Russia), left Tetuán on 4 October, but did not arrive in time and Buharrax surrendered on the 10th, although the prisoners were correctly treated and evacuated to Tetuán. Adrú also fell, further west.

Meanwhile, further south around Xauén, the positions in Miskrella (to the south-east), were already stretched to the limit, having a mere glass of water per day. Miskrella nº 2 also fell on the 10th, and nº 3 retreated to Xauén, as did the Amegrí and Harrún posts. Meanwhile, the Group of Larache nº 4, under Lieutenant Colonel Mola was destined for its natural zone, to the south-west of the Protectorate for a truly deserved rest: the Regulares of Larache had suffered 1,291 casualties in the whole campaign; 50 percent of the unit. On 16 October General Castro Girona re-established the position of Miskrella nº 3, to connect the string of positions that were south of Xauén to the south bank of the river Lau.

At that time Spain had 121,000 soldiers in the whole Protectorate, 5,000 more than when Lieutenant Primo de Rivera staged the coup d'état in September 1923. So, it did not appear that his plans to abandon the war were working. On 16 October, Primo de Rivera deposed Aizpuru and took command of the High Protectorate himself to execute his planned evacuation without intermediaries. Finally, Primo de Rivera reorganised the entire western zone in preparation for the evacuation: the Larache District would remain under a general; Ceuta and Tetuán would report directly to the Ceuta Distric; General Castro Girona assumed the entire Xauén area; General Serrano Orive would take the sector from the Puente de Fomento, north of Xauén, to Hámara, in the central part of the Tetuán road; and General Federico Berenguer was to command the northern part of the road, as far as Ben Karrich, next to Tetuán. On 23 October Kalaa Alto (El Ajmás) was evacuated, and on the 25th, the seven surviving ghosts of Abadda Alto (Beni Ider) were also saved, earning several Laureadas. This post had miraculously survived thanks to rain in September.[14]

Franco, the Youngest General in Europe?

On 24 October, the withdrawal from Draa el Aseff and Bad el Hamman (defended by elements of the Llerena and San Quintín Battalions), and other 18 dependent positions, continued in the western end of El Ajmás (28km from Xauén). This retreat was made using two columns: one led by General Castro Girona, and the other from Alcazarquivir, to the west, already very close to the French line. General Berenguer hoped for the collaboration of French Commissioner Lyautey, but the latter, who despised the Spanish action in Morocco, did not bother to act. General Castro Girona left with a vanguard of the 1st, 4th and 6th Banderas under Lieutenant Colonel Franco, with the Regulares, and the Segorbe and Talavera Battalions. The expedition was carried out with Franco breaking the enemy resistance in the forest of Tenefa, the westernmost point of El Ajmás, liberating the garrisons. On returning at night, when Franco was covering the movement of Lieutenant Colonel Núñez de Prado's convoy, forming the rear-guard, the Riffian attack again took place on the left flank, the enemy harka descending from heights of up to 1,800 metres and harassing the convoy for kilometres until they reached Akarrat, close to the north bank of the river Lau. After evacuating this last position and entering Xauén, the 4th Bandera remained with bayonets fixed, covering the final withdrawal. At

Colonel Franco promoted to Brigade General in February 1926 for the merits of the October 1924 actions, becoming, at his 33, the youngest or one of the youngest Generals in Europe. (Gárate Córdoba)

Colonel Millán Astray, founder of the Legión, on horseback, talking with Colonel Góngora, commander of the Fondak column, moments before of being wounded and losing his left arm. (Fernández Riera)

Colonel Millán Astray, founder of the Legión and the Radio National of Spain, in a studio picture. This tough, mutilated and valiant soldier was also famous for his confrontation with the philosopher Miguel de Unanumo during the Civil War, shouting 'Death to the intellectuals!'. Paradoxically he fell in love with Rita, the cousin of another great philosopher, José Ortega y Gasset. Rita Gasset gave Millán Astray a daughter. Being trapped in an unconsummated marriage but do not wanting to repudiate his wife, Millán Astray took care of the girl as his niece and he also kept his relationship with Rita, but still he remained married. (Gárate y Córdoba)

that moment the Spaniards noticed the good quality of the Riffian trenches, which seemed to be made by professional sappers. The operation cost 125 casualties to the Legión, not counting the hundreds suffered by other units. For this action Franco was awarded the second Individual Merit Medal and would be promoted to Brigadier General (although not at this very moment, but later, on 3 February 1926), the youngest General in Europe, according to some, at the age of 33 on the date of his appointment. [15]

Meanwhile, the founder of the Legión, Millán Astray, still merely a lieutenant colonel, was promoted to colonel and sent to the Fondak of Ain Jedida, in Wad Ras, taking command of R'Gaia's column. The Yebala region was also in revolt: the column of General Saro was operating in Anyera, and that of Colonel José Góngora in Wad Ras. Then, Millán Astray joined the combat that Góngora's column was fighting on 26 October and was unfortunate that a bullet split the left humerus of the Legión's founder, it being necessary to amputate his arm for him to survive. This was his second combat wound (he would suffer up to four of them). Thus, Millán Astray would observe how his subordinate, Franco, gained in rank, and then surpassed him. Franco was controlling Astray's creation, the Legión, and would soon become a general, while he was still a colonel, and now

mutilated. Still, the friendship of these two men was never broken and remained for a lifetime.[16]

Abandoning Xauén

Finally, with most of the garrisons evacuated, preparations began to abandon Xauén. The five Banderas of the Legión (all except the 2nd) were concentrated in the city on 10 November under Lieutenant Colonel Franco. The outposts of Zoco el Arbaá were attacked, killing a cousin of Franco serving in the Battalion of Las Palmas de Gran Canaria. A few days before, on the 5th, with the operations paralysed by the rains, Primo de Rivera summoned all his generals (including Sanjurjo, now a General of Division, who, appointed again as General Commander of Melilla since May 1924 had come from there as his opinion was highly respected by Primo). The dictator informed the generals that the new Estella Line, in the rear, was being completed: in the Gorgues, south of Tetuán, by the General of Engineers García de la Herranz; by Alcazarquivir, by the column of Colonel García Boloix; and in R'Gaia, between Wad Ras and Tangier, by General Saro with the columns of Valdés and Góngora. With this new line 180 positions were going to be abandoned, so saving troops, half of them around Xauén.

Once the rear-guard was organised, on the 11th Uad Lau, at the mouth of the river, was evacuated. It was more complicated to withdraw the Sebt position, on the river, a little further south-west, but the Burgos Battalion managed to evacuate it by sea thanks to the help of General Saro's troops: the Regulares of Ceuta, the battalions of Mahón and Otumba, and the harka of Melilla under Muñoz Grandes, with 30 aircraft and naval assets for support,

General Serrano Orive, honest but hot tempered, was affected by a painful stomach ulcer. His rivalry with General Castro Girona led Serrano into a mad rush, relieving Xauén (Xaouén or Chefchaouen) but being was shot dead when he was evacuating the city. (Fernández Riera)

A machine gun section of the Regulares of General Castro Girona's column, in the Gorgues. (Fernández Riera)

disembarked in K barges (as used by the British Army in Gallipoli) on 15 November.[17]

The following night, the evacuation of Xauén began, directed by General Castro Girona. Castro Girona divided his forces between those who left, under the command of Lieutenant Colonel Núñez de Prado, and those who covered the rear (the five Banderas of Lieutenant Colonel Franco, with 2,006 men). On the 17th, only Franco's Legión remained inside, and placed straw dummies on the lookout posts and evacuated the city at dawn, at which time the 10,000 troops from Xauén were already in Dar Akoba, to the north, with the Legión in the rear, covering the retreat of the column. All these troops were marching towards Tetuán, step by step and in good order despite the constant Riffian firing, in the middle of a rainstorm. On the 18th, they arrived at Xeruta (Beni Hassan), marching very slowly to protect the large convoy. After leaving Xeruta, a large mass of Riffians began to concentrate near the village, so the 1st Bandera had to return to occupy it to protect the rear. At that moment, General Serrano Orive joined the rear-guard and a bullet struck his jugular vein, killing him on the spot. Thus ended his days the brave General, a rival of Castro Girona. He was a noble man whose ulcer made him foul-mouthed and hot tempered, and whose eagerness for promotion led him to expose himself too much. Meanwhile, the 1st Bandera was surrounded, so the Legión Captain Pablo Arredondo stayed behind with the 1st Company holding the line, his unit annihilated to the last man, although allowing his comrades to escape. He was awarded the Laureate.

The fighting continued along the road: near the Zoco el-Arbáa (Beni Hassan), the Riffians began to concentrate, and Colonel Claudio Temprano Domingo led a charge with the 3rd Squadron of Regulares of Ceuta that cleared the road again, in the process, the colonel died on horseback and won the Laureate.[18] That day alone the Legión suffered 200 casualties. In a few minutes, Commandants Carmona of the Regulares of Ceuta, and Losada of the Arapiles Battalion were killed. Then, a tremendous panic followed, with the Arapiles, the Regulares and even some Legiónnaires rushing into Zoco el-Arbáa. General Serrano Orive's replacement, General Federico Berenguer Fusté, was also wounded in the thigh when he left Zoco to help those returning. Thus, General Castro Girona had to take command of the entire Xauén column, now sheltered in Zoco el Arbaá, halfway to the Tetuán road. His grouping now included five Banderas of the Legión, the Regulares of Tetuán, Ceuta and Alhucemas, 22 infantry battalions, nine batteries, six squadrons, and three companies of engineers: in total some 12,000 soldiers. After this panic, the Disaster of Annual was once again in the air and on the mind of every soldier... [19]

After the disaster, the Spaniards remained for three weeks in Zoco el Arbaá, harassed by the Riffians, who, however, did not attack. The Moors were waiting for General Castro Girona's departure before firing again. In Europe, seeing another disaster, French Prime Minister Édouard Herriot and Britain's Neville Chamberlain discussed the recognition of the Republic of the Rif, something that was an aim of French foreign policy. On 10 December, the Spanish column left again to the north, arriving at Taranés, harassed by the Riffians and suffering another 237 casualties just in the Legión, but with the morale recovered. In order not to overload the marching column, General Castro Girona had been sending troops ahead, from the Zoco and then from Taranés. So, the battalions of Asia, and Madrid, among others, were in Zinat, and those of Valladolid, Arapiles, Ceriñola, Córdoba, Castilla, and Gravelinas were already in Ben Karrich, on the outskirts of Tetuán. On the night of the 12th the retreat of the bulk of the column began. Two of the Banderas, the 1st and 3rd, were in the vanguard, to unblock the road, and the other three on the right flank under Lieutenant Colonel Franco, covering the heights of Keri-Kera (Beni Hosmar) where the Riffians were expected to attack. Lieutenant Colonel Núñez de Prado commanded the convoy and the left flank. At the same time, the air force bombed the hills to clear them of enemies. In any case, the action of the 10th might have been hard for the Riffians because they now hardly appeared. The column reached Zinat, and on the 15th, finally, Tetuán. The skill with which the retreat was carried out meant that General Castro Girona was promoted to Major General.[20]

In the end, unlike at Annual, the Spanish troops had overcome a nightmarish situation. Now they were fighting instead of fleeing, the natives did not desert, the commanders were experienced and determined, the Legión proved to be a decisive instrument, and in general the operations were made to ensure that no outposts were left to their fate, marching and fighting to evacuate them whatever the cost (even so, some 1,000 troopers could not be evacuated, and all but 160 dead men were taken prisoner).

How many casualties were there in these operations around Xauén? Exaggeratedly, some authors speak of 15–20,000 casualties, almost half of the troops available in the western zone, while others speak of 'only' 2,000 dead. Tussell, more moderately, speaks of 10,000 casualties. According to this last writer, the Legión alone had 1,899 casualties between July and December. The Regulares at Alhucemas had around 1,000. To these we must add the losses of the other units

of Regulares, which were also shock units, perhaps another 1,000, and as many others from the positions that had not been rescued. If we add those of the Peninsular battalions, which did not bear the brunt of the action but many of their companies were annihilated in their positions, we may reach 1,000–2,000 more. Therefore, we may say about 6,000–7,000 casualties in total, a similar but slightly lower number to the 8,000 of Annual. However, the difference to Annual was that the casualties in the eastern zone occurred all at once, in only one or two months, while in Xauén it was a trickle over six months, between July and December. Moreover, the army was not destroyed and continued fighting until it achieved its final objective. So, despite the retreat, morale was high and the fighting spirit intact.[21]

5
1924: The Withdrawal in Larache District

While these events were taking place in Xauén, the retreat to the Estella Line also took place in the west, including in El Raisuni's territory (now allied with Spain). This district belonged to the General Commandant of Larache, formerly under General Emilio Barrera Luyando, and since September under the previously defeated General Riquelme, who assumed the command taking with him the 2nd Bandera of the Legión. This unit was based in Zoco el Jemís de Beni Arós on 18 September. The Zoco would become one of the bases of operations on which most of the retreats would be made by General Riquelme, who this time would amend his tarnished reputation after his bad performance in Xauén.

Table 9: Identified units in the Larache District (September–December 1924)
2nd Bandera of the Legión
4th Group of Regulares of Larache (from October)
Regulares de Alcazarquivir
3rd Mehala of Larache
Mehala Ermiki
Harka of El Malili
Harka of Muñoz Grandes
Harka Alcazarquivir
60th Ceuta Regiment
2nd Brigade of Cazadores (probably), made of:
7th Ciudad Rodrigo Cazadores Battalion
5th Tarifa Cazadores Battalion
1st Cataluña Cazadores Battalion
18th Talavera Cazadores Battalion
10th Las Navas Cazadores Battalion
1st Barcelona Cazadores Battalion
1st Reus Cazadores Battalion

Battalion Ciudad Real
Battalion of Jaca
Battalion of the 7th Soria Regiment
Battalion of the 24th Bailén Regiment
Battalion of the 76th Victoria Regiment
Battalion of the 38th León Regiment
Battalion of the 6th Saboya Regiment
Battalion of the 14th América Regiment
Battalion of the 40th Covadonga Regiment
Battalion of the 7th Sicily Regiment
Battalion of the 74th Tenerife Regiment
Battalion of the 33rd Sevilla Regiment
Battalion of the 26th Luchana Regiment
Battalion of the 45th Tetuán Regiment
Battalion of the 23rd Valencia Regiment
21st Cazadores of Alfonso XII Cavalry Regiment
16th Cazadores of Albuera Cavalry Regiment
29th Cazadores of Taxdirt Cavalry Regiment

The Withdrawal in the Central Zone of the Larache District
On the 21st, the positions north of Beni Issef (south of Beni Arós and west of Xauén) were withdrawn with the Ciudad Rodrigo Battalion, covered by Colonel García Boloix's column. Another column under Lieutenant Colonel Sáez Retama, formed by the Mehala of Larache and the local harka also moved to their aid from Taatof, to the southwest (Ahl Sherif). On the 26th the evacuation of Beni Arós (south of the Zoco el Jemís) began, as the positions of Sumata, covered by the column of Colonel Prats with the 2nd Bandera of the Legión, and the battalions Tarifa, Sevilla, and Luchana. On 26 September, three DH.9As of the Napier Squadron took off from Auámara, Larache, to protect the advance of Colonel Prats' column, which was trying to

Table 10: Columns of the Larache District under General Riquelme (September–November 1924)

Location	Commander	Composition/notes
Alcazarquivir Sector	Colonel García Boloix	21 September: evacuation of Beni Issef 23 October: From Jolot to Turkuntz (squadron Taxdirt, squadron Talavera, Jaca and Reus battalions) 28 October: to Aulef (Beni Gorfet) 10 November: Ahl Serif: To Messerah (Ahl Sherif): León, Saboya, Ciudad Real, América, Covadonga, Sicily, Cataluña and Tenerife Battalions (16 cannons and 4,145 men)
Jarrub river; Taatoof (Ahl Sherif)	Colonel González Carrasco	October: Jarrub river (Regulares of Larache, Tarifa, and Las Navas Cazadores, León, and Tetuán battalions) 10 November: Taatoof (Ahl Sheriff): three Tabors Regulares of Alcazarquivir, harka of Alcazarquivir, 2nd Bandera of the Legión, Las Navas, Tarifa, Tetuán and León battalions, squadron Albuera, two batteries
Sumata and Beni Arós	Colonel Prats	26 September: Evacuation of Sumata and south of Tazarut (Beni Arós): 2nd Bandera of the Legión, Tarifa, Sevilla, and Luchana Battalions 12 October: Zoco el Jemís (Beni Arós): 2nd Bandera of the Legión, Las Navas, Sevilla and Luchana Battalions, Mehala and harka of Larache

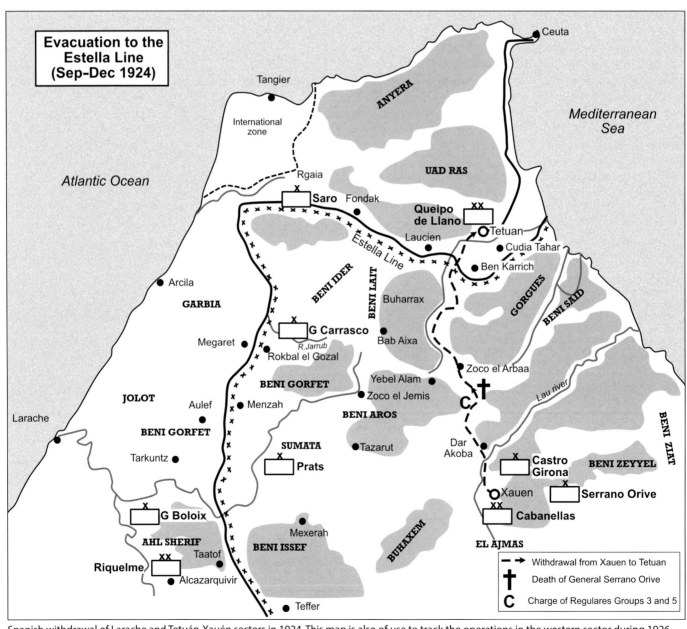

Spanish withdrawal of Larache and Tetuán-Xauén sectors in 1924. This map is also of use to track the operations in the western sector during 1926. (Map by Mark Thompson)

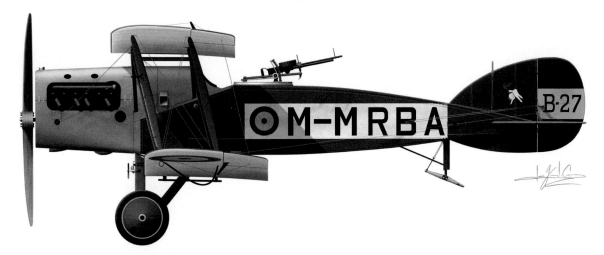

The first modern fighter-bomber deployed by the Spanish *Servicio de Aeronáutica Militar* in Morocco was the Bristol F.2B Fighter. On their transfer to Spain in 1918, all had their engine cowlings painted in mid-grey, fuselage and top wing surfaces in dark olive green, and clear-doped fabric on wing under-surfaces. Assigned to the *2° Escuadrilla Ligera*, they initially wore pseudo-civil registrations, and these were retained for quite a while after. The small flying bird applied white, applied on the fin, was probably the personal insignia of the crew to which this example with the individual serial number B-27 was assigned. (Artwork by Luca Canossa)

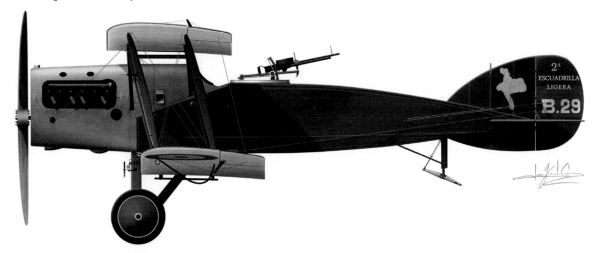

As the Rif War went on and on, Bristol F.2B Fighters of the *2° Escuadrilla Ligera* were deployed to Melilla air base in Morocco in 1922. Over the following months, the quasi-civilian registrations were removed and even the national insignia on their rudders toned down. This example was left in dark olive green overall (with wing under-surfaces in clear dope), while the unit insignia and the individual serial number were reapplied in light grey on the ruder. Personal insignia in the form of a dancer was applied on the fin: sadly, photographs show the latter already badly bleached by the sun and sand, and thus details remain obscure. Bristol F.2Bs became the first Spanish aircraft to deploy gas bombs, in the form of C-5 weapons filled with 20kg of yperite. (Artwork by Luca Canossa)

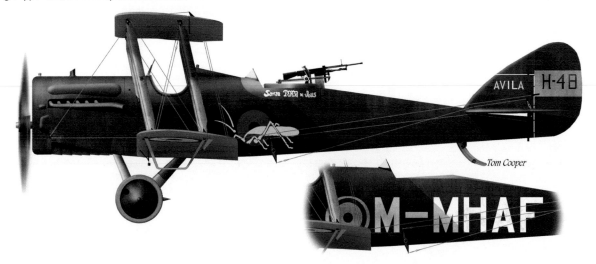

Airco DH.4s had originally entered service in 1916 and were manufactured in large numbers during the First World War. Spain acquired 45 in 1919, mostly with the help of donations from the population and thus most wore the names of Spanish cities on their fin; illustrated here is *'Avila'*; another known example was *'Vigo'*. All were painted in dark green overall, with wing-undersides in clear dope. National markings were applied at least on the top of the upper wing and fuselage undersides: photographs are not clear in regards of their possible application on undersides of the lower wing. The ruder was entirely covered by the Spanish national colours and contained the aircraft's individual number. Pseudo-civilian registrations (shown inset) were removed by 1920. The example illustrated here was nicknamed *'Santa Teresa de Rolls'* (a play upon the name of famous poet and Saint of Avila, Santa Teresa de Jesus), and wore personal insignia in the form of a large white insect. (Artwork by Tom Cooper)

Amongst 45 DH.4s were several DH.4Bs armed with a forward-firing Vickers machine gun installed on the side of the forward cockpit, and a double Lewis machine gun in the rear cockpit. They wore similar colours and insignia to the DH.4s, and were assigned to the Expeditionary Squadron forward deployed to Melilla. Their actions against the Rifians, starting in 1920, proved anything but easy: the aircraft usually had to range well over the Mediterranean Sea before turning south to attack from an unexpected direction, with the engines almost at idle. Usual tactics were to bomb first, then return for a strafing run with both forward and rear machine guns. Much to the delight of contemporary Western press, they instigated numerous massacres of the local population by regularly striking markets densely packed by civilians and livestock. Losses were heavy, with 34 out of 45 DH.4s lost, 13 shot down by the Rifians. (Artwork by Tom Cooper)

Hard on the heels of DH.4/4Bs, Madrid acquired a batch of Airco DH.9s. This variant originally entered service in 1917, and more than 5,000 had been manufactured in Great Britain and the USA by November 1918. The DH.9 was highly appreciated for its robustness, simple maintenance, and a range of 1,000km while carrying a load of 300kg. The Spanish *Servicio de Aeronáutica Militar* deployed them to Morocco while painted in dark green or dark olive green on upper surfaces and sides. Wings were originally painted in green on upper surfaces but left in clear dope on the lower surfaces, before upper surfaces were either painted in white, or their green colour was bleached by the sun. Most had their entire fin painted in yellow. The swastika symbol, having no connection here to Nazism, was used by several aircraft of the DH.4 Napier squadron. (Artwork by Tom Cooper)

Spain acquired Fokker C.IV light bombers as a result of a Military Aviation contest in 1923, and then had them manufactured under licence by the Spanish company Loring at the works in Carabanchel, in Madrid. Deployed to Morocco in 1925, they served with the Fokker Group at Melilla, commanded by His Highness Don Alfonso de Orleans y Borbón. Their engine and metal surfaces along the upper fuselage were left in bare metal colour (dulled by weathering), while the fuselage was painted in dark green. National markings were worn in four positions: the ruder was painted in Spanish national colours and wore the type identification (C.IV) and the individual number of the aircraft. (Artwork by Tom Cooper)

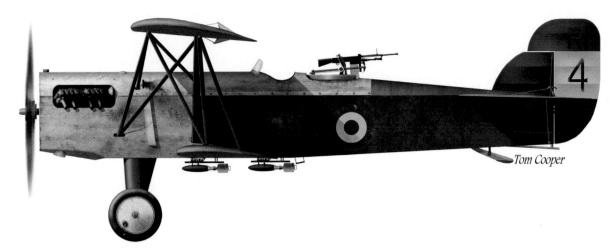

Experience from the Rif War prompted Madrid into commissioning Loring to develop a heavily modified version of the Fokker C.IV, designed to serve as a 'long-range colonial bomber'. Manufactured at Carabanchel, this received the designation R.1. The first aircraft of this type reached Morocco in 1926 and were promptly deployed in an intensive campaign of air strikes on Riffian towns and villages: having a range of 800km, they proved capable of reaching any corner of Spanish Morocco, and thus the Riffian Republic. Like the Bristol fighters, Loring R.1s were frequently equipped with gas bombs, including C-1s (with 50kg of yperite), C-2 (with 10kg of yperie), C-3s (26kg of phosgene), and C-4s (10kg of chloropicrin). (Artwork by Tom Cooper)

The first Spanish Breguet XIXs were manufactured in Spain (up to 203 examples) by the Spanish CASA company, founded precisely for this purpose on 3 March 1923. The first arrived in Africa in June 1925. This example, in dark olive grey and with the number 4 on the rudder, saw much action in 1926–27, towards the end of the war. According to Permuy, between 1924 and 1927 all the usual details of individual aircraft applied on the ruder began disappearing, step by step, except for a character denoting the type and the individual number of the airframe. By 1926, all aircraft had been renumbered individually, without any other details, as shown here. (Artwork by Tom Cooper)

Spain acquired about 140 Breguet XIVA2s (observation version shown here) and up to 40 Breguet XIVB2s (bomber version), mostly with the help of donations from the public. All had their front fuselage either left in bare metal, or painted in light grey, while the rest of the airframe and both wings were either in clear dope, or in sand colour. This example was bought with money donated by the citizens of Manila in the Philippines (formerly a Spanish colony for more than 300 years), after the Annual Disaster, in late 1921. The aircraft was not only named *Manila* (see fin), but also received a corresponding inscription on the fuselage, applied in imperfect Spanish: '*Les españoles de Manila al Ejército de África*' (it should have been '*Los*') (*The Spanish from Manila to the Army of Africa*), and an illustration of Don Quixote and his horse. (Artwork by Tom Cooper)

As far as is known, all Spanish Breguet XIVs were powered by the Italian-made Fiat A.12 engine. The first eight reached Spanish Morocco in September 1919, equipping a flight each at Tetuán and Larache. Eventually, all were rotated into and out of the war and no fewer than 30 were written off: 18 were shot down while 12 crashed. This example was sponsored by donations from the citizens of Madrid and thus named *Madrid* on its fin. On its arrival in Spanish Morocco, it still wore the pseudo-civilian registration, of which the prefix M designated Spain, while the M in the suffix designated it as a military aircraft. The remaining three letters denoted the manufacturer (B for Breguet) and the individual aircraft: FI stood for aircraft No. 70, also applied on the ruder. Notable is the ladder made from metal, enabling quicker embarking and disembarking of the observer/gunner: this became widespread by 1922. (Artwork by Tom Cooper)

Another Breguet XIVA2 with gaudy insignia was this example, aircraft number 74. The inscription *Ciudad Real* on the fin identifies it as donated by the citizens of a town in the La Mancha area (the land of Don Quixote), while the inscription on the fuselage reads, '*Initially [paid] by the Manchego people*'. Clearly visible is the roundel overpainted in black: this became a widespread practice in around 1921, even if the roundel was more often just toned down, but still visible. The standard armament consisted of a single- or twin Lewis 7.92mm machine gun manufactured by BSA in Britain, installed in the rear cockpit. Apparently, very few Breguets had bomb shackles under the fuselage. (Artwork by Tom Cooper)

The first amphibious aircraft operated by the *Aeronautica Militar* were 16 Savoia S.16s acquired in 1921. They were deployed in Spanish Morocco starting in March 1922, based in Atalayón in Melilla, and operated as bombers. Another batch of 16 were designated as the S.16bis and manufactured in Barcelona equipped with the excellent Spanish-made Hispano HS.12Fb engine of 300HPs for the *Aeronáutica Naval* – the Spanish Naval Aviation. Several of these served on the seaplane tender *Dédalo*, and took part in the landing at Alhucemas, where one was shot down around 30 September while engaging in an episode of flying 'the Spanish way'. Originally finished in silver dope overall, many received a light overspray of dark grey over time. The insignia J is somewhat controversial: this prefix was originally reserved for the Hanriot HD.1, though only one was acquired and lost in 1923, thus, it is possible that the letter was subsequently reused on Savoias. (Artwork by Tom Cooper)

The Supermarine Scarab was a military version of the civilian Sea Eagle amphibian, equipped with a pusher engine. In addition to the ability to land on water, it could land on land, and is shown here with its wheels raised. Spain acquired 12 to serve aboard the seaplane tender *Dédalo* as bombers and reconnaissance aircraft. Although often shown with their fuselages painted in blue, these were actually left in the natural colour of varnished wood, while the wings, tailplane, and elevator were left in clear-doped fabric. Like other British-made aircraft sold to Spain in the 1920s, they wore pseudo-civil registrations in large black letters on a large white rectangle on the rear fuselage – and retained these for most of their service with the Spanish Navy. (Artwork by Tom Cooper)

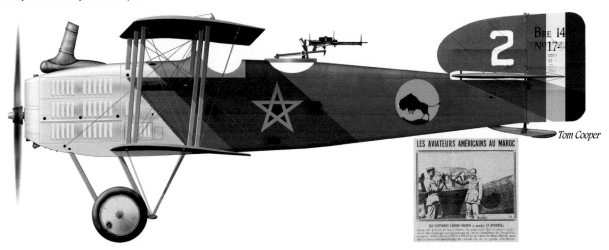

In April 1925, when the Riffians attacked into the Protectorate of Morocco, due to the lack of their own pilots and in an attempt to win over the US public to their side, Paris scrambled to recruit former members of the Lafayette Squadron and thus came into being the *Escadrille Chérifienne*: officially a unit of the Moroccan Armed Forces and equipped with Breguet XIVA2 fighter-bombers. This saw intensive action through the rest of that year, and was involved in the massacre of Chefchaouen (Xauén). Details of the appearance of its Breguets differ widely but the most authoritative reports stress the use of the *vert protective* (green, FS34108) on the fuselage and wings, as shown here. Single-digit serials were applied crudely on the fin, and several aircraft received not only the Cherifian insignia below the cockpit, but also a blue disc with a jumping buffalo on red ground, as just visible in the contemporary newspaper report shown inset. (Artwork by Tom Cooper)

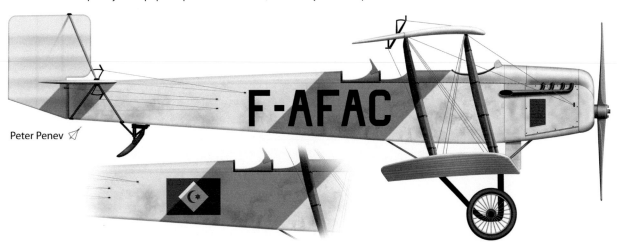

The Riffians tried several times to form their own aviation. Amongst other attempts, Abd el-Krim tried to buy three Dorand AR.2 aircraft from the bankrupt French company SRAT. The Riffian negotiators found one of them suitable to fly, probably No. 4, registration F-AFAC, and it was flown to the Rif on 24 December 1923. The Spanish aviation was able to locate and destroy it on the ground in an action that marked the first ever destruction of an aircraft by another aircraft in all of Africa. This attack was undertaken by DH.9s of the 3rd Group and led by Lieutenant Ansaldo, the future commander of the Nationalist Bomber Aviation during the Spanish Civil War. Notably, the aircraft was delivered to the Rif still wearing this pseudo-civilian registration: the application of the Rifian flag on its fuselage – as shown inset – is hypothetical: it is unlikely that any was ever applied. (Artwork by Peter Penev)

In April 1922, the Spanish converted the British-constructed but German-flagged merchant ship *Neuenfels* into the seaplane tender *Dédalo* – the first aircraft carrier of the Spanish Navy. Setting sail for Ceuta on 3 August 1922, the ship initiated operations against the Riffians just two weeks later. On 26 July 1924, the ship embarked seven Scarab amphibians in Southampton, in Great Britain. Because these proved too large to be stored inside the hull, they had to be parked on the deck. A storm on 25 August then washed away five and damaged two others. Thus, *Dédalo* supported the Alhucemas landing with six Savoia S.16s, six Macchi M.18s, an SCA airship (shown as anchored on the forward mast) and only six Scarabs. (Artwork by Anderson Subtil)

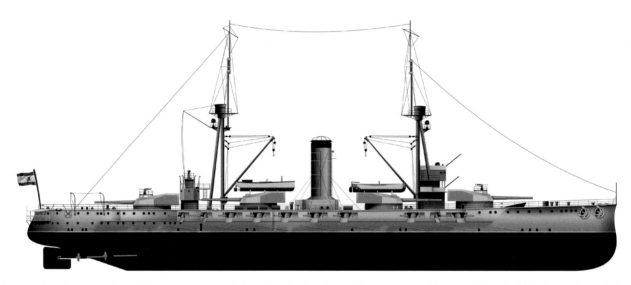

The Spanish dreadnought *Alfonso XIII* was the second of three España-class battleships constructed in Great Britain in 1910 for the Spanish Navy with the aim of reconstructing the fleet after the losses of the Spanish-American War. Each displaced 15,700 tons at normal load, or 16,450 tons at full load, and was armed with eight 305mm (12in), 20 120mm (4in), and four 3-pounder guns, and two machine guns. While *España* ran aground and sank at Cap Tres Forcas (north of Melilla) in 1923, *Alfonso XIII* supported the Alhucemas landings in September–October 1925 together with sister-ship *Jaime I*. Renamed *España* in 1931, the ship went to the Nationalists during the Spanish Civil War, while *Jaime I* was secured by the Republicans – but both were lost during that conflict. (Artwork by Anderson Subtil)

This is a reconstruction of a Type K landing craft used in the Landing of Alhucemas, the first multinational landing operation including land, air and naval assets under a unified command structure. The landing was a success and was studied by Allied forces when planning amphibious operations during the Second World War. Originally, these vessels were British *X-Lighter* landing craft, first deployed in the Gallipoli landings in 1915. Spain acquired 26 from Gibraltar in May 1924. Each could carry 300 troops in the hold, and disembark them over its forward ramp, on occasion still some 50 metres short of dry land. (Artwork by Anderson Subtil)

This Renault FT-17 tank has a Giraud turret, equipped with a Hotchkiss M1914 8mm machine gun and it seems that the 37mm Puteaux cannon and the octagonal Renault turret were not used by Spain in Africa. Its armour was 8–22mm thick, and the speed was only 7.8km/h. The Renaults had a disappointing start in Spanish Morocco in February 1922 when two were lost, but in 1925 they were the first tanks to participate in an amphibious operation. They proved successful in the Malmusi Mountains, and they were crucial for the breakthrough of the Rifian front lines after the Alhucemas landing. (Artwork by David Bocquelet)

This Renault command vehicle was equipped with a TSH station (*telegrafía sin hilos* or wireless telegraphy). Eleven were bought in 1919, followed by six in 1925. Each company of Renault infantry assault tanks of the Spanish Army operated at least one example. The camouflage pattern shown here was inspired by a drawing by Alcañiz Frescon Editores but may have been similar to that of the standard FT-17. (Artwork by David Bocquelet)

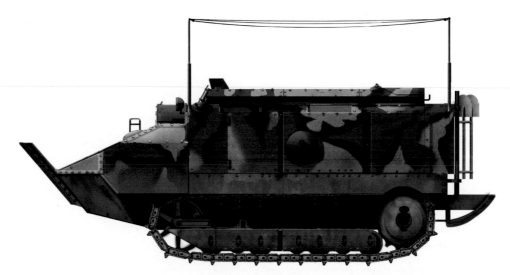

The Schneider CA1 heavy tank was the heaviest armoured vehicle of the Spanish Army during the Rif War. Altogether six were acquired: each had a crew of seven and was armed with a single 75mm gun and two 8mm machine guns. They were operated by the Artillery Assault Gun Battery and deployed in combat for the first time in support of the Renaults during the Battle of Tunguntz on 17 February 1922. (Artwork by David Bocquelet)

This native Moroccan non-commissioned officer of the Regulares – after the Legión, considered the best unit of the Spanish Army in the 1920s – is shown here mounted on a horse. His assignment to a cavalry unit is indicated by his white turban instead of the red *tarbuch*. The red colour on his cape, the cuffs of the jacket, and on the sash, defined him as a member of the Group of Regulares of Melilla; the Regulares of Tetuán wore indigo blue; Ceuta light green; Larache dark blue; and Alhucemas amaranth red. Other parts of his dress include a chickpea-coloured zouave jacket and breeches, hazel-colour leggings, and boots. He is shown armed with a 9mm Astra Model 1921 (or Model 400) pistol. (Artwork by Renato Dalmaso)

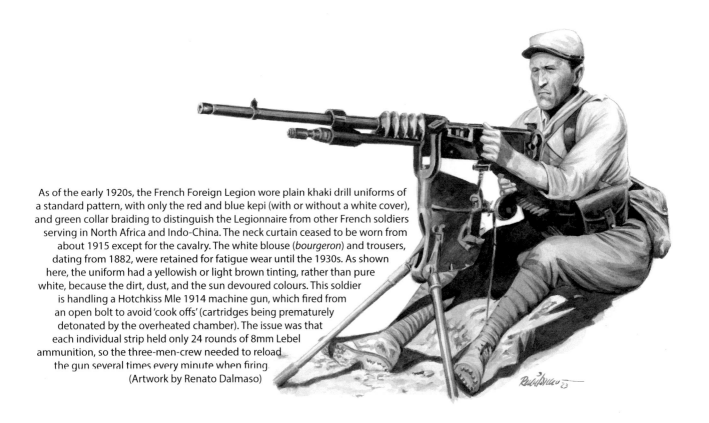

As of the early 1920s, the French Foreign Legion wore plain khaki drill uniforms of a standard pattern, with only the red and blue kepi (with or without a white cover), and green collar braiding to distinguish the Legionnaire from other French soldiers serving in North Africa and Indo-China. The neck curtain ceased to be worn from about 1915 except for the cavalry. The white blouse (*bourgeron*) and trousers, dating from 1882, were retained for fatigue wear until the 1930s. As shown here, the uniform had a yellowish or light brown tinting, rather than pure white, because the dirt, dust, and the sun devoured colours. This soldier is handling a Hotchkiss Mle 1914 machine gun, which fired from an open bolt to avoid 'cook offs' (cartridges being prematurely detonated by the overheated chamber). The issue was that each individual strip held only 24 rounds of 8mm Lebel ammunition, so the three-men-crew needed to reload the gun several times every minute when firing. (Artwork by Renato Dalmaso)

This officer of the Spanish Legión or *Tercio de Extranjeros de la Legión* is shown wearing a summer campaign uniform, without jacket and only the light green shirt (often worn open); with darker breeches with green leggings, and the (very comfortable) Valencian espadrilles instead of booties, which proved more appropriate for the heat and the rough terrain. His belt is the British Mills style acquired in Gibraltar, and he is shown armed with a Spanish-made Mauser 1916 Model rifle, in 7.65mmx53mm calibre, and an Astra 1921 Model 9mm pistol. On his head, he wears the typical Elizabethan barracks cap with a red tassel: this proved highly popular and was soon in widespread use – including by the commander of the Legión and future dictator of Spain, Francisco Franco. (Artwork by Renato Dalmaso)

There are not many references about the Mehala Jalifiana, and in some cases the uniform is confused with – or is similar to – that of the previous Policía Indígena. The jacket and breeches were greenish grey, with high black boots and leather belts. Nevertheless, on campaign these were frequently replaced with brown belts, Valencian espadrilles and leggings as shown here. They could wear a red cap or *turbach* (similar to the famous Fez cap) like that of the infantry of the Regulares (as in this picture), or they could wear a sand-coloured *candora* or turban, and/or a *chechia* (a peakless red cap in the shape of a skullcap). Over the greenish grey uniform, a dark brown *chilaba* or djellaba could be worn, with or without fine white stripes (seen here without), or a *chilaba* in the same beige or sand colour of the Regulares. The Mehalas were also shock troops, like the Legión and Regulares, but they were more lightly armed than their colleagues. Also, despite being instructed by Spanish officers, they were mainly led by Moroccan officers and, in theory, were part of the army of the Sultan of Morocco that was cooperating with the Spanish authorities to suppress the Riffian rebellion; in reality, they acted under the Spanish commanders and followed their instructions. They carrier the Spanish Mauser 7.65mmx53mm of the 1893 or the 1916 models. (Artwork by Renato Dalmaso)

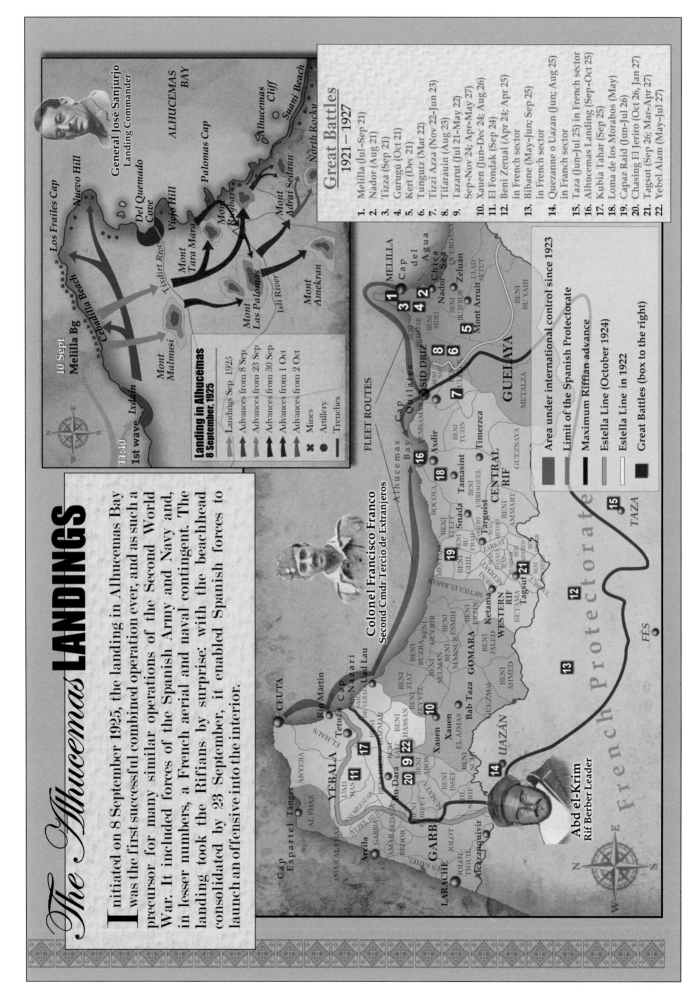

The Alhucemas LANDINGS

Initiated on 8 September 1925, the landing in Alhucemas Bay was the first successful combined operation ever, and as such a precursor for many similar operations of the Second World War. It included forces of the Spanish Army and Navy and, in lesser numbers, a French aerial and naval contingent. The landing took the Riffians by surprise: with the beachhead consolidated by 23 September, it enabled Spanish forces to launch an offensive into the interior.

General José Sanjurjo
Landing Commander

Colonel Francisco Franco
Second Cmdr Tercio de Extranjeros

Abd el-Krim
Rif Berber Leader

Landing in Alhucemas 8 September, 1925

- Landings Sep 1925
- Advances from 8 Sep
- Advances from 23 Sep
- Advances from 30 Sep
- Advances from 1 Oct
- Advances from 2 Oct
- Mines
- Artillery
- Trenches

Great Battles 1921–1927

1. Melilla (Jul–Sep 21)
2. Nador (Aug 21)
3. Tizza (Sep 21)
4. Gurugú (Oct 21)
5. Kert (Dec 21)
6. Tunguitz (Mar 22)
7. Tizzi Azza (Nov 22–Jun 23)
8. Tifarauin (Aug 23)
9. Tazarut (Jul 21–May 22)
10. Xauen (Jun–Dec 24; Aug 26) Sep–Nov 24; Apr–May 27)
11. El Fondak (Sep 24)
12. Beni Zerual (Apr 24; Apr 25)
13. Bibane (May–Jun; Sep 25) in French sector
14. Quezanne o Uazan (Jun; Aug 25) in French sector
15. Taza (Jun–Jul 25) in French sector
16. Alhucemas Landing (Sep–Oct 25)
17. Kubia Tahar (Sep 25)
18. Loma de los Morabos (May)
19. Capaz Raid (Jun–Jul 26)
20. Chasing El Jeriro (Oct 26, Jan 27)
21. Tagsut (Sep 26; Mar–Apr 27)
22. Yebel Alam (May–Jul 27)

Legend: Area under international control since 1923; Limit of the Spanish Protectorate; Maximum Riffian advance; Estella Line (October 1924); Estella Line in 1922; Great Battles (box to the right)

(Map by Anderson Subtil)

evacuate the Tahar Barda and García Acero posts. From the air the DH.9s detected some trenches that they attacked immediately, but when leaving the first pass Napier No. 63 of Lieutenant Gómez Spencer received several hits, one in the thigh of his observer Captain Ochando Chumillas. When Spencer wanted to return to take him to a hospital, Captain Ochando made a tourniquet and told him to continue, so Spencer made three more passes until Ochando ran out of bombs. When he returned, Captain Ochando, that had barely survived in the operations in Xauén, entered a coma and then died, earning a posthumous Laureada.

Captain Ricardo Burguete, son of General Burguete, with his aircraft. Gauging by the shape of the engine and the fin, this was probably a DH.9. Burguete was wounded in the belly on 9 October but was able to land and save his aircraft, being decorated with the Laureate. (Fernández Riera)

On the 28th this withdrawal was continued by the garrisons of the Soria and Cataluña Battalions and the companies of the Ceuta Regiment that were south of the eagle's nest of El Raisuni, in Tazarut (Beni Arós). These were escorted by the Tarifa, Sevilla and Las Navas Battalions, the 2nd Bandera, the harka of El Malili, and the Mehala of Larache, the column arriving at Zoco el Jemís.[1]

At that moment, however, a risky situation was brewing. General Riquelme had taken the bulk of the Larache Command's troops inland for evacuations, so that the coastal bases were cut off from the Command's two main bodies of troops: those of Beni Arós, to the north, that were isolated from the Megaret (Garbia) rout to the west, their exit route; and the troops in Mexerach or Messerah (Beni Issef), to the south, whose route from Teffer (Ahl Sherif) and Alcazarquivir (Jolot) was also cut off. In need of reinforcements, on the 8th the two tabors of Lieutenant Colonel Mola's Larache Group arrived by sea at Arcila (Garbia), coming from Dar Akobba. With these troops and the Mehalas of El Malili and Ermiki, Colonel González Carrasco organised a shock force for the Larache District. At the same time, the operations counted on the air support of the Aumara Squadron (Jolot), between Larache (Jolot Tiguil) and Alcazarquivir. In one of those air missions, on 9 October, the aircraft of Captain Ricardo Burguete Reparaz was hit when bombing the enemy harkas that were attacking the positions of the road from Tatoof (Ahl Sherif) to Alcazarquivir, in Yayuca and Denna. Captain Burguete had taken off with an armoured aircraft (which disabled the observer's controls) to reconnoitre the Riffian positions of Beni Arós, and near Maxherat he located the enemy, flying low through the thicket to bomb it, and then descended further to strafe it. Burguete received a wound in the side, and another in the belly but continued his mission until his ammunition was exhausted, at which point he managed to land at Taatof, earning a Laureate.

Then, the evacuation of Bab es Sor was organised, on the line of communication between Beni Ider and Beni Arós. These outposts were defended by troops of the Cazadores of Soria and the harka of El Melali. Back on 3 October the convoy of the Cazadores of Barcelona had already had problems when arriving. Its evacuation was achieved on the 12th, with two columns: that of Colonel Prats with the 2nd Bandera of the Legión, the Battalions of Las Navas, Sevilla and Luchana, the Mehala of Larache and a harka, from Zoco

El Raisuni, who, after several times changing sides and surviving to the limit, ended his days abandoned by his follower El Jeriro and the Spaniards, becoming prisoner of Abd el-Krim, where he died. (via Villalobos)

el Jemís (Beni Arós) to the south, linking with the column of Colonel González Carrasco, from Rokba (Beni Arós), that had 700 Regulares in the vanguard under Lieutenant Colonel Mola. This column came from the north, through the Jarrub river.[2]

The Raisuni, Abandoned

Around 23 October a column under Colonel García Boloix with a squadron from the Taxdirt Regiment, another from Talavera, and the Jaca and Reus Battalions, had to move from the village of Jolot to the north-east, to Takunz or Tarcuntz, to control the village of Beni Gorfet, which showed signs of rebellion. The Mallorca Battalion was left at the outpost of Jolot.

The next day, Colonel García Boloix evacuated or supplied several positions around Aulef (Beni Gorfet) defended by Cazadores of the Ciudad Rodrigo Battalion. In the Sumata kabyle, to the east, there were still several positions in danger, and the Riffians isolated Beni Arós from the coast. So General Riquelme now focused on evacuating Zoco el Jemís (Beni Arós), that was being defended by the Bailén Battalion, and by many elements of the relief columns that departed from there. The operation was carried out on 30 October. However, when passing through Bab Sor, the 2nd Bandera of the Legión and the harka of Muñoz Grandes had to break the Riffian line at bayonet point, and the column of Colonel González Carrasco with the Regulares of Larache, Cazadores de Tarifa, Cazadores de Las Navas, León, and Tetuán Battalions, had to move forward in support from Rokba (Beni Arós) on the Jarrub river. Once the way was cleared, several more positions in the north-east, defended by the Battalion La Victoria, were evacuated by another column under Lieutenant Colonel Margarida del Pozo with the Valencia Battalion, a squadron of Alfonso XII, and a company of Cazadores of Barcelona.

The positions on the Jarrub river, the last remaining positions in Beni Arós, were then abandoned. These outposts had their headquarters in Rokba el Gozal, the base of Colonel González Carrasco's column. Carrasco led the withdrawal of the heavy convoy, which included all the impedimenta and war material evacuated from the Beni Arós positions, arriving at Megaret (Garbia), to the west, on 30 October. In the end Colonel González Carrasco had evacuated 26 positions in his retreat, suffering 200 casualties in four skirmishes. With his departure, El Raisuni, at times an enemy and now a friend of Spain, was left alone in Tazarut, east of Beni Arós, awaiting the arrival of Abd el-Krim's warriors, who would put an end to his life.[3]

Table 11: The Aviation in Africa (Summer–Autumn 1924)
1st Group (Tetuán, then to Melilla in autumn 1924)
Two Breguet XIV squadrons (Tetuán, then to Melilla in autumn 1924)
2nd Group (Larache)
Two Breguet XIV squadrons
3rd 'Rolls' Group (Melilla, then Tetuán since September, then to Larache)
Three DH.4 Squadrons (Melilla, then Tetuán since September, then to Larache from September)
'Napier' DH.9A Squadron (Melilla, then to Larache)
4th Group Light Group (Nador, Melilla)
Two Bristol F.2B squadrons (Nador, Melilla)
One Fokker C.IV squadron (Nador, Melilla, since December)
One Nieuport Ni.29 fighter squadron (Nador, Melilla, since September, replacing the Martynsides)

A Breguet XIV. (Sánchez & Kindelán)

A row of Fokker C.IV, manufactured by the Spanish Lohring Company (the famous engineer Barrón worked there). These aircraft operated in Morocco in 1924–25 (Sánchez & Kindelán)

The Lucus Line

Once the central zone of the district, between Tetuán and Arcila, was abandoned, the southern zone then retracted towards Alcazarquivir. For this purpose, Colonel González Carrasco's column was sent to this area again, to help the column in the area, under Colonel García Boloix. The garrisons of Ahl Sherif, to the east, were supplied and maintained by Colonel García Boloix as a buffer to protect Alcazarquivir (Jolot). The evacuation took place in the Beni Issef kabyle (with its main base of Messerah, further east). For this, Colonel González Carrasco departed from Tatoof (Ahl Sherif) on 10 November with three tabors of Regulares of Alcazarquivir and its harka, the 2nd Bandera of the Legión, the battalions of Las Navas, Tarifa, Tetuán and León, a

A detailed view of the cockpit and the machine gun position of possibly a Breguet XIV (note the engine). Unusually, the crew consists of three members (only the XIV T was transformed into a transportation aircraft with three crew members). (Sánchez & Kindelán)

squadron of Albuera, and two batteries. On the right of the road would go Colonel García Boloix, covering the march to liberate the encircled Messerah outpost. Again, General Riquelme coordinated both columns from Tatoof, in the rear. In the advance the Spanish also counted on aviation and tanks. Another column under Sáez of Retama was covering the lines of communications as the other troops advanced, up to Teffer, to the south-east. In the end, Colonel González Carrasco, after advancing 45km, arrived at Messerah on the 12th, and from there all the surrounding posts were evacuated by troops of the León, Saboya, Ciudad Real, América, Covadonga, Sicily, Cataluña and Tenerife Battalions, 16 cannons and 4,145 soldiers in all. The aviation was again essential to know the situation of the garrisons, but it had to lament certain material losses: around 6 December, Captain Sampietre's aircraft crashed, fortunately near Aulef (Beni Gorfet), in Spanish territory and without the loss of his life. Finally, the position of Messerah, along with all the garrisons of Beni Iseff (30 positions), was evacuated on 9 December, all the troops arriving safely at Tatoof (Ahl Serif) on the 16th. For this achievement Colonel González Carrasco was promoted to Brigadier General.[4]

In the end, the Estella Line, configured by Primo de Rivera as a new front after the withdrawal, was had positions as follows: it started in the Mediterranean, in the less steep part of Beni Hozmar, south-east of Tetuán; from there it continued westward covering almost all of Wad Ras, reaching almost to the Atlantic at Cuesta Colorada (Garbia), next to the Tánger (Tangier) border; from there it turned south following the Garbia border along the Jarrub river, reached Beni Gorfet and then Jolot and Ahla Sherif until the French border. In the end the manoeuvres of retreat under enemy fire to achieve this new line of fortifications had been brilliantly carried out by General Riquelme, for whom nobody cared. But this defensive approach would change when Abd el-Krim made the biggest mistake of his life: attacking the French zone.

The Aviation in Africa at the End of 1924 and Beginning of 1925

With the near destruction of the DH.4 Rolls Group in the Xauén relief and evacuation operations, the situation was so complicated that the Spanish commanders foresaw that it was vital to reactivate the aviation in Larache again, beginning with its aerodrome. To equip the Larache aerodrome several DH.9 aircraft were sent from Melilla, and also the DH.4 Rolls Group from Tetuán, but the Breguet XIVs remained in Tetuán.

In December the air force in Africa was joined by the first Fokker C.IVs of González Gallarza's squadron, manufactured by the Loring factory in Carabanchel, Madrid. Also, an eight-aircraft Nieuport Ni.29 fighter squadron under Captain Francisco Vives Camino arrived in Melilla in September 1924, replacing the Martynside fighters. Their purpose was to destroy the alleged new-born Riffian air force, but once the enemy aircraft were destroyed on the ground, the Nieuports had nothing to do but training until November 1925, when they returned to Spain. Finally, the Breguet XIV Group known as 'La Bámbula' returned to the eastern sector in autumn 1924.[5]

Two views of a Nieuport Ni.29 C.1 fighter, that arrived in September 1924, probably due to the rumours that the Riffians were creating their own air forces. (Canario Azaola files, via Permuy)

6

1925: The Offensive against France

In 1925, the Spanish forces were on the defensive in both the west and east of the Protectorate, as instructed by Primo de Rivera. In the west, the harka of M'hammed Abd el-Krim and El Jeriro (brother of the supreme Riffian commander of the same last name), formed by Yebalis, Gomaris and Riffians, entered the holy city of Xauén. On 23 January they penetrated Beni Arós and assaulted Tazarut, capturing El Raisuni, who was condemned to death. He was not executed but died as a prisoner of Abd el-Krim. This was a sad end for El Raisuni, who had been on the verge of destruction at the hands of the Spaniards for more than 10 years, to meet his end at the hands of another Moroccan, Abd el-Krim, a newcomer confronting his supremacy in the Yebala and Gomara.

At the same time, the kabyle of Anyera, next to Ceuta, in the rear of the Estella Line, revolted. To put them down, on 30 March a fleet sailed from Ceuta, which disembarked the 4th and 6th Banderas and a tabor in Alcazerseguer, with air cover, putting down the revolt.

Meanwhile, in the eastern zone, in January a punitive action was carried out with tanks and aviation against unruly villages in

Tafersit, which brought calm to the eastern front until May. Then, it was learned that the Riffians were preparing a revolt in the Spanish rear: an enemy harka of 1,000 warriors was being concentrated in Izumar, near Annual (Beni Ulixek), in the northern sector, and even began fortification works. General Sanjurjo, moved his troops in a line between Dar Quebdani (Beni Said), to the south, and Afrau, on the coast, to the north, to prevent any infiltration. As infiltration was precisely the plan of the Riffian troops, seeing it now impossible, the harka withdrew.[1]

Abd el-Krim Attacks France

Returning to spring 1924, Abd el-Krim had tried unsuccessfully to occupy the village of Beni Zerual, the so-called granary of the Rif, in the valley of the river Uarga, which had not yet been occupied by France. Marshal General Lyautey (Marshal since 1921), in order to avoid new penetrations, in the second half of the year established a line of 60 defensive posts north of the Uarga, following the Spanish border, about 60km north of Fez. The main centres of the line were

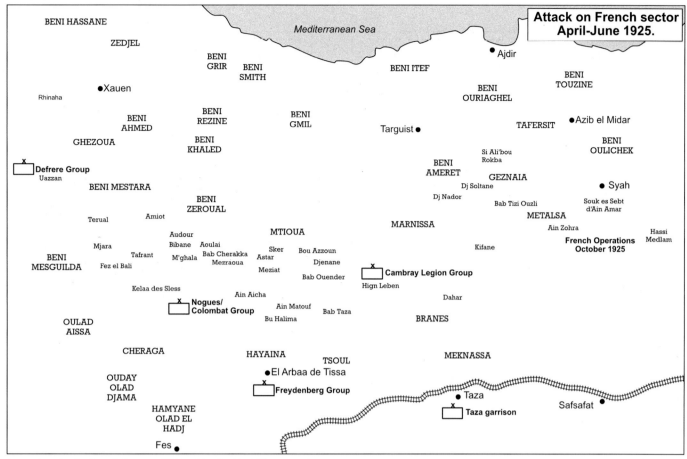

Operations in the French Sector of 1925. (Map by Mark Thompson)

Terual, Biban, Taunat and Kifan, from west to east. The motives of the Riffian attack on France are not clear. According to some authors Abd el-Krim had to equip the more and more numerous kabyles that joined him, and he could only do so by taking the armament from conquered positions, now something impossible to do with the new Spanish defensive lines. This impossibility to provide arms and ammunition, in the Riffian mentality, would imply a serious lack of leadership and prestige that would end in massive desertions and the dissolution of the Riffian forces. According to other sources, Abd el-Krim was aiming to force France to recognise the Rif Republic and the expansion of its hinterland. He did not realise that he had just brought together two neighbours, Spain and France, who had hitherto been unfriendly towards Morocco, and who had previously fought for primacy in the region.

Although Marshal General Lyautey began to foresee the imminent Riffian offensive, he still had insufficient troops: the 61 battalions in French Morocco during the Great War had been reduced to 40 or 42, and 15 artillery batteries. He requested and received eight or nine more battalions by 30 April, and with the other 9 reserve battalions he already had, he would form three mobile groups of 12,600 soldiers in all, of 700 men per battalion. However, his forces would be smaller than expected, as the battalions actually numbered between 400 and 600 soldiers. At the end of May 1925, he had 77 battalions, 25 squadrons, 31 batteries and 16 squadrons of aircraft.[2]

Abd el-Krim penetrated again in Beni Zerual on 13 April 1925 at five points: M'hammed, his brother, with the Qaids Budra, Bu Lahia, Alluch and Ben Azug did so from the east, from Targuist, in the western Rif, including regular troops of the nascent Riffian army (two tabors, 500 soldiers), accompanied by 2,500 warriors from the Central Rif and Senhaya; Lyazid ben Salah, Qaid of Beni Erzin, attacked from the north-east with 800 warriors from the Gomaris

Beni Erzin, Metiua, and Beni Khaled; Mohammed Moharrax attacked from the north with another 800 warriors from Beni Zeyyel, Beni Selman, and Ajmás; Mohammed el-Meslahi attacked from the north-west with 1,500 warriors from Ajmás, Guezaua, Beni Khaled and Beni Ahmed; and finally, Suleiman el-Mestaui attacked from the west with warriors from Beni Mestara. The moderation of these Riffian numbers for this great offensive against France, about 6,000–7,000 warriors in all, gives us a more realistic figure of the troops that Abd el-Krim's followers could really put into the field. The pro-French Sherif Abderrahman el-Darqaui (or Derkaui) tried to resist at Amiot, but he was forced to burn his positions on the 16th and to cross the Uarga river into the French zone with his 600 warriors. Beni Zerual was conquered in three days. The only French reaction was to bombard the Riffians with 18 aircraft from Beni Malek, and a slight movement of troops towards the Ouarga by General Chambrun.

Until now the Riffian attack had overrun the French allies, but not the French troops themselves, though this changed soon. First, the French positions began to notice how their wells (generally outside the posts) were occupied or besieged by the Riffians, as had happened before with Spain. On the 19th, the Taleghza and Bab Cherakka posts were attacked, and the pro-French Riffians who were in their rear crossed over to the rebels: these were 350 Beni Urriaguelese cousins of those of the Spanish zone, and fractions of the Sless, the Jaia, Senhadya, Raghioua and Mezziat Kabyles in the period until 27 April. Then, the Riffians concentrated in two groups: one moved against Uazzan, to the west, and the other to the south against the French posts of the middle Uarga. On the 22nd they attacked the main post of Bibane, which protected the north of Fez (south of the Gomara region), using four pieces of artillery to take this blockhouse. This finally raised the alarm with Lyautey. As

Table 12: French Mobile Groups April–June 1925

Date	Commander/Group	Location	Composition
April	Front commander: General Chambrun, then Daugan from 24 May	Spanish-French frontier	4–5 mobile groups (see below)
April	Colonel Nogués, then from 27 April General Colombat's Mobile Group	Central sector: Ain Aicha, middle Ouarga, north of Fez	Four battalions, a squadron and three batteries. 27 April: five battalions, two squadrons and four batteries (3,500 soldiers) 13 May: 10 battalions
April		Eastern Sector: Taza	six battalions, three squadrons and three batteries
May	Colonel Freydenberg	Central-east sector: Upper Ouarga, El Arbaá de Tissa (Hayaina)	Six battalions, two squadrons of Spahis, and four batteries
May	Colonel Cambay (with Lieutenant Colonel Giraud)	East Sector: High Leben, north-west of Taza	French Foreign Legion Group: up to four battalions, three batteries and a Goum. 21 May: 6 battalions
June	General Defrère	West Sector: Ouezzane	

the French sources themselves recognise, Lyatuey, 'blinded by his condescension towards the Spanish, he had forgotten that in 1924 the army of Spain had been modernised and equipped with efficient units'. He himself stated, in his own words 'it will result in the whole country an impression and feeling that the Riffians are able to beat us and to have on us the same successes as on the Spanish'.[3]

Bibane Resists?

General Chambrun formed two observation groups, one to the north of Fez under Colonel Nogués, in Ain Aicha and Sless formed by four battalions, a squadron and three batteries, in the centre of the French line; and another for Taza with six battalions, three squadrons and three batteries, in the east, near Algeria. Chambrun thought that the main attack would come from the Fez sector, so he prepared to place his troops on the two roads that went from Beni Zeroual and M'tioua to Fez. To carry out the deployment, Colonel Nogués' column left Ain Aicha heading west, to Fez el Bali, reinforcing on 27 April General Colombat's new Mobile Group now with five battalions, two squadrons and four batteries, 3,500 soldiers in all, that was being formed to cover the middle

French troops in a position in Morocco, near a medical post. (Keystone-France/Eyedea, via Courcelle & Marmié)

French troops advancing through the bush with their artillery. (Deroo collection, via Courcelle & Marmié)

French Prime Minister, Paul Painlevé, to the left, visiting the front in French Morocco, with Marshal General Lyautey, to the right, his face half covered like a Moor. (Service Historique de la Defense, via Courcelle & Marmié)

Ouarga. Another Mobile Group, under Colonel Freydenberg with six battalions, two squadrons of Spahis, and four batteries would protect the upper Ouarga, and would go from Tissa (Hayaina) to the north to cover the gap left by Nogués at Ain Aicha, on 2 May. And finally, a French Foreign Legion Group was created for the High Leben under Colonel Cambay, reinforced with troops from Lieutenant Colonel Giraud to add up to four battalions, three batteries and a Goum. Between the end of April and the beginning of June, Morocco had received 19,600 infantrymen in some 28 battalions, and also a battalion of 45 tanks, a squadron of motorised machine guns, six squadrons of cavalry, 19 batteries of artillery, four heavy batteries, and six squadrons of aircraft.[4]

The main threat was against Bibane, located in the massif of the same name that dominated the valleys of Audour, Aoulai and the Ouergha, in the central-western sector of the French line. By controlling Bibane, all the routes leading to Fez could also be controlled. The Middle Ouarga Group of General Colombey's 'White Rats', in Fez el Bali, with his vanguard led by the brilliant Colonel Nogués, would carry out a series of desperate actions to maintain or evacuate the French positions in the area, similar to what had happened in Xauén a year earlier. Audour was supplied, but the advance to the Bibane massif was repulsed after heavy casualties on 5 May. The Aoulai post was on the point of succumbing, and the only measure possible to encourage its defenders was to notify the garrison by telegram that they had just received the Legion de d'Honneur. On the 13th, General Colombey was reinforced, now numbering 10 battalions, including two of the Foreign Legion units, and six batteries, and he marched again from Tafrant, to relieve Bibane, to the east. Colonel Nogués finally managed to supply the post at the cost of 110 casualties, but when they departed Bibane was again under siege. General Colombey was then able to march south-east and evacuate M'Ghala, but he found the entire Outzagh garrison wiped out and cut to pieces. Further east, the Foreign Legion came under enemy fire and evacuated Aoulai, abandoning all the heavy equipment of the post.

Further east, Colonel Freydenber's High Ouerga Group found itself in a similar situation. Freydenberg marched to the Taounat (Meziat) post, the epicentre of the whole defensive system in the area, led by the 6th/1st REI (*Regiment Etrangere de Infanterie*) of the Foreign Legion. This elite unit managed to break through the front and enter into the post. From there, they helped to evacuate the

other forts, to the east: Bou Soultan was dynamited and abandoned, as well as Bab Ouender, on 7 May, managing to save the five soldiers defending the post.

Meanwhile, General Chambrun organised an offensive to clear the posts of the upper Ouerga on 21 May once he had received reinforcements at Ain Aicha: Colonel Freydenberg would advance east on the right bank of the Ouarga, and the Cambay Group on the left bank. After a great artillery barrage and air bombing, Colonel Freydenberg's 11 battalions advanced and liberated Moulay Ain Djenane and Bou Azzoun, but the Cambay Group, with six battalions, only reached Mediouna. [5]

On the Verge of Collapse

The French now considered the need to evacuate all the posts, but for the moment Lyautey was opposed to this measure, to avoid panicked scenes like that at Annual. These forts, thought Lyautey, should be held with the support of aviation. So, 10 squadrons of eight aircraft each were located on this northern front, equipped with Breguet XIV A.2s and Farman F.60 Goliaths of the navy. Colonel Armengaud, commanding the 37th Aviation Regiment, moved his aircraft as close to the front as possible. At the same time, the just arrived General Daugan took command of the front on the 24th. The next day, Colombey's Group had to lead a new supply convoy to Bibane, in the central sector. The convoy only arrived after an epic charge by some companies of the 1st REI of the Foreign Legion, and at the cost of 402 casualties.

Meanwhile, General Daugan was organising a counteroffensive when his plans were cancelled by a new attack by Abd el-Krim's forces, led by his brother M'hammed who reinforced the Moroccan warriors with some of his Riffian Regulares, and after a new Riffian push, on 2–3 June all the French posts north of Taounat (Meziat), Astar and Sahela fell. Also, Sker and Mezraoua were blockaded, and further west the Riffians crossed the Ouerga around Ain Aicha, to infiltrate and march south to Sidi Allal al-Haj, just 11km from Tissa (Hayaina), capital of the Upper Ouarga region, north-east of Fez.

Colonel Freydenberg organised a counterattack with the 6th/1st REI to regain the Taounat positions, but after suffering 231 casualties in the end he was not able to avoid the fall of the two posts at Sker and Merzraoua. At the same time, to the west, General Colombat was not able to prevent the final fell of Bibane on 5 June: all his 54 defenders perished in the fort. The last message from defender Sergeant Berney, asked the artillery to bombard his own post while he was agonising and was unable to even write his own full name. On 7 June Audour was evacuated by the 54 soldiers of its garrison in a suicidal sortie made by Lieutenant Franchi, and then Archikarne post fell.

The Riffian Offensive Expands to the West and East

At the same time, the Yebalis of El Jeriro joined the fight to attack Ouezzane, at the western end of the French front, crossing the Lucus on 8 June. The sector was a salient called the 'bird's beak' that had been left in the air after the Spanish evacuation to the Estella Line. So, Ouezzzane was the northernmost of sector of the French the line. Colombat's Group was sent there, but they might divert to protect the Ouazzane (Ahl Roboa) airfield itself, at Beni Malek. Towards 15 June General Defrère's new Mobile Group came to the rescue of the 'bird's beak', but the French group was totally surrounded before reaching Rihana, near Ajmás, Gomara. Only the appearance of three aviation squadrons saved the French forces from destruction.

At the same time, the posts continued to fall: Beni Derkoul, on 14 June, in the central sector, was destroyed after Sub-Lieutenant

French heavy artillery enters action to smash the Riffian positions. (L'Illustration, via Courcelle el Marmié)

French Renault 17 tanks crossing the Uarga river. (Manríquez García)

from France, and several independent battalions from Algeria). In addition, these were reinforced with the elite of the French army: several individual companies of the 6th and 7th/1st REI Foreign Legion battalions, the 2/2nd REI, 3/3rd REI, and the 4th REI, as well as the 1st Foreign Cavalry Regiment REC. Also, the 37th Air Regiment would double its number of machines from 80 to 160 aircraft.[6]

In any case, by the end of June, the 300km French front was about to collapse. With the bulk of the Riffians entrenched in Bibane, but free of immediate enemies after taking the French position, Abd el-Krim was able

Lapeyre blew up the post with dynamite with all the materiel. Further west, 800 warriors infiltrated Beni Mesguilda, in the French rear, approaching the crossing of the Ouarga river at Mjara, and causing the revolt of the whole kabyle against France. The posts and relief columns in Beni Mesguilda did not cease to be attacked by the rebels, so in the end a Mobile Group of 5,000 men had to be created with reserves from Fez and Meknes to control the kabyle.

In the course of June, another 14,000 French troops arrived in Morocco. In the first six months of the year, Lyautey had received 36 infantry battalions (including two Senegalese Tirailleur (Sharpshooter) regiments from Tunisia, four other regiments

to move to other sectors and extend the offensive. The desperation was such that Lyautey requested the use of mustard gas or hyperite, known euphemistically as Howitzer No. 20. The government authorised the shipment of the gas, but demanded an explicit approval each time it was going to be used and only as a last resort. It is not known if the French finally used it or not.

The new area chosen by the Riffians for the next attack was that of Taza, at the eastern end of the front. Its strategic importance was enormous, as it controlled the route to Algeria and touched the Middle Atlas. If Abd el-Krim broke the front it would cut the communications between Oujda (Uxda) and Fez, and once he reached the Atlas, he would put a second mountain range between the Riffians and the French. M'hammed was detected on the night of 22–23 June crossing the French lines with 5,000 warriors between the posts of Ain Matouf and Bu Halima, followed by artillery. One by one the French garrisons were annihilated: Kef el-Ghar on 29 June, Dahar on 1 July, Leben on the 4th. Colonel Giraud's column, despite fighting all day on the 3rd, did not manage to stop the offensive. In the fighting zone, the Tsoul and Branès Kabyles went over to the Riffians, like the Riata tribesmen, who

Table 13: French Deployment July to September 1925		
Date	**Units/ Commander**	**Location**
July	General Naulin	
September	Group West (General Pruneau)	Ouzan
September	128th Division (General Hergault)	Ouzan
September	135th Division (General Pruneau)	Ain Dfali
September	Group Centre (General Marty)	Fez
September	3rd March Division (General Gaureau)	Mjara and Fez el Bali
August	2nd March Division (General Billotte)	Arbaá de Tiza and Ain Aicha
July	Group Eastern or 19th Corps (General Boichurt)	Taza
July	11th March Division (General Simon)	West of Taza
September	1st March Division (General Vernois)	Taza
September	Reserve	
July	Moroccan Division (General Marty)	Fez
September	1st Spahis Brigade	Fez

would join the rebels in the Beni Ouarain massif. Now the front was already a few kilometres from Taza. A Riffian incursion made the Hayaina and Cheraga tribesmen flee to Fez.

The French reacted by sending all the available reserves for Taza: there were only two companies of Zouaves left. General Cambay, in panic, recommended abandoning Taza and retreating east through the Moulouya towards Algeria. After much discussion, Generals Lyautey and Daugan finally prevailed, and fearing a panic similar to that at Annual, decided to hold out until reinforcements arrived. On 5 July, Billotte and Giraud's mobile groups launched counterattacks at Bab Taza, north-west of Taza, and at Kifane, to the north, succeeding in punishing the Riffians and stopping their advance for the time being. Taza itself was supplied with between 60 and 90 days of food to withstand an eventual siege. At the same time, Marshal General Lyautey convinced the Sultan to declare his public support for France, and also raised a Moroccan Mehala of 6,000 troops to help the French forces.

Meanwhile, another minor offensive by Abd el-Krim in the central sector, between Kelaa des Sless and Ain Aicha made the allies of Cheraga and Fichtala flee to Fez. The danger had passed, however, as massive reinforcements in the form of divisions began to arrive from Algeria and France itself. Between 7 and 15 July France evacuated the Ruhr to deploy three of its divisions in Morocco, and by the 11th, a new 19th Army Corps had been formed in eastern Morocco with the Moroccan Division in Oujda, the 11th Division, an infantry regiment, and a battalion of the Foreign Legion. General Naulin arrived with these troops, replacing General Daugan. By 24 July General Naulin had 50,000 troops in the three sectors of the northern front. All this overwhelming deployment was the work of one man: the Marshal General of France Philippe Pétain, the hero of Verdun.[7]

Pétain Arrives
By the month of June, some 43 of the 66 French positions had been annihilated by the Riffians. Abd el-Krim's forces took 51 guns, 200 machine guns, 5,000 rifles, and 35 mortars. According to some quite optimistic and unreliable data, the Riffians lost only 43 warriors.[8] Taza, on the frontier with Algeria, was under threat, and all the aircraft at the Ain Meduina airfield had been destroyed. Some sources speak of 11,000 French casualties, and 2,500 dead and missing, but perhaps the number of rifles lost (5,000) gives

Marshal General Philippe Pétain in the French Morocco. (Service Historique de la Defense, via Courcelle el Marmi)

French Marshal General Philippe Pétain, the hero of Verdun and the saviour of French Morocco with his massive delivery of reinforcements, pictured in 1941. He was also the architect of the French-Spanish alliance that defeated Abd el-Krim. Pétain ended his days in jail due to his collaboration with the Nazis and the deportation of a hundred thousand Jews for extermination. De Gaulle tried to exonerate him somewhat with the expressive words 'Old age is a shipwreck'. (via Desperta Ferro Magazine)

us an indication of the real number of casualties: 1,285 dead, and 5,306 wounded, that is, not as many as Annual, but similar to those lost by Spain in Xauén. However, the Xauén evacuation took place during almost half a year of fighting, while Annual happened over about two months, and the French disaster in just three. Thus, the negative image of the Spanish army and contempt for the Riffian danger faded away. The prestigious French army had been just as badly defeated by raggedy ragamuffins as its northern neighbour in Morocco had been.

The defeat led to the resignation of Marshal General Lyautey, who had been hostile to the Spaniards, and he was replaced by Marshal General Pétain, who was to have an excellent relationship with Spain. In fact, this resulted in a cooperation agreement signed in Madrid on 25 July 1925. Pétain, the hero of Verdun, took the Riffian threat seriously and called for a total force of three army corps with six divisions and a reserve. The Marshal would also sympathise with the new Spanish officer corps of the Legión and the Regulares, especially with Franco, whom he considered the spearhead of a kind of Spanish Risorgimento.[9]

Marshal General Pétain arrived at the most needed time: in Taza, in the east, near Algeria, the mobile groups were totally isolated in the middle of enemy territory, and Colonel Giraud's group, north of Kiffane, was almost out of ammunition. On 17 July the Riffians infiltrated along the Fez-Taza route and managed to cut the railway and telephone on the 29th. The 7th/1st REI of the Foreign Legion, recently arrived from Algeria, was launched immediately to the front, on the night of the 24th to save the post of Bab Moroudi. At that moment Abd el-Krim changed the axis of his offensive and fell on the west again, in Ouezzane. Colonel Freydenberg was sent between 8–13 August to cover the Rharb plain, under a 50-degree sun, taking by assault the Adjen and Sarsar massifs with the support of Renault tanks, used for the first time by the French in Morocco. The offensive was supported by Spanish troops under General Riquelme, who joined at Lucus, and a Spanish-French air force bombed Amezzou.[10]

Finally, on 16 August the French counteroffensive was launched in the Taza sector. General Naulin formed a manoeuvre mass of 17,000 soldiers in 25 battalions with the arrival of the 2nd Division. These troops were formed in four columns to subdue the village of Tsoul and regain all the posts lost since April. Then, on the 26th, 16 battalions fell on the Branès Kabyle, with 155mm heavy artillery and tanks, crushing it. With such forces the Riffians could only flee.

In the meantime, more French troops were coming: the 128th Division, coming from the Ruhr, had just landed in Casablanca, and two more Spahis brigades were expected. General Naulin was thus able to organise three army corps: Group West (General Pruneau) with the 128th (General Hergault, at Ouazan) and 135th (General Pruneau, at Ain Dfali) divisions; Group Centre (General Marty) with the 3rd (General Gaureau, between Mjara and Fez el Bali) and 2nd (General Billotte, between Arbaá de Tiza and Ain Aicha) Marching Divisions; and the Eastern Group (General Boichurt) or 19th Corps with the 11th (General Simon, west of Taza) and 1st (General Vernois, in Taza) Marching Divisions; the Moroccan Division (General Marty) remaining as a reserve in Fez; and a Cavalry Group (General Jonchay) with the 1st Spahis Brigade.

On 11 September, some 24 battalions were operating in the Tafrant sector, and 20 battalions in the Taounat sector. At the end, the old French lines of April were reached. The Pro-French Qaid El Derkaui was re-established at Amiot, and after a bombardment of the Bibane massif by 14 aircraft squadrons, the old post was recaptured on the 16th. The Riffian resistance was now rather weak as the bulk of the Riffians had retreated to the Spanish zone due to the Alhucemas landing. The Xerifian Squadron, with the support of the French air force, even began to bombard Xauén. As we shall see later, there were probably only some 6,000 Riffians fighting now against the French, some 2,000 in each of the west, central and east sectors.[11]

7
1925–26: The Landing of Alhucemas

Marshal General Pétain and Prime Minister and Lieutenant General Primo de Rivera's new plan consisted of a Spanish-French cooperation to make a pincer advance to crush Abd el-Krim between two lines of fire. In the south, the French would march along the Uarga line to the north-east, linking up with the Spanish forces already in the upper Kert. To the north, the Spanish would make a landing in the Bay of Alhucemas, at Bocoya and Beni Urriaguel Kabyles, attacking the Riffians from the rear. However, for the time being, Primo de Rivera maintained his position of limited action. In his mind the Spanish forces after the landing would occupy the Riffian capital, Axdir, but then to halt their advance to begin negotiations for peace with Abd el-Krim.

The planning of the landing, in just a couple of months, was due not only to the brilliant work made by the General Staff officers but also due to the experience acquired after several attempts in the past. In 1913, General Francisco Gómez-Jordana had already carried out studies to execute a landing in Alhucemas, as well as in 1921 and 1922. Now, another Gómez-Jordana, the son of the former General, would inherit his father's plans, improving them for 1925. General Jordana planned to land a force of 20,000 soldiers with air, naval and armoured support at Ixdain and Morro Nuevo. The invaders would have to face what Jordana estimated to be some 10,000 Riffians equipped with 100 cannon and many machine guns. In truth these were only some 2,100, as we shall see, although later they would probably reach 10,000 warriors after receiving a large number of reinforcements. The Spaniards would create a bridgehead to land the entire contingent, and from there march against Axdir (Beni Urriaguel), the capital of Abd el-Krim. To carry out the operation, Jordana studied in depth the Allied landing in Gallipoli in 1915 so as not to make the same mistakes of the Great War. General Primo de Rivera was at first hesitant about the operation, as he remembered the failure of the British. In fact, he was several times on the verge of cancelling the operation, but finally the plan was presented to Pétain who gave his approval on 21 August, in Algeciras, Spain.

The Naval Component

The French Marshal put an important French naval air contingent under Primo de Rivera's command: the battleship *Paris*, the cruisers *Strasbourg* and *Metz*, two monitors and two destroyers, a tug with a captive balloon, and six Farman Goliath seaplanes from Bizerta, Algeria.[1]

To these forces, Primo de Rivera would add two battleships (*Alfonso XIII* and *Jaime I*); four cruisers (*Méndez Núñez*, *Blas Lezo*, *Victoria* and *Extremadura*), three destroyers (later reduced to one); one aircraft carrier (*Dédalo*) equipped with six Savoia SIAI S.16s, six Macchi M.18s, and six Supermarine Scarabs; six gunboats, 11 coastguards vessels, five torpedo boats; seven fish-guards; one captive balloon and an armed dirigible. The Scarab was a British seaplane whose only customer was the Spanish Navy with 12 machines ordered. These aircraft had a record of bad luck; while still in England, the commander of the Group, Frigate Captain Pedro de Cardona, crashed an example against a ship when he was taking off. Then, the *Dédalo* departed from Southampton on 26 July 1924 with all the Scarabs on deck, as the aircraft were too large (only by some centimetres) to store them inside the hull of the ship. So, on 25 August a sea wave struck five machines, and disabled two others. The number of Scarabs available for Alhucemas in 1925 were reduced to six.

To transport the troops and land them some 26 K landing barges, four tugs, two transports, two water tankers, and three motorboats were concentrated as landing craft. These had to be used to carry the troops to the beaches, after being moved from the larger transport elements. Some 27 vessels were requisitioned from the Transmediterranea Company, including three hospital ships, and six fast petrol ships, three launches for transporting the wounded and four smaller boats. The K barges, used by the British at Gallipoli, were rotting in Gibraltar after the Great War, and Primo de Rivera had acquired them a year earlier, foreseeing the possibility of a landing. After being refitted, some of them armoured and many reinforcing their landing ramps to support armoured cars and heavy material, they were ready on 30 March 1925. It should be remembered that Primo de Rivera at that time was planning to withdraw from Africa, but as a man of foresight, he always considered several options at the same time, never ruling out the landing as an alternative, even a year before it took place. These details reflect the meticulous work of an excellent General Staff, near improvising the landing when it was finally necessary. Alhucemas was the first multinational landing in history under a single command, coordinating air (130 aircraft), naval (132 ships, including an aircraft carrier), land and armoured elements. For this reason, it would be studied for later landings by the Allied forces during the Second World War, such as those in Sicily and Normandy.[2]

The Air Component

As for the air component, in addition to the six French and 18 Spanish aircraft embarked, Primo de Rivera would have 15 Bristol F.2Bs and six Potez XVs as fighters; 25 Breguet Br XIVs, 15 Fokker C.IVs, 15 Breguet XIXs, six De Havilland DH.4s, four DH.9 A reconnaissance and bombing aircraft; eight Savoia SIAI S.16s and seven Dornier Do-J Wal reconnaissance seaplanes; and three Junkers F 13 ambulances. The ground aviation, under General Jorge Soriano Escudero, was organised in three *Escuadras* (groups of squadrons, or wings): the 1st *Escuadra*, with the 1st and 2nd Breguet Groups, that had two squadrons in Tetuán and another two in Larache; the 2nd *Escuadra*, with the 3rd De Havilland-Napier-Potez Group (with one squadron each of DH.4 Rolls, DH.9 and Potez XV A-2 types) and the 4th Bristol Group, both in Melilla; the 3rd *Escuadra*, with the Fokker Group, and another Group of new Breguet XIX sesquiplanes, both in Melilla; and the Independent Atalayón Group of Dornier Wal and SIAI S.16 bis M seaplanes. Regarding the Potez Group, some 12 Potez machines were ordered the previous year, some of them arriving on 16 June 1924 in Melilla, under captains Pascual Girona, Ricardo de la Puente, and Rafael Gómez-Jordana. The 15 Do-J Wal were ordered from CMASA in Italy (Germany was banned from manufacturing them due to the Treaty of Versailles) in April 1923, arriving in Melilla near immediately. Concerning the Breguet XIX, up to 203 were built by the Spanish CASA company, that was founded for this purpose in March 1923. In June 1924 the first three samples arrived, that entered in combat one year later, under Captain Díaz Sandino.

Sadly, amongst the projectiles gathered for the aircraft there were also bombs loaded with yperite or mustard gas. It seems they were used sporadically. Hidalgo de Cisneros, future commander-in-chief of Republican aviation during the Civil War, would say somewhat callously 'I don't know if the yperite caused damage in the enemy camp. It seemed that the Moors were gargling [with it].' From 29 August, fearing that the Riffians had acquired aircraft, the aviation added one or two white bands to their fuselages to distinguish them, something also done in the Normandy landings.

The Land Component

The landing forces, would be a reinforced division under the command of General Sanjurjo, made up of two brigades: the brigade of General Leopoldo Saro y Marín, or Ceuta Brigade, formed by a company of 10 Renault FT-17 tanks, two Legión Banderas (6th and 7th), three Tabors of Regulares of Tetuán nº 1, the harka of Muñoz Grandes (900 warriors), the Mehalas of Tetuán and Larache (600 men), three battalions of Cazadores de África (3rd, 5th and 8th), and three batteries of artillery (one of them of 105mm howitzers),

Field Marshall Pétain and General and Dictator Primo de Rivera during the meetings in Algeciras where the Alhucemas landing plan was approved. (via Marín Ferrer)

A stern view of the seaplane tender *Dédalo* with a total of 18 S.16s, Macchi M.18s and Scarabs. (via Marín Ferrer)

Another view of the Seaplane carrier Dédalo, crowded with aircraft. Originally, this was the British-built but German-operated steamer Neuenfels, captured in 1918 and turned into a seaplane carrier in 1922. (via Marín Ferrer)

not know how or where he was going to be attacked. In any case, he foresaw the possibility of a landing at Alhucemas, so he reinforced his positions there, erected trench lines and placed the bulk of his artillery in this sector. However, Abd el-Krim's attitude was not only defensive, but in order to confuse any potential Spanish deployment, he decided to attack the capital of Spanish Morocco: Tetuán, south of Ceuta. The offensive would again be led by El Jeriro, Abd el-Krim's man in the west, who knew the area perfectly well having been a follower of El Raisuni years before, whom he betrayed. El Jeriro he counted on 3,000 warriors from Beni Hozmar for the offensive. These troops were made of his own kabyle, reinforced with machine gunners and Riffian artillerymen, adding eight 75mm cannons and one 105mm gun. El Jeriro began the attack by assaulting a line of 10 fortified posts located in the Gorges mountains. Some 400 Spanish soldiers were there, all of them being coordinated by the position at Kudia Tahar, north of Beni Hozmar, on the road south of Tetuán. Kudia Tahar itself was defended by only 137 men of the 5th Infante Regiment and a Schneider mountain battery, and, once again, the water well was outside the post, 2km away,

about 7,500 men in all; and the brigade of General Emilio Fernández Pérez, or Melilla Brigade, formed by a Marine Infantry Battalion, two Legión Banderas (2nd and 3rd), three tabors of Regulares of Melilla nº 2, the Harka Varela (600 warriors), the Mehala of Melilla (600 men), 16th Cazadores Battalion, the 2nd Battalion of the 68th África Regiment, the 1st Battalion of the 59th Melilla Regiment, and two batteries (one of howitzers), about 9,000 soldiers in all.

In Ceuta and Melilla there were 1,500 more soldiers in each district as a reserve, and also in the Peninsula there were 10 more battalions, three groups of 105mm howitzers, a group of 155mm, and another group of 75mm. The artillery amounted to 15 batteries of 155mm, 105mm, and 75mm howitzers, and two of 150mm mortars. Of these units, some nine batteries were installed in the Rock of Alhucemas, an islet property of Spain located less than a kilometre from the Riffian coast, which acted as an excellent 'floating' battery.[3]

Abd el-Krim's Reaction: Kudia Tahar

Abd el-Krim was informed of the recent Spanish-French alliance, and he also knew that a joint offensive was imminent, but he did

at the Aduar de Dar Gassi. The position itself was no more than a wall 1.6m high, surrounding just seven tents.

On 3 September El Jeriro cut the road to the well and began to bombard the position. The Riffian gunners were experienced men, and in half an hour they destroyed three of the Spanish artillery pieces, and by the end of the day had already inflicted 59 casualties. The burning Spanish tents were seen from Tetuán, so a very small relief column of 130 soldiers was sent to rescue the post, the rest of the troops were fixed on the Estella Line, and the organisation of the landing had left the front without immediate reserves. Half of this column managed to enter into the post. The next day, the last intact part of the position was destroyed. A new relief column of 600 soldiers from Ben Karrich under Colonel Hernández Francés marched to the north only to be repulsed after suffering 48 casualties, his commander being hit in the belly.

It was then decided to use to air power to save the post, and on 5 September some 16 Breguet XIXs arrived at Tetuán from Nador, Melilla. The Breguets then flew 211 support missions over Kudia Tahar, dropping 428 bags of supplies and 552 bombs. On the 9th,

Table 14: Aviation for the Alhucemas Landing (September 1925)

General Soriano Escudero	Number of machines	Location
1st Escuadra	25 Breguet XIVs	Tetuán
1st Breguet Group		Larache
Two Breguet XIV squadrons		Larache
2nd Breguet Group		Tetuán
Two Breguet XIV squadrons		Tetuán
2nd Escuadra		Melilla
3rd De Havilland-Napier-Potez Group		Melilla
One DH.4 Rolls squadron	6 DH.4s	Melilla
One DH.9 squadron	4 DH.9As	Melilla
One Potez XV A2 squadron	6 Potez XVs	Melilla
4th Bristol Group		Melilla
Two or three Bristol F.2B squadrons	15 Bristols	Melilla
3rd Escuadra		Melilla
Fokker Group		Melilla
Two or three Fokker C.IV squadrons	15 Fokker C.IVs	Melilla
Breguet Group		Melilla
Two or three Breguet XIX squadrons	15 Breguet XIXs	Melilla
Independent Atalayón Group		Atalayón/Melilla
One Dornier J Wal squadron	7 Do-J Wals	Atalayón/Melilla
One SIAI S.16 Bis M squadron	8 S.16s	Atalayón/Melilla
Naval Aeronautics		
Seaplane Carrier Dédalo		
One Savoia SIAI S.16 Bis M squadron	6 S.16s	*Dédalo*
One Macchi M-18 squadron	6 M.18s	*Dédalo*
One Scarab squadron	6 Scarabs	*Dédalo*
French Forces		
6B2 Squadron	4-6 Farman F-60 Goliaths	Probably at Melilla

Regiment, Intervention of Beni Hozmar, harka and Mehala of Tetuán, and a 70mm battery.[4] The command of these three columns was given to General Sousa, whose initial assault was repulsed, but then, on the 12th, with the support of 36 artillery pieces, the Spaniards of Colonel Balmes reached the watering place of Dar Dassi, and from there they broke the lines of El Jeriro, saving Kudia Tahar at the cost of 120 casualties. In the attack the Spaniards took 126 enemy corpses. After this diversion both Primo and Sanjurjo returned to the main front of Alhucemas. In the operations for Kudia Tahar nine soldiers won Laureates, two more than those of the entire Alhucemas landing, and is evidence of how hard and bitter was the heroic defence of the post.[5]

The Alhucemas Landing

On 7 September Primo de Rivera began the operations for the landing. Firstly, the North African Squadron with two cruisers, the gunboats and the light and transport elements of the fleet departed from Ceuta, taking General Saro's reinforced brigades on board. This unit was divided into four columns and a reserve. The first column, the vanguard, would be under Colonel Franco with a tank unit, one tabor of the harka of Larache and two tabors of the harka of Tetuán, a tabor of the Mehala of Tetuán, 6th and 7th Banderas of the Legión, the 3rd Cazadores Battalion, elements of the machine gun, mortar and engineer sections of the 6th Cazadores Battalion, two sapper companies of the Tetuán Battalion, and 1st Mountain Artillery Battery with 75mm guns; the second column under Colonel Martín with the 1st and 2nd Tabors of Regulares of Tetuán, the 5th Cazadores Battalion, two companies of the Larache Battalion, elements of machine gun, mortar and engineer sections of the 6th Cazadores Battalion, 2nd Battery of Mountain Artillery with 70mm guns; the third column under Lieutenant Colonel Campins with the 3rd Tabor of Regulares of Tetuán and 8th Cazadores Battalion; and the headquarters and reserve with the Asmani and Solimán harkas. At the Martín River, east of Tetuán, the auxiliary harkas of Asmani and the Jatabi, 232 warriors in all, were picked up. At the same time the Training Fleet with two battleships, two cruisers, the destroyers, and the water carrier) departed from Algeciras, Spain, also picking up General Primo de Rivera at the Martín River. Finally, a third fleet sailed from Melilla with one battleship, two cruisers, and two French monitors, and the requisitioned Spanish transports, with General Sanjurjo.

Captain Suarez Somontes' Breguet No. 15 managed to supply the post despite the fact that his observer, Lieutenant Nombela, was hit in the spine, winning another Laureate. In addition, all the aviation of the 1st Squadron of Tetuán and Larache was also used. In spite of everything, the post of Nador 3, merely at 300 metres from Kudia Tahar, defended by 21 soldiers of Sergeant Azcoz, was overwhelmed. Its 10 survivors, all wounded except two, were able to escape thanks to Azcoz, who, half naked and with several wounds, was left alone to cover the retreat. When he was about to be killed, Azcoz threw himself off a cliff and miraculously saved his life, reaching the Nador 1 post, winning the Laureate.

Despite this diversion at Kudia Tahar, General Primo de Rivera kept his nerve and did not suspend the landing, so just two days later the Alhucemas operation began. On the 10th, Primo de Rivera finally withdrew two Legión Banderas and a tabor of Regulares from Alhucemas, which together with General Sanjurjo moved to Tetuán to save Kudia Tahar. For the first assault, three columns were made that would depart from Tetuán: the 1st Column under Lieutenant Colonel Balmes coming from Alhucemas with two Banderas of the Legión and a tabor of Regulares of Melilla; the 2nd Column under Colonel Perteguer with two battalions of Regiments 35th Toledo and 60th Ceuta, a company of Cazadores and a 105mm battery; and a third one with a tabor of Ceuta, a battalion of the Serrallo

Table 15: Alhucemas Landing forces (September 1925)
Reinforced Division
General Sanjurjo
Ceuta Brigade (7,500 men)
General Saro y Marín
Company of 10 Renault FT-17 tanks
6th Bandera of the Legión
7th Bandera of the Legión
Group of Regulares of Tetuán nº 1 (3 tabors)
Harka of Muñoz Grandes (900 warriors)
Mehala of Tetuán (600 men)
Mehala of Larache (600 men)
3rd Arapiles Battalion of Cazadores
5th Segorbe Battalion of Cazadores
8th Tarifa Battalion of Cazadores
Two 75mm batteries
One 105mm battery
Reserves
Ceuta: 1,500 men
Melilla: 1,500 men
Peninsula: 10 Battalions
Melilla Brigade (9,000 men)
General Emilio Fernández Pérez
Marine Infantry Battalion (675 men)
2nd Bandera of the Legión (600 men)
3rd Bandera of the Legión (600 men)
Group of Regulares of Melilla nº 2 (three tabors of 500, 530 and 530 men)
Harka Varela (600 or 750 warriors)
Mehala de Melilla (600 or 750 men)
16th Battalion of Cazadores de África (860 men)
2nd Battalion/68th África Regiment (1,200 men)
1st Battalion/59th Melilla Regiment (1,296 men)
One 75 mm battery (210 men)
One howitzer battery (210 men)
Artillery
3 groups of 105mm howitzers
1 group of 155mm
1 group of 75mm
2 batteries of 150mm mortars
Alhucemas Rock
5 batteries of 155mm (20 pieces)
2 batteries of 105mm (4 pieces)
2 batteries of 150mm mortars (4 pieces)

An aerial view of the post of Kudia Tahar attacked by the Riffians to distract the Spaniards from the Alhucemas landing. (via Sánchez & Kindelán)

Captain Rodrigo in a parade in Melilla with his Regulares, celebrating the successful stand of Kudia Tahar. (Carrasco & de Mesa)

The coffin of Lieutenant Colonel Hernández Francés, commander of the 1st Mehala of Tetuán, killed by his wounds in Kudia Tahar. (Carrasco & de Mesa)

The three fleets joined together off the coast of Alhucemas. Then began preparations to launch the first landing wave, consisting of 8,000 soldiers, each one equipped with 200 rounds of ammunition, two cold rations of meat, and two canteens. These would be followed by transports and cisterns with 3,400 water vats and the hospital. The fog and bad weather at dawn caused the landing to be postponed for 24 hours, which was used as an opportunity to bombard the coast with battleships and cruisers.

It is difficult to determine the Riffian deployment on the coast, but there were probably about seven groups of about 300 warriors, two cannons, and four machine guns, each. That is, about 2,100 soldiers with 14 cannons and 28 machine guns. However, Abd el-Krim expected the landing further east, on the wide and clear beaches of Sfiha and Suani, where he must have placed about four of these groupings, leaving only about three on the heights that closed the bay to the west, which is where the landing actually took place. We can deduce something of the Riffian deployment due the location of the Riffian batteries (each of two guns instead of the customary four) detected by Spanish intelligence: from west to east, there was a battery at Punta de los Frailes, another at Morro Nuevo and another one at Morro Viejo; all of them in the landing area although somewhat to the east, except for the first one. Outside of the landing area, were the batteries of Adrar Sedum, Rocosa, Castillo of Muyahedi, Loma, and Prisioneros (all already on the beach of Sfiha, outside the attack area). Therefore, the choice of the landing point, apart from the main Riffian defensive deployment, was a new success of the Spanish General Staff.[6]

The next day, at 0600 the French fleet bombarded La Rocosa and Suani beach, to fool the Riffians and make them concentrate their forces there. Then, at 0820 the Spanish ships began the bombardment of Ixdain and Punta de los Frailes, the actual landing place. At 1140 the tugboats began to pull the K barges. The Riffian fire contested the invasion and caused five dead. One kilometre away from the coast the barges were released, which under the power of their own engines reached the beaches of Ixdain and Cebadilla, near the promontory that closes the Bay of Alhucemas on its western side.[7]

The first barge was K 23 carrying the 24th Company of the 6th Bandera of the Legión, followed by the harka of Muñoz Grandes. Some 50 metres away from the shore the ramps were lowered, and the soldiers descended with the water up to their chests and their arms raised, holding their weapons and ammunition high, with Colonel Franco at their head. Just at the moment of landing, the 2nd Bristol F.2B Squadron (Álvarez Buylla) appeared to protect it, followed by the 1st Fokker C.IV Squadron, the Napier and Rolls squadrons (DH.9s and DH.4s), and the Dornier Wal seaplanes under Ortiz Muñoz. Commandant Muñoz Grandes covered the right flank and centre of the beach (west), while Franco's 6th Bandera marched on the left (east). After taking Monte Rocoso, two machine guns and a Riffian cannon, and forming a minimal bridgehead, General Saro himself disembarked to organise the rest of the advance. At the end, only two landing barges were disabled in the entire landing. Then, the merchant ships disembarked the medical equipment and ammunition, covered by the fire of the fleet and the air force (some 40 aircraft were flown that day).[8]

Consolidating the Beachhead

With the arrival of further reinforcements, General Saro organised two lines of advance: Martín's column was deployed to the west, and the column of Colonel Franco was to act in the east. At the same time,

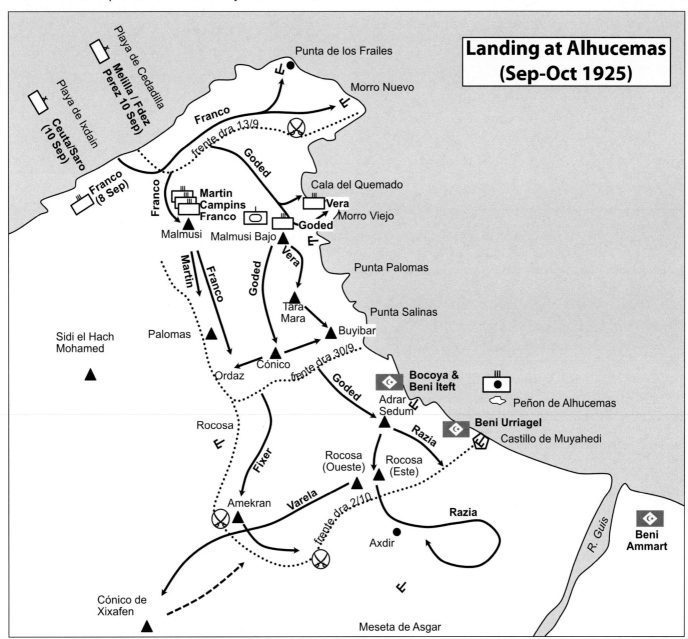

Landing at Alhucemas (Sep-Oct 1925)

(Map by Mark Thompson)

The battleship *Alfonso XIII* bombing the Alhucemas coast with its eight 305mm guns. (via Marín Ferrer)

A Riffian machine gun crew. Machine guns were sometimes operated by disguised foreign mercenaries. (Desperta Ferro Magazine)

Abd el-Krim's Riffian warriors during 1925. (Desperta Ferro Magazine)

Riffians handling an artillery piece. (Hulton Deutsh Collection/ Corbis via Courcelles & Marmié)

the beach of Ixdain, difficult to access, was abandoned. Henceforth, for the moment only the beach of La Cebadilla was used. With the western flank covered by Muñoz Grandes' harka, successive reinforcements extended the bridgehead eastwards: the Mehala of Larache now landed, and advanced against Morro Nuevo, to the south-east, to take a new landing beach. Morro Nuevo, on the other side of the Alhucemas promontory had to be conquered in order to be able to expand the beachhead. With just one beach, the Spanish forces would not have enough space to receive reinforcements to break the front, so they could be cornered against the coast by the Riffians, as happened to the British at Galipolli. The Mehala was supported by the 7th Bandera (newly created in June 1925), which joined the 6th Bandera in its advance to the north-east against the Frailes, at the tip of the Alhucemas salient, taking three Riffian guns

and a machine gun. These just captured positions were defended by the Spaniards by creating a perimeter with barbed wire, trenches, and machine gun posts to prevent counterattacks.

Then, the 3rd Battalion of Cazadores de África disembarked, reinforcing the western sector of Commandant Muñoz Grandes. Muñoz Grandes advanced against the fortifications of Mount Malmusi, which were defended with artillery that fired firing piercing shells. At the same time, the newly landed sections of sappers cleared the beaches of mines so that they could receive the second landing waves, the first two tabors of Martín's column. The 2nd Battery of Mountain Artillery was carrier ashore on the shoulders of the troopers at 1305. Muñoz Grande's harka took the first slopes of Malmusi mountain to secure the landing. The barges then returned to pick up the third wave, formed by Campins' column, which arrived in the early morning of the 9th, forming the reserve for the other two columns. The 3rd Tabor of Regulares de Tetuán No. 1 went to reinforce the right (Martín's column) and the 8th Battalion of Cazadores went to the left (Franco's column).

At the end of this day the Spanish had suffered 103 casualties and one aircraft shot down. The aircraft was DH.9 A No. 68 of Napier Squadron, which fell into the sea, although its crew was rescued. The Dornier Wal No. 2 piloted by Ramón Franco, the brother of the future dictator, suffered an engine breakdown, but the seaplane was saved. From then on, the air support began to diminish until it finally disappeared due to the bad weather, until 16 September, and the tides and waves prevented the seaplanes from landing in the bay. On top of that, several transports and the battleship *Paris* were hit by enemy fire, although without suffering great damage. For this

The first wave of the landing led by Colonel Franco, that was short by some 50 metres of the beach, so Franco's Legión had to walk with the water at chest height under the enemy fire. Note the K landing barges, and the black dots (the soldiers) moving to the beach. (via Marín Ferrer)

the squadron in a faluche that served as their base. At the end the landing had been a success, but the question remained as to whether the Spaniards would manage to break through the front and march inland, or be cornered on the coast, as happened at Gallipoli.[9]

Spain and its First World War

The First World War consisted, on its western front, typically of terrible trench warfare, in which the advances were measured by metres, from hill to hill, with a massive artillery support, gas, and aviation, against an enemy protected behind barbed wire lines, redoubts and positions covered by machine gun and cannon fire. Spain had been spared of all these terrible scenes by its neutrality, but now, sadly, its turn had come.

reason, fearing that the aircraft carrier *Dédalo* could be bombed, it was moved to Melilla, taking all its aircraft (including the French ones) to Atalayón, Melilla. On the good side, the Dornier and Savoia seaplanes of the Military Aviation anchored among the ships of

On 9 September, the 3rd Howitzer Battery was emplaced and began counterbattery fire to destroy the Riffian artillery, and the Renault assault tanks were finally landed. The tanks were left on the right (or west) flank, next to the Tetuán Regulares. The Riffian fire was very intense, and the cruiser *Méndez Núñez* was hit, forcing the heavy ships to move away from the coast, while the French fleet left the battle scene for good. Two Dornier Wal seaplanes were also lost, one by enemy fire and the other by engine failure, but without suffering losses in personnel.

A view from the beach of the first waves of the landing. (via Marín Ferrer)

A K landing barge with the Regulares jumping directly on to the beach instead of wading through the sea, in this picture of reinforcements arriving after the first waves. (via Marín Ferrer)

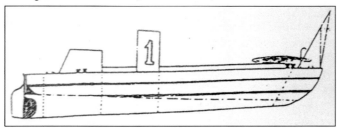

A sketch of a K landing barge, first used by the British in Gallipoli where they were referred to as X-lighters, and acquired by Spain from stocks at Gibraltar. (via Marín Ferrer)

After the first waves of troops had landed, heavy equipment was landed by freighters. (Desperta Ferro Magazine)

Cargo unloading from a barge. (Desperta Ferro Magazine)

A view of three DH.9 aircraft. One of them, number 68, was shot down by Riffian fire during the landing. (via Sánchez & Kindelán)

A detailed view of the nose of a Dornier Wal seaplane. While piloted by Ramón Franco, brother of the future dictator, aircraft number 2 was damaged on landing, but at least its hull was recovered. (via Sánchez & Kindelán)

as we saw at the beginning of this chapter. Luckily, they would return to Alhucemas on the 19th.

On the 11th, the artillery duel at Alhucemas increased as Abd el-Krim took advantage of the break to reinforce his artillery in the sector. Also, at about 2200 he launched a large night counterattack with 800 Riffians all along the line, with rifle fire and grenades, especially on the eastern flank. His troops reached the so-called Casamata del Cañón, on the Morro Nuevo Peninsula, where they occupied the position after putting the entire garrison to the sword. Varela's harka and the Mehala of Melilla made a counterattack and regained the position.[10] Finally, the Riffians abandoned their counteroffensive around 0500.

On the 12th, the Spaniards created a second and a third line of trenches in their rear which they connected to the front line by covered roads, and again at 2300 the Riffians launched another night counterattack in the eastern sector. The Spaniards counted on this occasion with naval fire and illumination via searchlights to disrupt the offensive.

The static artillery duel between both contending sides continued for 10 days. On the 16th there were already six Spanish batteries (four of 70mm mountain artillery and two of 105mm howitzers) on

On the 10th, three Spanish artillery batteries were already in the front line, which were also supported by the nine batteries on the islet of Alhucemas. Then, the disembarkation of General Fernández Pérez's Melilla Brigade began. This unit was made up of Mehala troops who were deployed in the extreme left (or east) of the line. The situation remained stationary, since as we have seen, generals Primo de Rivera himself and Sanjurjo had to depart to Tetuán with three battalions (whose landing was cancelled) to save Kudia Tahar,

Soldiers of the 7th Bandera of the Legión, a new unit that practically had its baptism of fire in the Alhucemas landing, seen here, with a captured Schneider 75mm gun. (Desperta Ferro Magazine)

Future Dictator Franco, with his brother, Ramón. After the Rif War, in 1926 Ramón Franco flew his Do Wal named *Plus Ultra* more than 10,000 kilometres from Palos in Spain to Buenos Aires, Argentina, becoming a national hero. Paradoxically, he was a Mason and a supporter of the Republic, collaborating in the exile of King Alfonso XIII. During the Civil War blood ties weighed more heavily and he became a supporter of the rebels and he crashed and died in a Cant Z-506 in 1938. (via Gárate Córdoba)

land. This time, methodically, the counterbattery fire and the aviation destroyed the Riffian batteries one by one: on the 13th, Mount Malmusi was bombed, and on the 17th both the Spanish and the French seaplanes attacked the Riffian shelters built into the rock. From that day on, there was an increase in the use of C-5 bombs loaded with mustard gas, dropping a total of 466 munitions by the end of the operations in October. This type of terrible armament was used sporadically to beat very difficult positions where Riffians were hidden in rocks or caves and far from the Spanish troops.

Finally, on the 22nd a Spanish offensive reconnaissance was carried out to test the state of the Riffian force and its best defended positions. The Moors of the harka of Muñoz Grandes attacked at 0500 from the west, and that of Varela from the east, but the Riffian fire was very powerful, so that both units withdrew after two hours. However, Abd el-Krim's key position was discovered: this was the fortified Mount Malmusi, to the south-west. Abd el-Krim had organised several points of concentration of warriors from the interior, at Adrar sed-Dum (for the warriors of Bocoya and Beni Iteft); on the beach of Sfiha (for those of Beni Urriaguel); and on the river Guis, east of Axdir, (for those of Beni Ammart); so that the Riffian positions were reinforced at least by the troops of these kabyles.

On the night of the 22nd to the 23rd, the Riffians attacked the camp of the harka of Suleiman el Jatabi, cousin of Abd el-Krim, to capture it. The assault had not success as Varela's harka reinforced the other pro-Spanish harka.[11]

The Armoured Assault on Malmusi

On the 23rd, some 12,000 Spanish soldiers already disembarked began the assault on Mount Malmusi. The Saro Ceuta Brigade was made, west to east, of the following columns: 1st Column, under Colonel Martín consisting of 1st and 2nd Tabors of Regulares of Tetuán, 5th Cazadores Battalion, and two 105mm batteries; 2nd Column under Lieutenant Colonel Campins consisting of 3rd Tabor of Regulares of Tetuán, 8th Cazadores Battalion; and 3rd Column under Colonel Franco with a tank company, two tabors of the harka of Tetuán, a tabor of the harka of Larache, 6th and 7th Banderas of the Legión, 3rd Cazadores Battalion, and a 70mm battery. The Melilla Brigade was made up of Colonel Goded's column of the harka of Melilla under Varela, 2nd Mehala, 2nd and 3rd Banderas of the Legión, 16th Cazadores Battalion, a 70mm battery, and a sapper company; and the reserve under Colonel Félix Vara, consisting of the Regulares of Melilla Group, Marine Infantry Battalion, and a 70mm battery.[12]

The Ceuta Brigade of General Saro would make the main effort, attacking the Malmusi Alto (High Malmusi) from the beach of Cebadilla, to the south-west, with the columns of Franco and

A view of the Spanish fleet with several freighters, barges, and a fabricated dock, unloading reinforcements and heavy equipment. (via Marín Ferrer)

A detailed view of one of the docks designed and built on the Alhucemas beaches to land further reinforcements. (via Marín Ferrer)

aircraft (four shot down and three damaged and grounded) between the 17th and the 23rd. To ensure a continuous air presence over the frontline, some six to eight aircraft were permanently in the air, especially the Fokker Group under the Royal Prince Alfonso de Orleans. The Prince spent three consecutive hours in the air over the enemy targets and under heavy Riffian fire.

At 0700 the Spanish artillery fire began on the Malmusi and on the second Riffian line of las Palomas, in the rear, to prevent them from sending reinforcements. Half an hour later colonels Franco and Campins left their positions for

Campins. Martín would make only a demonstration to distract enemy forces. Goded's column of the Melilla Brigade would attack along the coast from Morro Nuevo to Morro Viejo and Malmusi Bajo (Low Malmusi), to the south-east. Generals Sanjurjo and Primo de Rivera were left at Cebadilla beach to coordinate the operation. Air cover would be provided by the Rolls (DH.4) and Fokker Groups and the Potez Squadron, and the coastal areas would be supported by naval fire, both from the west and east. However, due to the heavy Riffian fire some ships took up to 40 hits, so only the battleships were able to stay on the line to provide fire support. Everything tells us that air support was massive and brutal, as 21–23 September accounted for about 33 percent of all bombs dropped on Alhucemas up to October. The air force had been reinforced with Breguet XIVs and XIXs from Tetuán after the Kudia Tahar operations. In any case, the air activity suffered heavy losses, as the Spanish lost seven

the assault, advancing preceded by the Renault tanks. In the centre the harkas of Tetuán and the Mehala of Larache moved against the slopes, and further west, towards the coast, Campins' 3rd Tabor of Tetuán deviated to encircle the enemy position. Despite heavy fire, these units reached the summits fixed as their first objectives, but then the Riffians blew up a minefield and most of the pro-Spanish Moroccans had to retreat. The Riffians then slipped down from the crags and made a counterattack taking advantage of the confusion, but the Spanish officers had remained in their positions trying to repel the assault. The native troops, spurred on by the example given by their commanders, turned back and bayoneted the Riffians.

Further east advanced the 6th and 7th Banderas of Franco's Legión. They met resistance in a reed bed and a grove that was assaulted head-on by the 6th Bandera, while the 7th Bandera, with the tanks, surrounded an enemy fixed at the front, and annihilated

Before the assault against the Riffian entrenchments at Malmusi, two further Dornier Wal seaplanes were destroyed, one being shot down by Riffian fire. (via Sánchez & Kindelán)

them. At 1046 the advance to the highest peaks of the Malmusi Alto began, which the 6th and 7th Banderas and the harka of Muñoz Grandes crowned in only 10 minutes. Then, they continued through the so-called Cuernos (Horns) of Xixafen. At 1345 the 3rd Tabor of Regulares crowned the Loma del Almiar, protected with a mobile barrage of artillery. In the final clearing work among the rocks, 50 Riffian corpses were found.[13]

Meanwhile, the Melilla Brigade of General Fernández Pérez also began its advance from the east, with Goded's column divided on three axes of march: the one of the centre was made of the 2nd and 3rd Banderas of the Legión, and the Melilla Regulares. These were covered on its flanks by the Varela' harka (in the interior, to the west), and the Mehala of Colonel Martín Alonso on the outside, on the coast, to the east.[14] The reserve column under Colonel Vera, then moved his Regulares forward to the west, to connect with Colonel Franco and the Ceuta Brigades. In the meantime, in Goded's column, Colonel Varela advanced in the vanguard, having to take refuge in some ruined houses to protect himself from the Riffian fire. Even so, Varela recovered and pushed the Riffians to the Barranco (ravine) of Cardeñosa, in the foothills of Malmusi Bajo (Low Malmusi). Then, these Riffians were also attacked from behind and with armoured vehicles, collapsing and dissolving the Moorish line. At the same time, with naval fire support, the Mehala advanced to Morro Viejo, which it took at 0930. A point of resistance was left in his rear, in the Cala del Quemado, which was annihilated in a casemate-by-casemate assault by the Legión troopers.

For the rest of the day the troops rested until 1825 when new troops were deployed to consolidate what had been conquered. Now the Spanish lines included the Iber Loken and Tixdirt springs, which alleviated the water necessities of the army a little. The Riffians abandoned 165 rifles and left another 50 corpses, with 23 prisoners taken. With this ended the French air force operations in Alhucemas, as their four Farman F.60 Goliaths from 6B2 Squadron now departed, though his was compensated for with a new Breguet squadron that arrived from Seville. Then, the Breguet XIX Group was moved to the Melilla area.[15]

The Mehalas suffered heavily during the 1925 operations. In this picture, the soldiers on the left and right (Bel-Hosain and Bel-Achehed) were injured, and the one in the middle was killed in action. (Carrasco & de Mesa)

The Breakthrough to Axdir

The next Riffian defensive line, further south, was located along the Monte de las Palomas, and to the east the Monte Taramara. The Sanjurjo Division was then reorganised for the next assault: the Ceuta Brigade was organised into the 1st Group under Colonel Franco with two tabors of the harka of Tetuán, two tabors of Regulares of Tetuán, 6th and 7th Banderas of the Legión, a four-company sapper group, a 70mm battery and a 105mm battery; the 2nd Group under Colonel Martín with one tabor of Regulares of

A Renault FT-17 tank resting with some soldiers in the Alhucemas campaign. (via Marín Ferrer)

A French Farman Goliath. These heavy bombers were retired from the front after the assault on the Malmusi in the last days of September. (via Sánchez & Kindelán)

Tetuán, 5th and 8th Cazadores Battalions, a 70mm battery and a 105mm battery; and the 3rd Group of Lieutenant Colonel Losada with Mehala of Larache, 3rd Cazadores Battalion, a naval 76.2mm battery and a 105mm howitzer battery. The Melilla Division had Colonel Goded's 1st Group with the harka of Melilla, Mehala of Melilla, the 2nd and 3rd Banderas of the Legión, a 70mm battery and two sappers companies, and the 2nd Group under Colonel Vera with a group of Regulares of Melilla, a battalion from the África Regiment, a 70mm battery and a sapper company. On the 28th and 29th the aviation located up to 18 Riffian artillery pieces some five kilometres from Ait Kamara. Immediately, on the 30th, not leaving Abd el-Krim time to consolidate his lines, General Saro's brigade, preceded by Colonel Franco's column, after a land and naval artillery preparation and a furious aerial bombardment, advanced from the slopes of the Malmusi.[16] His vanguard consisted of the harka of Tetuán, followed by the Regulares. They were supported, to the west, by Losada's Mehala and Cazadores. Colonel Martín would be kept in the rear to connect, to the east, with the Melilla Brigade. Then the Spanish harkas crossed the dry riverbed of the river Tixdirt and occupied las Palomas with two companies of the Legión, supported by the fires of the Mehala of Larache and the Regulares of Tetuán. All of this was done despite an episode of friendly fire: the air force mistook the Mehalas and Regulares for Riffians and attacked them.

In any case, more than 60 aircraft took off, staggered by squadrons every 45 minutes. A Potez, a Fokker and a Savoia SIAI S.16 bis were lost while in the 'Spanish Flight', although luckily there were no personnel casualties. At 1145 Franco's troops were relieved by Martín's column that came behind with fresh troops. On the east flank, Colonel Goded's column advanced against Mount Cónico, and then to Ordaz, to his right, supported further east by Colonel Vera, that would take Taramara and Buyibar Heights. Colonel Félix Vera personally assaulted these two places with hand grenades, supported by two aircraft.

On 1 October the advance in the east was resumed. Fernández Pérez's Melilla Brigade would be preceded by two columns under the command of Colonel Goded. He assaulted the heights of Adrar Seddum, further south, the last obstacle to reach Axdir, the capital of Abd el-Krim. Goded had the 1st Regulares of Tetuán to the west, between Monte Cónico and las Palomas, followed by the Mehala of Melilla; then in the centre, Goded counted on the harka of Varela, followed by the 2nd Bandera of the Legión; and to the east, he had the three tabors of the 2nd Regulares of Melilla (with the 1st Tabor in the rear). Behind this force were the engineers and machine guns of the Melilla Battalion. Further in the rear, the 3rd Bandera, the Melilla Battalion, and the artillery were covering with their fire the advance from the positions gained the day before.

At 1000 the Spaniards crossed the dry riverbed of the Isli River to the west, that marked the end of Bocoya kabyle to the south, and the beginning of Beni Urriaguel. To the east, Adrar Saddum was crowned, and on the west, the Regulares of Tetuán, under the charismatic Colonel Fiscer (also written as Fixer), took Mount Amekrán, where they captured three cannons and two machine guns. The weak Riffian counterattacks were repulsed, and the Spanish line was consolidated. That same day, Lieutenant Senén at the controls of Bristol No. 15 located in Yebel Amekrán, west of Axdir, a group of Riffians carrying an artillery piece. Senén descended and bombarded the piece at an altitude of just 60m, destroying it, despite receiving a bullet in the head and then another in the wrist. Senén bandaged his wounds with his observer's tie and continued his mission. After landing, he lost consciousness but survived and won the Laureate.[17]

On 2 October, General Goded continued his advance. The forces of Varela's harka, on his left (east), occupied La Rocosa, a position north of Axdir itself, and the Mehala of Melilla linked up with Varela from Amekrán, on the right. In any case, in a last and desperate dash the Riffians managed to annihilate the Spanish advance guard at Casamata at night, but all of this was for nothing. The Riffian front was completely broken, and so the Spaniards spread out through Axdir, Sfiha beach and Suani, occupying Abd el-Krim's own house, who had abandoned the defensive lines. Four other cannons were captured. Now, the navy training fleet returned to Spain, although the battleship *Jaime I* and the cruiser *Méndez Núñez* remained in the North Africa Squadron.

Between 3–6 October the Spanish reinforced their lines, and on the 13th operations were resumed to rectify the lines and put an end to the Riffian pockets. This time two columns were formed under Colonel Vera's Group, the one of Lieutenant Colonel Balmes consisting of the harka of Solinán, the harka of Varela with two tabors, and the 2nd Bandera of the Legión; and the one of Lieutenant Colonel Pozas – future defender of Madrid on the Republican side – with a tabor of Varela's harka, a tabor of Regulares of Tetuán, two companies of Regulares of Melilla, and five of sappers. Both columns cleared the area surrounding Amekrán, between Rocosa, to the east, to Xixafen, to the west taking this last mount.

Unlike the Allies at Gallipoli, the Spaniards managed to break through the front, assaulting and taking the hills that dominated the landing beaches and then to penetrate into the interior, forcing the collapse of the Riffians. The war would last another year and a half, but everything would now consist of harassment and clearing actions. Spain had finally achieved its decisive victory by forcing the Riffians to do battle in the conventional way, as they had to protect their capital, the heart of their main kabyle, and their leader, that all were in a fixed position. In any case, the Alhucemas offensive was not a military stroll, as the Spaniards suffered 2,236 casualties in this month of operations (60 percent of them being native troops), that is, about a 15 percent of the 18,000 men landed. Of these, 361 were killed. The losses for the Riffians are not easy to calculate, as some sources talk about 1,000 casualties in all, while others state that just the number of deaths were 700, so with the injured and prisoners perhaps they could be similar to the Spanish total losses. Regarding the air force, eight aircraft were lost and seven more were damaged, although only one pilot was killed.[18]

Linking with the French Troops

Meanwhile, in the southern sector, faithful to Marshal General Pétain's commitment, the French resumed the offensive, this time penetrating into Spanish territory, although benefiting from the near absence of Riffian troops, as the bulk were now concentrated against the Spanish in Alhucemas. In the first phase, six battalions of the Dosse Brigade/1st Division, would expand the base for the offensive, in the north of Kifane, in the eastern sector. However, torrential rains on 27 September halted operations. Marshal Pétain, impatiently, went to the front to lead the offensive, sending General Naulin to the rear.

When the offensive resumed in October, the forces within Boichurt's Eastern Sector (including the 11th and 1st March Divisions, and cavalry) were as follows: the Western Group, some 12,000 troops with 23 battalions, two squadrons of tanks, two squadrons of cavalry, 900 Harkeans, and two squadrons of aircraft, had to march north from Kifane; the Central Group with five battalions, a Spahi marching regiment, 400 goumiers, 300 harkeen, a tank company and an air squadron, had to take Ain Zohra and support the flank of the Eastern Group. This latter group, under General Jonchay, in Hassi Medlam, in a flat terrain, would be formed almost entirely by cavalry (eight squadrons of the 1st Spahis Brigade, a tank company, six infantry battalions, 200 goumiers and two air squadrons) would march northwards, trying to expand his front as much as possible, then to shake hands with the Spanish forces, and finally moving diagonally westwards to cut the Riffian rear in Si Ali Bou Rokba (Geznaya).

The Western Group advanced without encountering resistance, reaching Nador, Bab Soltan and Tizi Ouzli (Geznaya and M'talsa) on 5 and 6 October. Seeing the ease of advance, the Central Group was then disbanded, and its forces distributed in the other two groupings. On the other hand, the East Group, stuck in the mud, could hardly advance, although it reached Souk es-Sebt de Ain Mar (M'talsa), linking up with the Spaniards. Finally, the 1st Spahis Brigade did manage to advance in depth, reaching Bou Rokba (Geznaya), but being totally

Soldiers of the Mehala of Melilla during combat operation in Alhucemas. (via Carrasco & de Mesa)

A mix of Regulares and Legión troops celebrating the taking of Axdir, with a captured flag of the Republic of the Rif. (via Marín Ferrer)

Two German mercenaries captured by the Spanish after taking Axdir. Probably these professional soldiers were contracted by the Riffians to handle the artillery pieces or the machine guns. (via Marín Ferrer)

Pétain Pushes Primo

As already mentioned, when Marshal General Pétain and Lieutenant General Primo de Rivera met, the Spanish dictator limited Madrid's intervention to the landing and capture of Axdir. According to Major General Gómez-Jordana, Military Director for Morocco and the Colonies, he and Primo preferred to defeat Abd el-Krim by so-called 'political action', by bribing or pressuring the kabyle leaders that would force Abd el-Krim to sue for peace, rather than by military operations. However, Pétain (supported by General Sanjurjo) managed to convince Primo de Rivera to continue the fight to the end with the argument that the Riffian leader had joined to the Third International and received the support of the French Communist Party, so that the survival of the regime in any form was a risk to the stability of the whole of Africa. Thus, on 6 February 1926, a new agreement was signed in Madrid to continue the operations until the surrender and expulsion of Abd el-Krim and the disarmament of all the kabyles. In the meantime, Primo de Rivera had continued with the clearing operations behind the Estella Line, and on 13 January he had completely subdued the rebel Kabyles of Anyera and El Hauz, which were threatening Ceuta and Tetuán, collecting some 2,000 rifles. This number of rifles also allows us to evaluate the real war potential of the Riffians in the area, in contraposition to the gross exaggerations made by the Spanish and French intelligence services.

As Abd el-Krim knew of the signing of the new Spanish-French Agreement, he decided to carry out a local counterattack that would delay the allied offensive and open room for negotiations. The Riffian leader decided to attack Tetuán again, capital of the Spanish Protectorate, which was still in the front line. Ahmed Jeriro placed some 1,000 warriors with 155mm heavy artillery in Bu Zeitung, with which he bombarded the city in February. The Spaniards tried at first to disperse the Riffian concentration with air strikes, but finally General Sanjurjo had to organise an operation to dislodge the rebels by taking Dar Rai (Beni Hozmar). On 4 March, Brigadier General Federico de Souza y Regoyos, with the support from 11 batteries under Colonel Perteguer Astudillo and naval fire, launched four or five columns against the Riffians. These were one on the left under Colonel Luiz Orgaz Yoldi,[20] with four tabors of Regulares, two battalions of the Serrallo Regiment, and a battery; one on the right under Colonel José Millán Astray (returned to service after another serious wound), with four Banderas, two battalions of the Ceuta Regiment, and a battery. These groups were flanked by Lieutenant Colonel Eduardo Sáenz de Buruaga on the extreme left,[21] with Beni Hozmar's Intervention, a tabor made from a friendly harka, and the 3rd África Battalion; and by Lieutenant Colonel Aureliano Álvarez Coque on the extreme right flank,[22] with the Mehala of Tetuán, and the 1st Battalion of Cazadores. In just three days the Spanish cleared the front and occupied Bu Zeitung, but not without losses: on 4 March, Colonel Millán Astray took Loma Redonda but when he was

isolated it was counterattacked and had to retreat to Ain Mar (M'talsa). The operation had cost 100 French casualties.

During the winter the French army was deployed as follows, from west to east: 128th Division in Ouezzan; 35th Division in Tafrant, Amiot and Ouled-Guezzar; 11th Division in Taunat, Muley and Ain Yenine; 1st Division in the Tsoul and Branès Kabyle; Moroccan Division, north of Kifane; and the 3rd and 2nd Divisions as a general reserve.[19]

fortifying it, he was shot in the face and injured again, now for the fourth time. The bullet destroyed Millán Astray's maxilla and left cheek; he lost his eye and suffered from vertigo for the rest of his life.

Meanwhile, Abd el-Krim had launched another offensive against the sector of Larache-Alcazarquivir, in the western end of the Protectorate, but the quick reaction of Brigadier General Riquelme (who had panicked in Xauén but was later rehabilitated in Larache) repulsed the attack with a column under Colonel José Asensio Torrado.[23] Torrado occupied the Ahl Sherif and Beni Issef kabyles, to the east of the western sector, thus abandoning the defensive Estella Line to begin offensive actions. The demoralisation among the Riffians was already something evident, and the 'political action' of the Intervention Service reached the figure of 1,703 rifles delivered by the kabyles to the Spaniards on 15 March. Probably the great majority of them must be attributed to the two subdued kabyles in the western zone.[24]

The Planning for the Final Offensive

The last chance of a negotiated peace for Abd el-Krim happened in Oujda (Uxda), when the representatives of France, Spain and the Rif met under the 'Green Tapestry', in the spring of 1926, without results. Following the failure of the Uxda Conference, between 18 April and 6 May the allies began their offensive. The truth is that there was little to discuss at Uxda, as it was proposed that Abd el-Krim should accept the Madrid Agreement: exile and disarmament.

Broadly speaking, the offensive would consist of a concentric advance from the north and east by Spain, and from the south by France, with the allied forces joining hands at Targuist. First, a column of 3,000 or 4,500 Spaniards under Colonel Pozas Perea would set out from Afrau (Beni Said), on the coast, in the area of the Melilla sector, marching to the west to occupy the Tensaman kabyle.[25] His column was made up of native idalas, harkas and mehalas, the 18th Cazadores Battalion and a battery. In the Central Rif, in the recently conquered Axdir (Beni Urriaguel), Major General Castro Girona had now 28,000 Spaniards of the Alhucemas landing grouped in five columns: those of Brigadier General Ángel Dolla Lahoz in the reserve with two tabors of the Mehala of Tetuán, the 4th and part of the 7th Battalion of Cazadores, a Bandera of the Legión, and six batteries, for 4,700 soldiers in all; on his right flank was Colonel Benigno Fiscer's (or Fixer's) column of a tabor of Regulares from Larache, two Banderas of the Legión, the 7th, 8th and 9th Battalions of Cazadores, and four batteries, totalling 6,650 soldiers; Colonel Amadeo Balmes Alonso was deployed in the centre, formed by two tabors of the harka of Tetuán, a tabor of the Regulares of Larache, a Bandera of the Legión, the 3rd, 5th and 6th battalions of Cazadores, and two batteries, totalling 7,050 men; on his left was Colonel Emilio Mola Vidal,[26] formed by a harka and three tabors and two squadrons of the Regulares of Melilla, two Banderas of the Legión, the 13th, 14th and 15th Battalions of Cazadores, and a battery, 7,050 soldiers in all; and Colonel José Monasterio Ituarte with the cavalry,[27] formed by a Mehala cavalry tabor of three squadrons, a tabor of Regulares, and two mounted squadrons of machine guns, about 900 horsemen in all. Defending the Axdir perimeter would be the 2nd Battalion of Cazadores, 16 companies of line infantry, four machine gun companies, and seven batteries, under Colonel Vázquez.

These forces would break through the main entrenched Riffian front, to the south, and advance through Asgar and Tafra following the valley of the river Nekor, until linking up with a second Spanish group coming from Azib de Midar, to the south-east (east of Beni Tuzin, next to M'talsa). This second formation was a force of between

General Franco, on the left, and Colonel Millán Astray reviewing soldiers of the Legión. (Carrasco & de Mesa)

Colonel Millán Astray, several times injured (wounded in the chest in 1921, in the leg in 1922, an arm amputated in 1924, and an eye lost in 1926) but still on duty with his baton (and his adjutant) in the frontline again in 1926. (Carrasco & de Mesa)

8,000 and 12,000 Spaniards under Brigadier General Manuel González Carrasco with 1,000 natives of Intervention, three tabors and another tabor of cavalry of Regulares of Alhucemas, a Bandera of the Legión, two battalions of the África Regiment, the 16th Cazadores Battalion, the Mounted Mías of the Tafersit Mehala, four squadrons of the Alcántara Regiment, and six batteries, with 8,080 soldiers in all, in two columns under Colonels Miguel Campins and Miguel Ponte,[28] that would advance to the west, to Zoco el Telata de Eslef (Beni Tuzin), occupying the Alto Kert, and then would turn to the north by the mountain of Bu Ailma and the plateau of Teffer to link up in the valley of the Nekor with the Alhucemas-Axdir troops of Castro Girona. It was planned that with these two actions, Beni Urriaguel and Beni Tuzin kabyles would be subdued.

Protecting the left flank of Brigadier General González Carrasco there were 40,000 Frenchmen under General Marty. His North Taza Group would advance also, to cover the Spaniards. This army corps, formed by three divisions, would go up to the north from the valley of the Ouarga river, in Geznaya. From west to east, the 1st Division under General Vernois, would go from Bab Sultan (Geznaya) to the heights of Tamersga, on the border of Beni Urriaguel with Beni Ammart, occupying the latter village. The Moroccan Division under General Pierre Ibós, in the centre, would depart from Nador (Geznaya) towards Zoco el Jemís, on the south slope of the Yebel Haman mountains, clearing all the Geznaya, and then diagonally penetrating via Beni Amart until arriving at Targuist, eliminating this last Kabyle. And finally, the 3rd Division under General Edmond Dosse, to the east, would link up with the Spanish occupying the

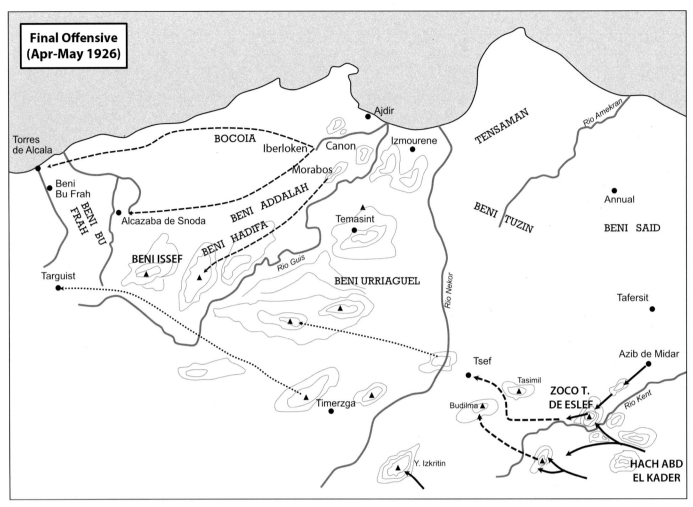

Final Offensive (Apr–May 1926)

(Map by Mark Thompson)

south of Beni Tuzin and the upper river Kert up to the Telata de Telef, and to the river Nekor.

Further west, three other French divisions under General Julien Dufieux, would remain on the defensive. These formed the Fez Group, another 40,000 troops: the 128th Division at Ouezzane or Oussán, south of the Lucus, facing the Yebala; further east the 4th Division, between Gezawa and Beni Zerwal, facing the Gomara; and finally, the 2nd Division, which would advance in a more limited way to the north-west through Beni Zerual, and to the north-east through the Senhaya. The six divisions had 72 battalions. Of these, 56 units were present on the front line in June, of which only six were European French, three others of the Foreign Legion, and the bulk being Mahgrebi troops: 24 of Algerian Tiralleurs and five of Moroccan Tiralleurs.

In total the allies had 120,000 soldiers and 150 aircraft ready for offensive operations, not counting the thousands of Spanish troops that would remain on the defensive on the Estella Line in Tetuán, Ceuta and Larache, as well as those of the Melilla District, and the French along the border. In fact, of these troops in the western area, some 8,000 Spanish would attack also in Ceuta-Tetuán, and another 6,000 from Larache. In all, some 52,000 Spanish would participate in the final offensive, being 21,100 shock troops (Legión, Regulares, Harkas, Mehalas, etc) and 30,900 conscripted soldiers. In addition, there were another 17,000 recruits being trained in the Spanish Protectorate, to be available if needed. So, the total number of Spanish and French troops in Morocco could be perhaps some 250,000 men. Of these, finally some 90,000 would participate in the offensive: 52,000 Spaniards and 40,000 French.

In order to carry out the attack, General Goded, Sanjurjo's new chief of staff, explained that it was a question of:

an overall plan to be developed without halts or setbacks within a given period, and this required a total change in our system of war [...]. It was no longer possible to apply the system of positions, but rather the one of columns, that in their advance, were not to use fortification except in combat for cover, but without establishing permanent fortified posts, which were only to be set up in small numbers and as support points.

In addition, like the French Mobile Groups, General Goded created mixed columns formed by about three infantry tabors and one of cavalry, accompanied by mountain artillery. These columns were more agile and with more firepower than their French counterparts.[29]

In front of the Spanish and French troops, on May 1926 Abd el-Krim counted on his incipient Riffian army and the warriors of 37 complete kabyles and part of other four half-occupied ones. If we take into account the population of the Rif and apply a mobilisation rate of 7 percent, similar to that of Revolutionary France (that even could be too much) we have about 750 warriors per kabyle. So, the total number of armed Riffian warriors would be around 29,000 fighters, in fact half the 60,000 warriors estimated by French and Spanish intelligence. Their artillery, calculated on the basis of the number of examples taken from the Spanish and French by the Riffians, according to the same governmental calculations, could be around 150 pieces and 250 machine guns.[30] The main deployment of this force, perhaps half of it, some 14,000,[31] were located in front

Table 16: The Final Spanish-French Offensive (May 1926)

Commander/grand unit	Composition	Strength	Location/objectives
Castro Girona	All forces in Axdir area	28,000 men	Axdir, advance through Asgar and Tafra following the valley of the river Nekor
Fiscer (/Fixer) (killed), later Castillo	One tabor of Regulares of Larache, two Banderas of the Legión, 7th, 8th and 9th Battalions of Cazadores, four batteries	6,650 men	West of Axdir, to envelop Morabos Hill through the west
Dolla (Reserve)	Two tabors Mehala of Tetuán, 4th and part of 7th Battalions of Cazadores, a Bandera of the Legión, six batteries	4,700 men	Right-centre (west of Axdir), in front of Morabos Hill, then to Tamasint
Balmes	Two tabors of the harka of Tetuán, one tabor Regulares of Larache, one Bandera of the Legión, 3rd, 5th and 6th Battalions of Cazadores, two batteries	7,050 men	Axdir, enveloping Morabos Hill from the east
Mola	Harka of Melilla, three tabors and two squadrons Regulares of Melilla, two Banderas of the Legión, 13th, 14th and 15th Battalions of Cazadores, and a battery	7.050 men	Left-centre (east of Axdir), to Loma del Cañón, then to cross river Guis
Monasterio, (Cavalry)	Cavalry tabor (3 squadrons) of Mehala, 1 tabor of Regulares, two mounted squadrons of machine guns	900 horsemen	Left of Axdir (east of Axdir), on the coast, to Sfiha beach, then to cross the Nekor
Vázquez (Axdir Garrison)	2nd Battalion of Cazadores, 16 line infantry companies, four machine gun companies, and seven batteries		Axdir perimeter
Melilla District			
Pozas	Native idalas, Harkas and Mehalas, the 18th Cazadores Battalion and a battery	3,000–4,500 men	Afrau (Beni Said), to Tensaman
González Carrasco	1,000 natives of intervention, three infantry and one cavalry tabor Regulares of Alhucemas, one Bandera of the Legión, two battalions of the África Regiment, 16th Cazadores Battalion, Mounted Mías Tafersit Mehala, four squadrons of the Alcántara Regiment, and six batteries	8,080 men	Azib de Midar (Melilla District), to Zoco el Telata de Eslef (Beni Tuzin), occupying the Alto Kert, then north to link up in the valley of the Nekor with the Alhucemas-Axdir troops of Castro Girona
Campins	Column under González Carrasco		
Ponte (cavalry)	Cavalry column under González Carrasco		To link with Pozas, in the north, then to Castro Girona's Axdir-Alhucemas forces
French Forces	Six divisions, with 72 battalions (56 units on the front line in June: including six French, three Foreign Legion, 24 Algerian and five Moroccan Tiralleurs, Senegalese)		
North Taza Group (Marty)	Three divisions	40,000 men	Taza, and linking with the Melilla District Spanish forces
Dosse	3rd March Division		Linking up with the Spanish, occupying south Beni Tuzin, higher river Kert up to the Telata de Telef, and river Nekor
Ibós	Moroccan Division		Nador (Geznaya), marching to Zoco el Jemís (Yebel Haman mountains, Geznaya, and then to Targuist and Beni Amart)
Vernois	1st March Division		Bab Sultan (Geznaya), to the heights of Tamersga (border of Beni Urriaguel with Beni Ammart)
Fez Group (Dufieux)	Three divisions	40,000 men	Ouasan-Fez, on the defensive
	2nd March Division		Fez, to Beni Zerual, and the Senhaya
	4th March Division		Between Fez and Oussán (between Gezawa and Beni Zerwal) facing the Gomara
	128th Division		In Ouezzane or Ouassan, south of the Lucus, facing the Yebala

of the bridgehead of Alhucemas-Axdir, in two lines of trenches that went from the conical Mount of Xixafen, in the west, then to the sea, to the east, at the line of the Iberloken and Guis rivers. In this sector, the stronger of Abd el-Krim, the Riffians even had fortified posts supposedly designed against artillery and aviation. In front, there were twice as many Spaniards under Castro Girona, who had to break through this line of entrenchments. Once again, the First World War was returning to the Spanish troopers in this sector. Nevertheless, the Riffian situation in the other sectors was desperate, so they had not the slightest chance to win. On the rest of the front there were perhaps 6,000 warriors against the three French sectors; some other 4,000 Berbers were facing east, against Melilla; and another 4–5,000 were deployed to the west, guarding Larache and Ceuta, in the Yebala, Luccus (or Garb) and Gomara. Here, in the other sectors of the front, the numerical superiority of the allies could reach as much as some 12 to one against the French, or three to one against the Spanish in Melilla and Tetuán-Larache.[32]

Table 17: Likely Riffian Deployment

Location	Troops
Alhucemas sector: Conical Mount of Xixafen, in the west, then to the sea, to the east, at the line of the Morabos Hill, and Iberloken and Guis rivers	14,000 men
Melilla sector	4,000 men
French sector	6,000 men
Larache-Tetuán sector	4–5,000 men
Total	29,000 men, 150 cannons, 250 machine guns

The End of Abd el-Krim's Rif Republic

On 8 May, the 28,000 men of Major General Castro Girona in the Alhucemas-Axdir sector began the offensive after a bombardment made by, allegedly, 150 aircraft, but probably half this number. The right flank advanced south, inland, against the Loma de los Morabos (Morabos Hill), while the left flank advanced to the south-east, following the coast, with the support of the fleet. Colonel Fiscer(/Fixer), who intended to envelop Morabos Hill by going westward, became bogged down in the rocks, and had to be helped by Brigadier General Dolla's reserve column, which attacked the hill frontally. The gap between the two columns was covered by Colonel Balmes' central column, which in its advance overtook Brigadier General Dolla and occupied the heights overlooking the beach of Sfiha, east of the mountain. Then, Colonel Monasterio's cavalry, preceded by assault cars galloped towards the beach, clearing all the way to the east. By the end of the day, the Spaniards had suffered 540 casualties.

The next day, Colonel Balmes began the ascent to Morabos Hill, but the Riffians continued to hold out, so the casualties now amounted to 800 men. Lieutenant General Primo de Rivera hesitated, but General Sanjurjo decided to continue with the assault. At dawn on 10 May, Lieutenant Colonel Varela, with the Regulares from Ceuta and Tetuán, in Colonel Balmes' vanguard, managed to take the hill from the east, while Colonel Mola turned towards the centre and took the Loma del Cañón (Cannon Ridge) with the Regulares of Melilla and the harka of Tetuán. Finally, the front was broken after suffering 377 additional casualties, so a general advance in all this sector took place. In this phase of the battle, sadly Colonel Fiscer(/Fixer) was killed when he enveloped Morabos Hill from the west. His replacement, Colonel Castillo, deployed his troops there, to garrison the just conquered ridge.

Soldiers of the Mehala of Tafersit with a Spanish officer in 1926. (Carrasco & de Mesa)

Soldiers of the Regulares firing at the Beni Urriaguel Riffians. (via Marín Ferrer)

After Major General Castro Girona suffered 1,188 casualties in all this fighting (including two pilots conducting 'the Spanish Flight'), the next day Colonel Mola was able to cross the Guis River, and on his left Colonel Monasterio advanced with his horses to the river Nekor, to the east, on the coast. In the west, Brigadier General Dolla advanced south and occupied Tamasint, which was Abd el-Krim's headquarters, on the 17th. In the extreme south-east, in the Melilla sector, outside the Alhucemas-Axdir front that we have just narrated, Colonel Ponte, now in command of the cavalry, crossed the river Nekor to try to make contact with Brigadier General Castro Girona's troops.

With the front collapsing, Abd el-Krim abandoned Beni Urriaguel and fled to the west, to Snada (Beni Issef). Then, the first massive surrenders of Beni Urriaguel, Beni Tuzir and Temsaman warriors happened and these former rebels would soon reinforce the Spanish troops. At the same time, from the north-east, in Melilla sector, Colonel Pozas' column advanced almost without resistance until it reached Annual, and from there, they marched to the river Nekor, shaking hands with the Spaniards of Colonel Ponte that were marching also with the southern part of the Spanish troops in the Melilla sector. Also, both Pozas and Ponte's forces now linked the area of Alhucemas with the sector of Melilla by land for the first time.

Further south-east and south, on 8 May Brigadier General González Carrasco's forces and General Marty's North Taza Group advanced from Midar and the French border respectively. The Spanish troops took Zoco el Telata de Eslef, linking up with the French 3rd Division. After fortifying the area, on the 15th the allies resumed the advance to the north, to join those of Brigadier General González Carrasco with those of Major General Castro Girona,

Abd el-Krim surrendering to French forces including several Tiralleurs and members of the Foreign Legion with their white Kepis. (L'Illustration, via Courcelle & Marmié)

Another picture of Abd el-Krim just captured in Targuist, with Foreign Legion soldiers. (Albert Grandolini collection)

being harassed from the north by Major General Castro Girona, from the south by General Marty's French, and from the east by Brigadier General González Carrasco. The last Beni Urriaguelians surrendered between 29 May and 10 June, and further to the northwest Beni Iteff did so. Thus, after barely five years of existence, the Rif Republic, Abd el-Krim's dream, disappeared like the wind. In the operations up to the end of May 1926, the Spaniards captured 14,500 rifles, 113 cannon, six mortars and 216 machine guns, a reliable indication of the Riffian forces that opposed their advance from the Alhucemas-Axdir sector.[33]

Abd el-Krim between French soldiers. He was deported to the island of Réunion, close to Madagascar, with a generous annual salary. In 1947 he managed to escape to Egypt, where he headed the Committee for the Liberation of the Maghreb. Being close to a Communist, in 1956 he refused the offer of King Mohammed V to return to Morocco, dying in Cairo in 1963. (Service Historique de la Defense, via Courcelle & Marmié)

while the French under General Marty continued towards the west, occupying Targuist.

Overwhelmed on all sides, the Riffians tried a counterattack with barely 200 warriors to recover this village, being repulsed. On the 27th, Abd el-Krim, after leaving the Spanish sector, escaped to the French one, surrendering to General Marty near Targuist. It seems that the attack of several Spanish Do Wal seaplanes over Beni Iteff was instrumental in harassing the Riffian leader and forcing him to surrender. The last remnants of the Rif Republic's forces had taken refuge in Yebel Hamman, in the south of Beni Urriaguel,

Victory parade under the Arc de Triomphe. From left to right King Mulay Yusuf, Doumergue, Herriot, Primo de Rivera, Briand, and on the extreme right, turning his head to the left, Pétain. (Maurice Branger/ Roger-Viollet, via Courcelle & Marmié)

8

1927–27: The Submission of Gomara and the End of the War

Once Abd el-Krim surrendered to the French authorities the cooperation with France practically ended. Spain then continued the campaign to subdue the rest of the Protectorate which remained rebellious: this was part of the Yebala south of Tetuán, the east of the Garb or Larache, the whole of the Gomara, and the western Rif. Due to the particularly rugged terrain of the Gomara, with altitudes of between 1,500 and 2,000 metres it was impossible for a large conventional force to penetrate it, so a different approach was used. Under the direction of the brilliant General Goded, Lieutenant Colonel Oswaldo Capaz, who knew the terrain perfectly well and had many friends and contacts in the area, would penetrate with about 1,000 pro-Spanish Berber warriors (in the future they would form the 6th Mehala of Gomara) from the coast towards the interior 'as a real Mehala chief of the Sultan', 'living off the country, demanding provisions and hostages from the subdued kabyles', and counting on the support of the aviation to locate the position of the Spanish troops and provide them with air support and ammunition.

The Capaz Raid
On 12 June 1926, Lieutenant Colonel Capaz landed at Cala Iris, next to Torres de Alcalá (Mestasa, western Rif), and advanced along the coast penetrating the Gomara region, further to the west. Beni Guerir kabyle was subdued without a fight. Then, Capaz turned southwards to Beni Mansur, and finally to Beni Jaled. He then turned north and, again on the coast, he subdued Beni Selman and Beni Ziat or Siat kabyles. From there, Capaz marched further west, and on 11 July he forced the surrender of Beni Said Kabyle, now in the Yebala region. After leaving posts on the coast at Uad Lau

(Beni Said), Tiguisas (Beni Buzra or Buxera), M'ter and Punta de Pescadores (Beni Esmih or Esmin), Capaz marched south again, inland, to Amiadi, a mountain pass between Beni Esmih, and Beni Mansur. This pass gave access to Ajmás and Beni Khaled or Jaled, making these kabyles open for invasion. In the end, in just one month, Capaz had subdued the whole of northern Gomara, with nine or 10 kabyles, seizing 3,000 rifles.

However, Ahmed El Jeriro was still in control of the rebel western kabyles and attacked Uad Lau with warriors from Beni Hassan and Beni Hozmar (or Hosmar). At the same time, Ajmás and Beni Khaled kabyles (the last having rebelled again) tried to invade the north of the Gomara, but Lieutenant Colonel Capaz managed to repulse them. Then, Capaz left a tabor in Amiadi, and surprisingly abandoned the front. He marched through Beni Zeyyel and penetrated by surprise into Xauén (Ajmás), on 10 August, taking advantage of a Spanish concentric offensive that was developing to reoccupy the holy city, further west.

Indeed, in June the Jalifian (Xerifian) forces of Larache, under the command of Lieutenant Colonel Asensio, had begun the offensive against Xauén marching to the east and reoccupying Teffer (Ahl Sherif) on the right or north bank of the Lucus River, supported by the French on the other bank towards Tanacob. At the same time, a force under General Federico Berenguer himself, commander of Ceuta District, formed by three columns (under colonels Canís, Balmes and Martínez Monje, with vanguards of the Legión and Regulares) on 2 August, marched against the Riffians, from Tetuán, in the north. The offensive was lead on the ground by General Sanjurjo. The rebels were concentrated in Zinat (Beni Hosmar), but seeing the

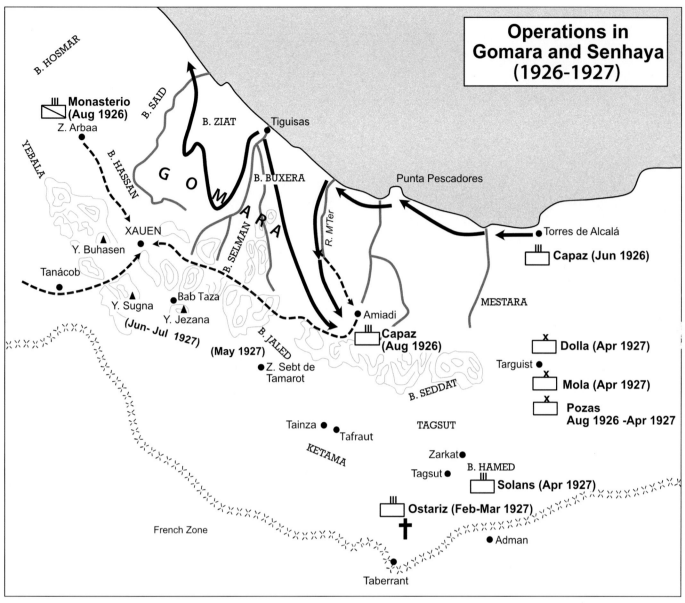

(Map by Mark Thompson)

mass that was falling on them, abandoned their positions. Colonel Monasterio's cavalry occupied Zoco el Arbaá (Beni Hassan) without a fight, and on 11 August the Spaniards entered Xauén unopposed to find that Lieutenant Colonel Capaz was already there. So, Beni Hosmar and Beni Hassan had now entirely submitted to Spain. Lieutenant Colonel Capaz, following the instructions of Goded, had created a school, and from then on, the Spanish military operations would try to be conducted according to these new tactics, more agile and similar to the way of making war of the rebel Riffians.[1]

Killing El Jeriro

Now the operations were cantered in the Yebala and the Garb (or Larache) regions, since Beni Ider, Beni Arós, Sumata, Beni Lait, Beni Gorfet, Beni Issef and El Ajmás (Gomara) were still held by rebels under El Jeriro. The Spaniards would launch a concentric offensive against El Jeriro from three sides: the right column, under Lieutenant Colonel López Gómez, with Lieutenant Colonel Valera as second commander with Interventions and Mehalas of Beni Mezauar and Wad Ras, Regulares of Ceuta, a Bandera of the Legión, a battalion of Cazadores, and a battery would cross Beni Ider from the north-west, from Dar Xaui; then a column of the left-centre of the harka of López Bravo and the Mehala of Coque, would depart

from Fondak de Ain Yedida, in the north, marching to the south to Zoco el Telata de Beni Ider to connect with the other columns; the column of the right-centre, under Colonel Patxot with five cavalry squadrons, a cavalry machine gun squadron, the Regulares of Tetuán, a Bandera of the Legión, a Battalion of Cazadores and two batteries) would attack from the east, departing from Ben Karrich, marching to Cudia Serviet, and then to Mount Buharrax; and finally, a small force under Captain Ferrer would cover the extreme left, in Beni Raten, and another under Captain García Figueras would protect the extreme right with the Intervention forces of Beni Arós, marching from Megaret to Rokba el Gozal. All these columns would be under General Gómez Morato, but General Sanjurjo would coordinate them.

It should be mentioned here that the harka of López Bravo, which had already penetrated Xauén, was formed by 1,000 or 1,500 Beni Urriagueles and Bocoyans. These Riffians, after being defeated, had no problem in fighting now for Spain, as long as they were left to plunder their enemies. The Riffians now would prove to be incredibly loyal to Spain after a decade and a half opposing her: in nine months these ex-rebels would suffer 1,000 casualties but would renew their forces twice over, suffering only three desertions in the

Lieutenant Colonel Oswaldo Capaz led a highly successful operation in the Gomara region that ended with the submission of 10 kabyles, known as the Capaz Raid. This would be the pattern on which all other offensives would be based: knowledge of the terrain, contacts with local Riffians, use of native forces and rapid and constant movements, living off the terrain and avoiding fixed positions. (Carrasco & de Mesa)

whole period.[2] So, it seemed that Spain finally had won the respect of the hard Riffian warriors.

On 3 November, the above-mentioned forces, the harka of López Bravo, with Jalifian forces, idalas, Regulares of Tetuán, two Banderas of the Legión and two battalions of Cazadores invaded Beni Ider kabyle in southern Yebala. During these operations El Jeriro was killed in a skirmish in Cudia Serviet (Servert) by the troops of Colonel Patxot, and so the Riffians asked immediately for surrender. Beni Ider, after being sacked, was subdued, together with Beni Lait, in December. Then, in January 1927, the forces of Larache occupied Beni Gorfet. So, all that remained opposed to Spain in the west was the mountainous heartland that was once the refuge of El Raisuni: Beni Arós, Sumata, Beni Issef and El Ajmás.[3]

Senhaja and Ketama: The Last Riffian Hope

Meanwhile, in the south of the western Rif region, next to the French border, Major General Castro Girona managed to attract the Ajamelich family, who controlled Ketama and the Confederation of Senhaja (the latter formed by seven small kabyles). Spain was invited to occupy the area, and on 12 August 1926, Colonel Pozas with four Mías from the Harka of Melilla, and warriors from Targuist, Beni Ghil and Beni bu Frah, and Captain Ostáriz with 500 natives, left from Targuist. Meanwhile, to the west, Lieutenant Colonel Capaz would guard the rebels of El Ajmás and Beni Jaled.

Colonel Pozas subdued Beni Seddat (north-west of Senhaja) and then went to Ketama, to the west. Captain Ostáriz, from the north-east, occupied Zarkat and marauded throughout Senhaja kabyles. However, on 22 August Lieutenant Colonel Capaz was attacked by forces of Beni Khaled and Ajmás under El Temsamani, a former ringleader of Abd el-Krim. Pozas, to the east, then abandoned his positions, which revived the Riffians who managed to isolate Capaz in Amiadi. However, the air force was able to supply Capaz with ammunition and gave him air support, so that by 12 September the Spaniard was once again in control of the situation. Then, Pozas and

Ostáriz reacted and occupied Ketama on the 23rd, and subdued Senhaja again.

Instead of dispersing in dozens of posts, the Spanish forces concentrated now in three points: Zarkat, Adman, and Tabarrán (Tagsut), between Ketama and the Senhaja, leaving only the pro-Spanish Moors in the controlled kabyles as a vanguard. The Ketama Riffians, however, with support from Beni Khaled and El Ajmás to the west (that remained unsubdued), rebelled again, now led by Ali el-Slitan or Sel-liten. The pro-Spanish warriors of Ketama were attacked by 1,000 men under Slitan on 5 February 1927, and Captian Ostáriz came to their aid from Senhaja with two Xalifian tabors, while again Lieutenant Colonel Capaz threatened the rear of Beni Khaled. Finally, Captain Ostáriz controlled the situation and was left in command of 2,000 warriors: the idalas of Senhaya and Ketama, and three tabors (one of cavalry) of the Mehala.[4]

In mid-March, an enemy harka was spotted penetrating through the south of Ketama, then towards Tagsut, west of Senhaya. Therefore, the local commander requested a Spanish garrison there and so the Spaniards sent a company of Regulares. However, it was all a trap and on 26 March the garrison was annihilated, except for one soldier who managed to escape and raise the alarm. Captain Ostáriz then marched to Tagsut with two tabors, when he discovered that the Riffians were attacking his rear in Tabarrant (Beni Bechir). The Tabarrant garrison luckily was able to retreat to the French lines, but Captain Ostáriz, who did not know about this, was ambushed by Slitan with a tabor when he was turning back to rescue the post, dying with 250 soldiers.

Two strong columns under Colonels Mola and Pozas, of 5,940 men consisting of two Mehala tabors, four Regulares, two Banderas of the Legión, a battalion and a battery; and 4,840 men of three Harkas tabors, three Mehalas tabors, two Regulares tabors, two Banderas of the Legión, a cavalry Mía and a battery, respectively, left from Targuist to control the situation. Another column was left in Targuist under General Dolla as a reserve, with 3,620 soldiers in two Mehalas tabors, one of Regulares, one Legión bandera, two battalions and two batteries. Both columns forked and then converged at Adman (Zarkat) and Tainza on 12 April, north-west of Senhaya. Then, a snow and windstorm broke out, the radio was cut, and the aviation was not able to fly. Colonel Pozas had 50 percent of his men with frostbite in just two days, and Lieutenant Colonel Solans' column, which had advanced through Beni Hamed and Beni Bechir to the south, was ambushed and suffered 30 percent casualties. In the end, Colonel Mola managed to resume operations and, with air support, on the 15th he managed to rescue Lieutenant Colonel Solans. Then, both columns together occupied Beni Bechir on the 18th, and then Tabarrant (Tagsut), further to the west. On the 28th, Colonels Mola and Pozas entered the city of Tagsut itself, which was sacked by the Spanish allies of Beni Said and Beni Tuzin. With all of Senhaya region pacified, Ketama also submitted. After that Colonel Pozas penetrated into Gomara to join Lieutenant Colonel Capaz. Slitan and Tensamani, being defeated, took refuge to the west, in El Ajmás.[5]

Ajmás: The Last Campaign

There were only pockets of resistance left in the western zone (Larache), and in the south of the Gomara and so the last Spanish effort was directed there: on 29 April the commander of Ceuta District, General Berenguer, launched 15,000 soldiers to clear Beni Arós, the old refuge of El Raisuni, which he achieved on 7 May with little resistance. For this purpose, three concentric columns departed: the one under General Souza with the local Intervention,

Captain Ostáriz (1) with the Qaid Tulú (2) and his native forces in March 1927 in the Senhaya. Soon after he would be betrayed, ambushed and killed. (via Carrasco & de Mesa)

Soldiers of the Mehalas and Harkas in the snow of the Gomara Mountains during the spring of 1927. (Alfonso Gordó, Biblioteca Nacional, via Villalobos)

Jaled, Beni Ahmed, and the east of Ajmás. His march was supported by another column under Colonel Mola, of 2,500 soldiers comprised of a tabor of the Mehala de Tafersit, another of the Regulares de Melilla, two Legión Banderas and a battery, in the area of Tamorot, and a reserve under Lieutenant Colonel Sáinz de Larín with two tabors of the Regulares de Tetuán, and a battery. Lieutenant Colonel Capaz and his supporting columns of Mola and Sáinz de Larín were able to surround the massifs of Yebel Alam and Buhaxem.

Once the rebels were isolated in the heights, then the Spaniards had to occupy these mountains. The first operation was organised to take Yebel Alam with four columns on 16 June: Colonel Balmes was in Ain Grana, with 6,650 soldiers consisting of the local Interventions of Beni Arós, Ahl Sherif, Beni Gorfet and Garbia, a tabor and cavalry of the Mehala of Larache, four tabors of Regulares of Larache, a Legión Bandera, the 4th and 6th Cazadores Battalions, and four batteries; Colonel Canís was in Timisar with 5,150 soldiers of the local Intervention of Beni Hassam, four tabors of Regulares of Ceuta, Tetuán and Alhucemas, a Legión Bandera, the 2nd and 3rd Cazadores Battalions and three batteries; Lieutenant

five squadrons and five tabors of Regulares, two battalions and three batteries, was on the right, departing from Mensak (Beni Gorfet); another column was under Colonel Balmes with local Intervention, two tabors and three squadrons of Regulares, a bandera of the Legión, two battalions, and two batteries, located in the centre, in Gozal (Beni Arós); and, finally, a column under Colonel Canís with a local Intervention and Wad Ras Battalion, the harka of Beni Urriaguel, five tabors, one Bandera and two batteries was on the left, departing from Buharrás (Beni Ider). For this offensive there was an additional reserve of six batteries. These columns fell on Sumata, which submitted between 13–23 May, and was sacked by the Beni Urriaguelese for not wanting the Riffians to hand over their 1,000 rifles. Finally, on the 26th, Beni Issef, further south, also fell.

At the same time, between 8–29 May, a column under Lieutenant Colonel Capaz, with 5,000 men consisting of the local Intervention, Bueno's harka, two tabors of the Mehala of Tafersit, three tabors of the Harka of Melilla, a tabor of Regulares of Alhucemas, another of Ceuta, a Legión Bandera and a battery, cleared the south of Beni

Colonel Álvarez Coque was in Bab Aixa with the harka of Beni Urriaguel and two Mehalas of Tetuán totalling 1,200 men; and, finally, there was a liaison group of 600 soldiers based in Hamades consisting of the local Intervention of Beni Ider and a tabor of the Mehala of Tetuán. These forces, with the personal supervision of the High Commissioner of Africa, General Sanjurjo, took the mountain after strong resistance on the 16th, and on 22 June they cleared the rest of the massif.

Finally, the summits of Yebel Sugna and Yebel Jezana, in the western Ajmás, were cleared between 28 June and 5 July, with 20,750 Spaniards concentrated for the offensive. Three groups were formed for this purpose: two columns were under Colonel Balmes and Lieutenant Colonel Asensio (future assailant of Madrid in 1936), departing from Tanacob, in the west Larache area with local Interventions, seven tabors and two Jalifian Mías, four tabors of Regulares, and a Legión Bandera; then, the columns of colonels Canís, Martínez Monje and that of Lieutenant Colonel Sáinz de Buruaga 'rubito' made the Xauén group, in the north with the harka

Rebel Riffians handing over their weapons in the Summer of 1927. (Alfonso Gordó, Biblioteca Nacional, via Villalobos)

of Beni Urriaguel, local interventions, three tabors of Jalifian forces, four tabors of Regulares and two Legión Banderas); and the Gomara group, in the east, divided into two columns under Colonels Mola and Lieutenant Colonel Capaz. Despite suffering 158 casualties, the Riffians were crushed, Temsamani surrendered, and el-Slitan fled to the French zone, where he surrendered. On 10 July El Ajmás surrendered all his weapons and was totally pacified. With this last act, the terrible Rif War, one that shattered three countries, Spain, France and Morocco, and that produced the fall of entire governments, after 18 years of suffering, had ended.[6]

The Last Flight

Coming back to the air activity, on 23 March 1926, Colonel Kindelán was appointed senior chief officer of the Air Service, still a branch of the Army. Around that date the aviation was reorganised. The 1st Tetuán Group and the 2nd Larache Group were reinforced by the Napier (DH.9A) and Rolls (DH.4) squadrons of the 3rd Melilla Group, and by the Breguet XIX and Loring R.I. groups of the Training Wing. The Loring aircraft was a machine redesigned by the ubiquitous Eduardo Barrón, inspired on the Fokker C.IV, with 30 examples built in Spain. In February 1926 the first samples arrived in Tetuán under Captain Francisco Arranz Monasterio, and they were integrated with the Breguets in the Sesquiplanes Group of Commandant Francisco León Trejo. The Lorings supported the operations of the harka of Capaz, in the Ketama range, and the reoccupation of Xauén on 10 August.

On 16 May, Lieutenant Martínez Ramírez was awarded the Laureate when flying Breguet No. 101 of the 2nd Squadron. He was attacking rebel groups at Sidi Benicar, when he descended to ground level through the Imamegait mountains when a bullet split his humerus and damaged the observer's controls. Ramírez still finished his mission by using all of his bombs and then landed. This officer's career is an interesting example of his indomitable character. In the past, assigned to pilot the Breguet XIV Group in Tetuán, his aircraft crashed on his first flight, and he was seriously wounded, taking five months to recover. On 8 July 1925, he returned to service and was shot down although he was able to be rescued with his observer

at sea. Then, in September, at Kudia Tahar, he was hit by enemy fire when flying, but after improvised emergency treatment he refused to be evacuated. Ramírez finally died at the end of the war, as an instructor, when he capsized a training aircraft.[7]

In the autumn of 1926, the aviation was reorganised again, and Lieutenant Colonel Gonzalo's Wing or Squad was formed, with three organic groups: these were the Western, the Eastern and the Seaplane Groups, adding the Bristol Expeditionary and the Expeditionary of the School of Instruction. The AME VI fighter, a Spanish version of the Bristol F.2B, designed by Captains Manuel Bada and Arturo González Gil, also arrived, forming two experimental squadrons. These ones, with the Bristols, were sent to Herráiz airfield, in Melilla, in spring 1926. Later, the Lorings of the R.1 Squadron/5th Expeditionary Group was moved to the Larache sector. In February 1927 the Loring R.I. Squadron and another Bristol squadron were repatriated, the AME VI and the DH.4 Rolls squadron were decommissioned, and a mixed squadron with DH.9 and Bristol remained.

On 4 July the last flight of the war occurred along with the last Laureate and the last fallen pilot. Facing difficulties in the assault on Yebel Hazzana, Captain Matanza Vázquez – commander of the airfield of Auamára, Larache, and of the 3rd Group of Breguet XIX – volunteered to act as an observer on Captain Suárez-Somonte's aircraft. The Breguet bombed and strafed the Riffian positions from low altitude. Then, Captain Matanza took a bullet wound in the chest, but he ordered the pilot not to turn around and he dropped his last bomb. When Suárez-Somonte finally landed, Matanza was dead. He was the last of the 79 airmen killed in the war, along with 139 aircraft destroyed. This was also the last flight of the war and the last air bomb dropped.[8]

A DH.9 manufactured by the Hispano Company in Guadalajara. These aircraft came from Melilla to reinforce the operations over the Gomara from Tetuán and Larache. (Salas Larrazábal)

9

The Fate of Abd El-Krim, the Rif and Morocco

Thus ended a ferocious 19-year war, which had served to modernise the Spanish army and create a caste of highly trained and prestigious officers, but at an extremely high cost, with little economic benefit and all to maintain the prestige of Spain worldwide after the great disaster of 1898. This group of brilliant commanders, including Cabanellas, Goded, Mola, Queipo de Llano and Muñoz Grandes for example, created strong bonds of friendship and camaraderie that would lead them, almost en masse, to join the rebellion against the government of the Republic just nine years later, led by Sanjurjo, and later by Franco. Curiously, the few African commanders who remained loyal to the Republic, such as Riquelme and Asensio, had also served together, which leads us to wonder to what extent camaraderie was not one of the factors that conditioned belonging to one side or the other?

As with Morocco, the country remained divided for a further 30 years, between the Spanish and the French protectorates. After Operation Torch liberated French North Africa from the Vichy regime in 1942 a large number of Moroccan soldiers fought valiantly with the Allies against the Germans, faithful to their French masters, but also with an eye in independence when US presidents Delano Roosevelt, and then Harry S. Truman, talked about the right to self-determination in the Atlantic Charter, that were also recognised in the United Nations Charter. The Kingdom of Morocco had been the first country to recognise the independence of the United States, so the US Government was especially sympathetic to the Moroccan aspirations.

The first opposition to the French regime could be seen when the new King of Morocco since 1927, Sultan Mohammed V, opposed implementing measures against the Jews that the Vichy French wanted to implement in Morocco to appease their Nazi lords in 1940. This was one of the first acts that marked the beginning of

a movement towards independence by Morocco. Also, between 1937–43 the nationalist Istiqal Party was founded, and the French authorities arrested all of their leaders.

The next stage occurred in 1947, when Mohammed V refused to sign a number of decrees drafted by the French authorities. On December 1950, as Mohammed V declared his support to the Istiqal Party and the Arab League, finally the French authorities surrounded his palace and arrested him, sending the King to exile in Madagascar and in the process converting him into a national hero. At the same time, thousands of Moroccan nationalists took refuge in Spanish Africa and the Spanish Sahara. Surprisingly, the Spanish authorities did not recognise the new pro-French appointed Sultan, did not stop anti-French activity on his soil, and even threatened to separate off his northern protectorate from Morocco. Finally, France, also having to fight the rebellion of Algeria and Mauritania and other colonies, recalled Mohammed V from exile, and granted the independence of Morocco on 2 March 1956. As the Spanish Protectorate had been created by the Spanish-French treaty in 1912, now that France was not the protector of Morocco, Spain had no rights to keep his northern protectorate, and on 7 April 1956 Madrid had to hand over to Morocco all the lands conquered from the Riffians after 19 years of terrible fighting. In any case, Spain kept Ceuta and Melilla and the rocks close to the coast, such as Alhucemas and Vélez de la Gomera, as they had not been part of this Protectorate but had been in Spanish hands for several centuries before.

The Fate of Abd El-Krim

After being taken prisoner, the French colonial authorities decided to deport Abd el-Krim to the island of Réunion, a French overseas possession near Madagascar. In Réunion, the French authorities provided him with a comfortable home and the perception of a

Nationalist 'brothers in arms'

General Miguel Cabanellas, who took Dar Drius by surprise in 1922 and led the rebellion of Zaragoza in 1936.

General Emilio Mola Vidal (centre), saved by Franco (left) in Dar el Akobba, 1924, then the director of the military uprising and head of the Army of the North during the Civil War, calling in this photo to ask for the support of his friend, General Franco.

General Manuel Goded, an intellectual, brilliant chief of staff and commander of the last 1925–1927 campaigns, he was defeated and executed in Barcelona in 1936.

General Queipo de Llano led the campaign to relief and evacuate Xauén in 1924 and commanded the Army of the South in the Civil War, seen here in Berlin in 1939. (Open source)

General Varela, who acted brilliantly with his own harka during the Alhucemas landing, later commanded one of the columns that tried to assault Madrid in 1936.

Paradoxically, Queipo and Cabanellas were Republicans and confronted King Alfonso XIII, but then they supported the military revolt of 1936. All of them were potential rivals to Franco to be the head the Nationalist Government in 1936, three of them, Mola, Goded, and Cabanellas, dying before the end of the war. (De la Cierva, unless stated otherwise)

Republican 'brothers in arms'

From left to right in the top photograph, generals Llano de la Encomienda and Pozas, the first came close to destruction in Tizi Azza in 1923, then commanded the Army of the North during the Civil War; and the second, Pozas, was near annihilated in 1927 in Senhaja, then commanded the Army of the Centre in 1936. (Libsa) General Riquelme, in the lower photograph, who was on the brink of disaster in Xauén, having to jump into a truck to escape. He was defeated in Toledo in 1936. (El Mundo) Riquelme served with Asensio Torrado, and both were defenders of the Republic during the Civil War. Also, all, Llano de la Encomienda, Pozas and Riquelme were far less successful during the Rif War (even, being all nearly defeated) than their Nationalists counterparts. Perhaps this difference in their behaviour during the Rif War set them apart from their fellow Africanists.

Sid Muley Hassan el Mehdi Ben Ismael, the 2nd Jalifa of the Spanish Protectorate, representing the Sultan of Morocco between 1925 to 1956. (Manríquez García)

King Hassan II appoints General Mohammed el Mizzián as a Marshall in 1970. El Mizzián saved the life of General Franco during the Rif War, becoming his friend for life, and commanded the elite 1st Division of Navarra during the battle of Ebro in the Spanish Civil War. There, he was accused of war crimes. He would later command the Moroccan forces when they smashed the Riffian rebellion of 1958. (Manríquez García)

King Mohammed V and Prince Hassan (future King Hassan II) review the National Liberation Army. (Manríquez García)

of Algeria. Nevertheless, he never saw again the proclamation of a Rif Republic.

generous annual salary. Spain demanded the extradition of Abd el-Krim but in vain. During his time in exile, the former guerrilla leader maintained his anti-colonial rhetoric. In 1947, after obtaining authorisation from the French government to move to the metropolis, Abd el-Krim managed to escape during a stopover in the Egyptian city of Port Said. The government of that country, headed by then King Faruq I, took him in as a refugee. From Egypt he headed the Committee for the Liberation of the Maghreb. In 1956, after the independence of Morocco, he rejected the offer of King Mohammed V to return with honours to his homeland.

In October 1958 a revolt happened in the Rif, in the old Spanish Protectorate, proclaiming the independence of the region, now from Morocco, and for the return of Abd el-Krim. Nevertheless, the revolt was suffocated by the son of King Mohammed V, the future King Hassam II, helped by General Mohammed ben Mizzián, a veteran of the 1936 Civil War who had commanded the Moroccan forces and then the elite 1st Division of Navarra during the battle of Ebro. After an offensive made by 30,000 Moroccan soldiers, that included Napalm bombing, that landed in Tangier and Alhucemas, taking then Tetuán and Xauén, the rebellion was crushed by April 1959. Abd el-Krim finally died in Cairo in 1963, shortly after seeing the complete decolonisation of the Maghreb after the independence

Bibliography

Note that all volumes are in Spanish, unless indicated otherwise

Books

Brenan, Gerald, *El Laberinto Español* (Barcelona: Plaza y Janés Editores, 1984)

Carrasco, Antonio, y de Mesa, José Luis, *Las Tropas de África en las Campañas de Marruecos* (Madrid: Almena Ediciones, 2000)

Courcelle-Labrousse, Vincent, and Marmié, Nicolas, *La Guerre du Rif* (in French) (Tallandier, 2008)

Fernández Riera, Vicente, *Xauén 1924* (Madrid: Almena 2013)

Fontenla Ballesta, Salvador, *La Guerra de Marruecos* (Madrid, La Esfera de los Libros, 2017)

Macías Fernández, Daniel, *A cien Años de Annual* (Madrid: Desperta Ferro, 2021)

Marín Ferrer, Emilio, *Atlas Ilustrado de las Guerras de Marruecos* (Madrid: Susaeta)

Nicolle, Dr David C., and Ali Gabr, Air Vice Marshal Gabr, *Air Power in the Arab World, Vol 4* (in English) (Warwick: Helion, 2021)

Pando, Juan, *Historia Secreta de Annual* (Madrid: Temas de Hoy SA, 1999)

Permuy López, Rafael A., *Los Pilotos de Caza de la Aviación Republicana, Vol 1* (Valladolid: Quirón, 2001)

Salas Larrazábal, Jesús, *Guerra Aérea, Vol 1* (Madrid: IHCA, 1999)

SHM (Servicio Histórico Militar), *Historia de las Campañas de Marruecos, Tomo IV* (Madrid: SHM 1991)

Velarde Silió, Jaime, *Aviones Españoles del Siglo XX* (Fundación Infante de Orleans, 2008)

Villalobos, Federico, *El Sueño Colonial* (Barcelona: Ariel 2004)

Articles

Albi de la Cuesta, Julio, ʹLa Noche Tristeʹ, *Desperta Ferro Contemporánea,* issue 30 (Madrid: Desperta Ferro, 2018)

Albi de la Cuesta, Julio, ʹPreludio de Alhucemasʹ, *Desperta Ferro Contemporánea,* issue 11 (Madrid: Desperta Ferro, 2015)

De La Rocha, Carlos, Maps in ʹEl Desastre de Annualʹ and ʹEl Desembarco de Alhucemasʹ, *Desperta Ferro Contemporánea,* issues 30 and 11 (Madrid: Desperta Ferro, 2015 and 2018)

De Mesa Gutiérrez, José Luis, ʹEl Desembarco de Alhucemasʹ, *Desperta Ferro Contemporánea,* issue 11 (Madrid: Desperta Ferro, 2015)

Gárate Córdoba, José María, *España en sus Héroes*, issues Special, 4, 7, 9, 11, 14, 15 and 16 (Madrid: Ornigraf, 1969)

Madariaga, María Rosa de, ʹLa República del Rifʹ, *Desperta Ferro Contemporánea,* issue 11 (Madrid: Desperta Ferro, 2015)

Muñoz Bolaños, Roberto, ʹLa Derrota de Abd el-Krimʹ, *Desperta Ferro Contemporánea,* issue 11 (Madrid: Desperta Ferro, 2015)

Muñoz Bolaños, Roberto, ʹLa Ofensiva de Fernández Silvestreʹ, *Desperta Ferro Contemporánea,* issue 30 (Madrid: Desperta Ferro, 2018)

Nogueira Vázquez, Carlos, ʹTácticas de Infantería en la Guerra de Marruecosʹ, *Desperta Ferro Contemporánea,* issue 11 (Madrid: Desperta Ferro, 2015)

Pando (ii), Juan, El Desastre de Annual, *Historia 16*, issue 243 (Madrid: Información e Historia, 1996)

Pando (iii), Juan, La Pesadilla del Gurugú, *Historia 16*, issue 247 (Madrid: Información e Historia 1996)

Sánchez Méndez, José and Kindelán Camp, Alfredo, ʹLa Aviación Militar Española en la Campaña de Marruecos 1909-1927ʹ *Aeroplano Especial*, 2011, issue 29 (Madrid: IHCA, 2011)

Yusta Viñas, Cecilio, ʹLa Aviación Militar Española, Nacimiento y Desarrollo Inicialʹ *Aeroplano Especial*, 2011, issue 29 (Madrid: IHCA, 2011)

Web Pages

Anuario Militar, < http://hemerotecadigital.bne.es/results.vm?q=paren t%3A0026917454&lang=es&s=23> accessed September 2021.

NOTES

Chapter 1

1   Pando (iii), pp. 19–20, talks about 16,000 men lost, but as explained in the previous volume 3,098 soldiers reported missing arrived in Melilla over the next few days. Pando also mentions exactly 144 posts. Also, it seems that the 6,000 soldiers that in theory were located in the own Melilla city existed only in the papers, as a draft of a payroll list found in the Picasso Files dated in the same 21 July talks about some 19,000 Spanish soldiers in the Melilla District, and not the some 25,000 mentioned in other payrolls some days or weeks before. In fact, in the city of Melilla there were only some 1,800 men on this date.

2   Mola Vidal would be the organiser of the military revolt of 1936.

3   Villalobos, pp. 229–231. Marín Ferrer, p. 191. Pando, p. 24, states 35,000 soldiers on 15 August. For information about the fate of the Regulares of Melilla see José Sánchez Regaña: http://desastredeannual.blogspot. com/2015/02/el-grupo-de-regulares-en-campana-1920.html.

4   Pando (iii), pp. 20–25.

5   Weyler was a very competent, prestigious, and tough man who near won the war with the Cubans in 1896–97 and had even planned to ferment rebellion in the Southern states of the United States during the Spanish-American War of 1898.

6   Pando (iii), pp. 20–23.

7   Pando (iii) pp. 20–23 and 32. The journalist Ramiro de Maeztu (his mother being of British ancestry), was firstly sympathetic to Fabian Socialism, turning then to conservatism. He was executed in 1936 by the Republicans during the Civil War.

8   Maura was Prime Minister at the time of the Barranco del Lobo disaster in 1909, see Volume 1.

9   He would go on to be the supreme Nationalist commander during the Civil War just before Franco.

10   Supreme chief of the rebellion in 1936, before Cabanellas and Franco.

11   Pando (iii), p. 26, for the numbers of the Army in Ceuta, Larache and Melilla, and the absence of tents. Villalobos, pp. 231, 297–298. The figures given by Villalobos seem to be wrong, as some columns with more units seem to have fewer troops than others with fewer units. Villalobos mentions Sanjurjo with only 5,800 men despite having nine battalion-type units; Berenguer with six units and 7,500 men; Cabanellas with six units and 6,000 soldiers; and Tuero with three units and 3,500 combatants.

Assigning 100 per company or battery, and about 700 per bandera, tabor or cavalry regiment, and about 900 per battalion, the figures vary: Sanjurjo would have about 8,300 soldiers; Berenguer about 6,200; Cabanellas 6,300; and Suero about 2,900. We have used these numbers. Marín Ferrer, p. 192.

12   Table made by the author, based on the units mentioned during this chapter, plus those mentioned in Mogaburo López, p. 39–46. This author mentions the Spanish Army's Orbat in the Peninsula and Africa in 1920 and 1930. From this author we know that the two Hussar cavalry regiments mentioned for Melilla were Pavía and Princesa, as there were no others in the army. The three other cavalry units are mentioned in other sources, and again Mogaburo helps us to identify them: the Farnese and Almansa Regiments were horsed not infantry. The África and Melilla regiments, were destroyed during the Annual Disaster and are not mentioned in the operations, but we know that they existed in 1921 and in 1926, so they were probably reconstituted, as happened with Alcántara Cazadores Cavalry Regiment. The infantry units probably served in garrison duties and not as maneuver elements. On the contrary, the San Fernando and Ceriñola regiments, also destroyed in the Annual Disaster, according to Mogaburo were not reborn until 1930 (p. 46), but, as we will see later, a kind of Cazadores battalion from each regiment was created, as the 15th Ceriñola Battalion. The engineer and artillery units are present in all orders of battle available for the Melilla Zone, so we understand that probably they were there also between August and October 1921. It is possible that another artillery regiment was present in the area, arriving from the Peninsula. We are not sure which regiments ones sent just a battalion from the Peninsula (the so-called Expeditionary Battalions) or whether they sent all their three battalions. The Valencia Regiment probably only sent one, as this unit is mentioned as a battalion, instead. Probably, the two resident Regiments for Melilla (África and Melilla) served here with their full three battalions. Finally, as there were between 21 and 25 battalions in the frontline during this period, it is also possible that other regiments served with their three battalions in this campaign, but not all of them.

13   Pando (iii), pp. 27–28.

14   Pando (iii), pp. 28–29.

15   Villalbos, p. 232. Marín Ferrer, p. 192. Pando (iii), p. 30, for the Riffian loses.

16   Pando (iii), p. 29.

17   Villalobos, pp. 233, speaks of 20,000 soldiers, but in view of the units mentioned it would be more like 14,000, which coincides with the numbers of the Sanjurjo and Berenguer columns. Marín Ferrer, p. 192. Pando (iii), p. 30, talks about 6,000 Riffians in all. The horrific details of Nador, also from Pando.

18   Villalobos, p. 233–234. Pando (iii), p. 32.

19   Villalobos, pp234–235. Marín Ferrer, pp. 194–195. Pando (iii), pp. 32–33.

20   Pando (iii), p. 34.

21   Pando (iii), p. 34–35.

22   Perhaps not surprisingly, in Sanjurjo's column were also the future main leaders of the revolt, including Franco and Cabanellas, which leads us to think that a relationship of friendship and trust had arisen between these men in those years that led them to easily agree upon the rebellion, later. They all knew each other well and knew what they were capable of. Nevertheless, Cabanellas, a Mason and a rightist Republican, would try to oppose Franco and the monarchists as a separate faction of the Nationalist forces, later during the Civil War.

23   Villalobos, pp. 235–236. Marín Ferrer, pp. 194–196. Gárate Córdoba, nº Especial, p. s/n for the detail of Uixán. Fontenla Ballesta, p. 378–379, for the Dar Drius operation and the Spanish air raids. Macías Fernández, pp. 240, 244–245 for the new units being created and the numbers of Spanish recruits.

Chapter 2

1   Nine infantry battalions, two regiments of cavalry and five of artillery – one fixed, three heavy and one light.

2   Villalobos, pp. 228–239. Fontella Ballesta, pp. 380–384. Macías Fernández, p. 244 for the repatriated troops. Marín Ferrer, pp. 197–200 for details of the tanks. Some sources mention the 3rd Bandera and others the 2nd, but as the 3rd one is not mentioned as arriving in Melilla until 1923–24, then it should be the 2nd Bandera.

3   Villalobos, pp. 239–240. Fontella Ballesta, p. 385–387. See Carrasco García & De Mesa, pp. 53, 72, 82–83, and 89, for the new indigenous units.

4   Gallarza would be the commander of the Nationalist bombers in the Civil War.

5   Sánchez & Kindelán, p. 88. For the Ansaldo and the F-50, see Velarde Silió, p. 63 and 41.

6   Sánchez & Kindelán, p. 89–90 and Fontella Ballesta, p. 384 and 402. For the Martinsyde, Bristols, Macchi, S.16, and S.13, see Velarde Silió, p. 56, 58, 60, 62 and 64.

7   Villalobos, pp. 240–241. Carrasco García & De Mesa, pp. 53, 72, 82–83, and 89, for the new indigenous units and the rise of Franco. Marín Ferrer, p. 201, and Gárate Córdoba Special No. p. s/n for Valenzuela and Millán Astray. See Macías Fernández, pp. 251–255 for the actions of Tizi Azza and the details of the order of battle, and Fontella Ballesta p. 405–406, for Silvela´s orders to not attack and the breach of them to save the convoy, and for the aviation and gas.

8   Sánchez & Kindelán, pp. 91–92. The details about the mission carried out by Kindelán in https://dbe.rah.es/biografias/11464/alfredo-kindelan-y-duany. See Fontella Ballesta, p. 409–410 for the first use of gas by aircraft, and Macías Fernández, pp. 256. Fontella says the 13th for the first bombing, and Macías the 14th.

9   Villalobos, p. 241. For the order of battle and some details of the operation, see Macías Fernández, pp. 257–260. See Fontella Ballesta, p. 411, for the anecdote about Boy and Franco, and for figures of troops and Riffian losses. Fontella contradicts Macías, as the first author says that the first unit landed was the harka of Beni Said.

10   Sánchez & Kindelán, pp. 91–92.

11   A qaid (variously spelled kaid or caid) is the title of a local chief.

12   The creation and destruction of Riffian aviation has been deeply investigated by Nicolle and Ali Gabr in Volume 4 of *Air power and the Arab World*, pp. 22–27, in Helion's Middle East at War series. Some information, mainly about Ansaldo, comes from Sánchez & Kindelán, pp. 93 and 81. These two Spanish authors include, and mix up, several rumours. According to this unconfirmed information, in March 1924 an aircraft acquired by Abd el-Krim was discovered in Bocoya by an aircraft flying from Tetuán. According to some other rumours, the Riffians had acquired three Dural or Potez XV type aircraft in Algeria in 1921, which would be flown by the French mercenary Periel and two Bosnian pilots. According to other sources, Abd el-Krim also had three aircraft captured from the Spanish after forced landings: probably this is correct but refers to different moments on time: the Bristol in 1922, the DH-9 in 1923, and the Durand (not captured but bought) in 1924.

13   Sánchez & Kindelán, pp. 94–96, 83, 86 and 90.

14   Brenan, pp. 99–103.

15   Villalobos, pp. 241–242. For the aircraft numbers, see Fontella Ballesta, p. 422.

16   Villalobos, pp. 243–244. See Fontella Ballesta, p. 424–425 for the air operations. See Marín Ferrer p. 205 and Fernández Riera, p. 43–51 for the menu made of eggs.

Chapter 3

1   Villalobos, pp. 236–237. Marín Ferrer, pp. 196–199. Carrasco García & De Mesa, pp. 53, 72, 82–83, and 89, for the Legión Banderas.

2   Villalobos, pp. 237–238. Marín Ferrer, pp. 197. Carrasco García & De Mesa, pp. 53, 72, 82–83, and 89, for the new indigenous units and the Legión Banderas.

3   Fernández Riera, pp. 18–22. Villalobos, p. 237. For the reorganisation of 17 January, see Fontella Ballesta, p. 402.

4   Not to be confused with the former Ceriñola Regiment.

5   Fernández Riera, pp. 22–28. For the aircraft, Sánchez & Kindelán, pp. 94–82.

6   Fernández Riera, pp. 30–31, 51–52.

7   Sánchez & Kindelán, pp. 94 and 82.

8   Villalobos, pp. 240–244. Fernández Riera, pp. 54–69, and 74–80 for details of these operations. Mola's Figueras Battalion is not cited by Fernández Riera, but is mentioned by Villalobos, who in turn does not cite one of the Tabors.

9   Beorlegui would go on to be the leader of the brilliant Navarran Brigades in the Civil War.

10   Fernández Riera, pp. 81–96.

11 Sánchez & Kindelán, pp. 94–96, 83, 86 and 90.

Chapter 4

1 Fernández Riera, pp. 97–104.

2 It is not surprising that Queipo became a 'republican' years later, rejoicing at the fall of Primo de Rivera and of the King afterwards, though this did not prevent him from taking up arms against the Republic in 1936.

3 Fernández Riera, pp. 104–111 and 125–126.

4 Fernández Riera, pp. 111–122.

5 Not to be confused with the destroyed San Fernando Regiment.

6 Fernández Riera, pp. 139–142, 132–133, 135 and 163.

7 Fernández Riera, pp. 145–148.

8 Fernández Riera, pp. 126–131. Villalobos, p. 245.

9 Fernández Riera, pp. 132–136.

10 Fernández Riera, pp. 149–154. Villalobos, p. 245, speaks very briefly of all these very interesting operations of August and September in only one page.

11 Miaja would be the defender of Madrid in 1936.

12 Mizzián became an intimate of Franco from now on, fighting later in the Spanish Civil War in the African shock units, and ending his days as Lieutenant General of the Spanish Army.

13 Fernández Riera, pp. 154–160. Apparently, Franco was very sparing in his report, which is not at all usual for him, and comments that his mission was not to save Abadda but to set up an intermediate camp. However, Fernández Riera dismantles this version on the basis of newspapers of the time and Mola's own memoirs.

14 Fernández Riera, pp. 163–174. The casualties of those of Larache, in Villalobos, p. 246.

15 Fernández Riera, pp. 174–178. The casualties of the Legión in Villalobos, p. 246. He hardly devotes any space to the action. On the date of Franco's appointment, Fernández Riera specifies this action as the cause, although the date is given in Gárate Córdoba, nº Especial, p. s/n.

16 Fernández Riera, pp. 179–180. Millán Astray's life is rather picturesque: having lost an eye and an arm in combat, he was a very active man and an 'enemy' of intellectuals. Millán Astray´s confrontation with Unamuno at the University of Salamanca during the Civil War became famous when the writer, a supporter of the Nationalists but disgusted by the repression, shouted at him in a speech 'You will win, but you will not convince' to which Millán Astray replied 'Long live to death, down with the intelligentsia!' However, despite his rudeness he was not an evil man. When the Falangists wanted to lynch Unamuno for his words, Millán Astray himself, and Franco's wife, Carmen Polo, escorted him so that nothing would happen to him. More paradoxical is his private life. When Millán Astray got married, his wife confessed to him that she had taken a vow of chastity, so he could not consummate the marriage. Despite this, he remained married. Then, against all odds, Millán Astray fell in love with the cousin of another intellectual, the philosopher José Ortega y Gasset. Millán had a stable relationship with Rita Gasset, and had also a daughter with her, so Rita, became officially her aunt.

17 Fernández Riera, pp. 180–186, 188. The K barges were ex-British X-Lighter landing craft built in 1915–16.

18 According to some sources, only six horsemen followed him, among them el Mizzián, who had saved Franco and would lead the Moroccan troops in the war of 1936.

19 Fernández Riera, pp. 186–196; Villalobos, pp. 246, mentions the straw man trick.

20 Fernández Riera, pp. 197–204. Villalobos, p. 246, speaks only briefly of the campaign.

21 Fernández Riera, pp. 244–247. Villalobos, p. 245–246.

Chapter 5

1 Fernández Riera, pp. 209–216. For the air actions, Sánchez & Kindelán, pp. 94–96, 83, 86 and 90.

2 Fernández Riera, pp. 209–219. For the air actions of Burguete, Sánchez & Kindelán, pp. 94–96, 83, 86 and 90.

3 Fernández Riera, pp. 219–224.

4 Fernández Riera, pp. 226–235. We are not sure about these Regulares of Alcazarquivir. Perhaps the source refers to the 4th Group of Regulares of Larache. Or perhaps it simply refers to some tabors that were based in Alcazarquivir.

5 Sánchez & Kindelán, pp. 94–96, 83, 86 and 90. For the Nieuport Ni.29, Permuy, p. 7, and Velarde Silió, p. 81–82. Regarding the DH.9s, the sources talk about squadrons, but looking at orders of battle for 1922–1927 we see that there was never more than one 'Napier' Squadron, and some four machines in all, so we have replaced the word 'squadrons' with 'machines'.

Chapter 6

1 Villalobos, pp. 247–248.

2 Villalobos, p. 248. Courcelle & Marmié, p. 135 and 211. Total forces at end of May in SHM, p. 97.

3 Villalobos, pp. 249. Marín Ferrer, pp. 207–209. Courcelle & Marmié, pp. 150–151, for the time of the invasion speak of 800 M'hammed´s warriors in Targuist, and three columns entering Ben Zerual: some 1,500 rifles from the north-west, 600 from the north and 800 from the north-east. They also mention the 600 pro-French warriors of Beni Zerual fleeing. For the French reaction and desertions, see Courcelle and Marmié, pp. 149–152, and for Bibane, and Lyautey regarding Spain, see pp. 158–159.

4 Courcelle & Marmié, pp. 152–155, and p. 211.

5 Courcelle & Marmié, pp. 159–179.

6 Courcelle & Marmié, pp. 182–207 and 211. Legión and Senegalese units, in Herbert (Risings and Rebellions 1919–39, Foundry 2009)

7 Courcelle & Marmié, pp. 221–232 and 255.

8 For this author the amount could be 10 times larger.

9 Villalobos, pp. 249. Marín Ferrer, pp. 207–209. This last author speaks of 48 positions taken, and 2,640 dead and missing in two and a half months, reaching 11,000 casualties in total. Albi de la Cuesta, in Desperta Ferro Contemporánea no. 11, pp. 10–11, tells how Lyautey changed his position of total refusal to collaborate with Spain to defend a landing at Alhucemas by a mixed Spanish-Anglo-French force. According to Courcelle and Marmié, pp. 253, by 20 July the French had lost almost 6,000 men: 1,005 dead, 3,711 wounded and 1,007 missing. Later, in 1939, Petain would be the ambassador of France to Spain and the new fascist regime of Franco, and would lead the Vichy French Government in 1940, cooperating with the Nazis and ending his days in the jail after the war.

10 Courcelle & Marmié, pp. 253–254.

11 Courcelle & Marmiér, pp. 255–6 and 272–3. Order of battle completed in SHM, p. 101. For cavalry SHM mentions a brigade, not cited by Courcelle, but Courcelle later cites 1st Spahis Brigade within General Jonchay's Grouping, pp. 281–282. See note 86 for the estimation of 6,000 Riffians in the southern French sectors.

Chapter 7

1 Marín Ferrer, pp. 211–215. Albi de la Cuesta, Desperta Ferro nº 11, p. 10–11.

2 Marín Ferrer, pp. 214–216. De Mesa, Desperta Ferro Contemporánea no. 11, p. 21, about the comparison with the Normandy Landings. Marín Ferrer, p. 243, quotes Eisenhower himself. Air order of battle in Sánchez & Kindelán, p. 99. For the Scarabs, see Velarde Silió, p. 88.

3 Marín Ferrer, pp. 214–215, 218–219. SHM, p. 225–227 for the numbers of soldiers in the units in the Melilla Brigade that are drafted in the attached table. For the artillery batteries in Alhucemas in the table, see SHM pp. 199–200. The assault tanks may have numbered 11, as a company was formed with two sections of five tanks, plus one more tank as a command vehicle (DFC nº 11, p. 43). SHM, p. 194, talks of only 10 tanks. De Mesa, DFC nº 11, p. 20–21, also speaks of 11 tanks, cites the air groups, and mentions the artillery deployment on the islet of Alhucemas. Lázaro Ávila, DFC no. 11, p. 45, talks on the white bands and the fear of Riffian aircraft. He also seems to suggest that the black and white bands of the Allied aircraft in Normandy came from here, something doubtful but possible. On Hidalgo de Cisneros, footnote DFC nº 11, p. 47. For the organisation of the ground aviation, Villalobos, p. 302. His work, which we follow, differs from that cited by Lázaro Ávila, who speaks only of a Bristol Group, another of Fokker, and a third Breguet one, as well as a Napier Squadron (DH-9A), another of Potez and another of De Havilland Rolls (DH-4).

4 The commander of the first column, Colonel Balmes, was a rival of Franco in the Canary Islands during the 1936 revolt and would commit suicide (or

was assassinated), opening the road for Franco's departure from the Canary Islands to command the Army of Africa.

5 Marín Ferrer, pp. 214–218 and 229. SHM, pp. 62–63. Sánchez & Kindelán, p. 100 and 89. For the Potez XV, Do Wal, and Breguet XIX, see Velarde Silió, p. 84 & p. 75–76.

6 Marín Ferrer, pp. 218–221. SHM, p. 215–216, for the Spanish order of battle. The Riffian deployment has been deduced by the author on the basis of the following data: De La Rocha, in his map of the landing (DFC no. 11, pp. 20–21) identifies only five groupings, and all of them outside the landing zone: one at Sfiha, three at Suani, and another beyond the Nekor river, and he places three batteries (without groupings) in the landing zone, at Los Frailes, Morro Viejo and Morro Nuevo. He also tells us that each grouping consisted of between 200 and 400 soldiers, two cannons and three machine guns. That is, about 300 men on average. De Mesa, DFC nº 11, p. 17, speaks of 14 Riffian guns in the area, which would correspond to seven groups (two guns per group). And finally, in DFC nº 11, pp. 16 and 17, a map is reproduced, drawn up by the Geographical Commission of the General Staff of Melilla, in which it mentions a line of trenches erected on the beach of Sfiha, where the batteries or cañoneras, of Adrar sud-Dum, la Rocosa, Prisioneros and Loma are located; and it also mentions further west the cañoneras of Morro Viejo and Morro Nuevo. He does not mention the one at El Fraile, which is mentioned by De La Rocha. We do not believe that De La Rocha's deployment is 100 percent correct, since he mentions four groupings in an area where no batteries were located (Suani and Nekor beaches), while in Sfiha beach he only mentions one, when according to the General Staff plan there were four batteries there. Therefore, taking the six batteries mentioned by the General Staff, at two pieces each, we get 12 guns in six groups. However, as according to De Mesa there were 14, there must have been one more grouping in the area with its two pieces, which is probably the one at Los Frailes mentioned by La Rocha, and which we also know existed as it was taken on the day of the landing by the 6th Bandera, which took three guns there (perhaps one of them from the nearby Morro Nuevo). Thus, in total there were seven groupings totalling about 2,100 Riffian soldiers. In any case, there are other discrepancies: in SHM, pp. 199–200, the instructions for the Spanish artillery to destroy the Riffian artillery batteries are reproduced. In this case there three batteries are mentioned in Morro Nuevo (perhaps here is included the one of Los Frailes, mentioned in other sources), a fourth one in Morro Nuevo, and a fifth in Malmusi, a sixth in Taramara and a seventh in Buyibar (these three last ones not being mentioned in other sources). In any case, this report is also consistent with the seven Riffian batteries, but in this case four batteries were near the landing area instead of three, and a fourth one was in the line of further approach (Malmusi), only two of them being out of the landing area.

7 Strictly speaking, the landing was not in Alhucemas Bay itself, but outside it, slightly to the west, in the Kabyle of Bocoya and not in the Kabyle of Beni Urriaguel.

8 Marín Ferrer, pp. 218–223. Lázaro Ávila, DFC nº 11, p. 45–46. De Mesa, DFC nº 11, pp. 17 and 21. For Franco at the head of the landing, see Sánchez & Kindelán, p. 101.

9 Marín Ferrer, pp. 223–228. SHM, pp. 64–71. De Mesa, DFC no. 11, p. 17, speaks of four cannon and three machine guns taken on the first day, corresponding to the cannon and then three more taken, according to Marín Ferrer. Marín Ferrer speaks of two machine guns taken, so the third one mentioned by De Mesa must have been taken at Morro Nuevo. In total, therefore, there were one or two Riffian groupings there, which were destroyed. Lázaro Ávila, DFC no. 11, p. 45–46 for the aviation, together with Sánchez & Kindelán, p. 101.

10 Varela would be the assailant of Madrid in 1936.

11 Marín Ferrer, pp. 228–231. SHM pp. 64–71. For the figure of 800 Riffians, as well as the Moorish concentration points, see the map notes of De La Rocha, DFC no. 11, pp. 20–21. See De Mesa, DFC no. 11, p. 18, for the attack on El Jatabi. See Lázaro Ávila, DFC nº 11, p. 46 for the mustard gas. According to Marín Ferrer, p. 219, Spain was a signatory in Versailles in 1919 to the prohibition of its use, so it is not surprising that it was kept secret. Spain placed orders in 1921, influenced by the spirit of revenge for the horrors of Monte Arruit, but they were not executed, so finally Spain manufactured its own gas in Melilla by mixing various substances. Mustard gas was first used in artillery in 1922 (1923, wrongly in some sources), and then sporadically by the aviation, between 1924 (1925, wrongly, in some sources) and 1927.

12 Years later, Goded, another colleague of Franco, would join him in the 1936 uprising, but he would be defeated in Barcelona and then executed.

13 Marín Ferrer, pp. 232–235. SHM, pp. 74–75 for the Spanish Orbat. De Mesa, DFC nº 11, p. 18. See the notes to De La Rocha's map, DFC nº 11, p. 18 for the 12,000 soldiers disembarked. Lázaro Ávila, DFC nº 11, p. 46 states that on 21, 22, 23, 30 September and 1 October 56.98 percent of all the bombs were dropped at Alhucemas, so I estimate that about 33 percent occurred on the first three days mentioned. Sánchez & Kindelán, pp. 102–103.

14 Alonso would be liberator of Oviedo in 1936.

15 Marín Ferrer, pp. 234–236. SHM, pp. 72–81. De Mesa, DFC nº11, p. 18. Aviation in footnote of DFC nº 11, p. 46.

16 The projectiles consumed this day and the one following represented 22 percent of all the bombs used in this campaign.

17 Marín Ferrer, pp. 236–239. De Mesa, DFC nº 11, pp. 18–19. SHM, pp. 82–91. Lázaro Ávila, DFC no. 11, p. 46, states that on 21, 22, 23, 30 September and 1 October 56.98 percent of all the bombs were dropped in Alhucemas, so I estimate that about 22 percent occurred on the last two days mentioned. Sánchez & Kindelán, p. 103 and 90. Ordiales was the same madman who landed to defend a downed aircraft and the bodies of its crew. During the Civil War he would be killed for resisting joining the forces of the Republic.

18 Marín Ferrer, pp. 242–243. De Mesa, DFC nº 11, pp. 19–21. For the Riffian dead, see an estimation in DFC nº 11, p. 4. For Lázaro Ávila, DFC nº 11, p. 47, there were 16 aircraft lost, stating that eight were shot down. He probably also refers to those destroyed, either by accident or by enemy fire. See Villalobos, p. 265, for the thousand Riffian casualties.

19 Courcelle & Marmié, pp. 280–283. SHM, pp. 107–108 and 110.

20 Yoldi would be rebel commander of the Madrid front during in the Civil War.

21 Sáenz de Buruaga was known as 'rubito', or 'blonde hair', another rebel commander, this time in Andalusia during the 1936 Civil War.

22 Coque was also a rebel commander in the Civil War.

23 Curiously, both Riquelme and Torrado would later fight for the Republic during the Civil War in the Madrid-Toledo sector, as if comradeship in arms also forged a comradeship in politics.

24 Muñoz Bolaños, DFC nº 11, pp. 36–41. Albi de la Cuesta, DFC no. 11, p. 11. For the operations at Anyera, see De La Rocha's notes to the map, DFC no. 11, pp. 38–39. SHM, pp. 116, for the order of battle.

25 Perea would be a Republican defender of Madrid in 1936.

26 Mola Vidal would be commander of the rebel Army of the North in 1936.

27 Monasterio Ituarte was also a famous rebel commander that led the last cavalry charge in the history of Spain during the Civil War.

28 Ponte would be the rebel defender of Zaragoza in 1936.

29 Muñoz Bolaños, DFC nº 11, pp. 38–41. See the map by De La Rocha, DFC no. 11, pp. 38–39 for the deployment of the French forces, being completed with Muñoz Bolaños for the axes of march. See Villalobos, pp. 266–67 for Goded's words, and pp. 303–304 for the Spanish force breakdown. In SHM, pp. 125–126, the reader can find the French and Spanish deployment, that we follow mainly. See Muñoz Bolaños for the mixed columns. According to De La Rocha, there were 3,000 men with Pozas, but 4,500 for Villalobos; and González Carrasco's was made of 12,000 by De La Rocha, but 8,000 for Villalobos. See Courcelle & Marmié, p. 212, for the French battalionsd. For the numbers of shock troops and the conscripted ones, and the offensive troops in Tetuán and Larache, see Macías Fernández.

30 Marín Ferrer, pp. 244, speaks of some 50 kabyles and 60,000 warriors. De La Rocha, DFC nº 11, in the notes on his map, p. 38, speaks of 40 rebel kabyles and another 10 in the process of occupation and pacification, although he refers to the beginning of 1926, a date prior to the pacification of the Yebala, El Haus, Ahl Sherif and Beni Isef. Muñoz Bolaños also speaks of 60,000 Riffian warriors, 150 cannons and 250 machine guns. However, counting carefully the kabyles not occupied by Spain and France, the figures are lower: the 37 (or nearly so) intact kabyles, would be Tensaman, Tafersit, Beni Tuzin, Beni Urriaguel, Bocoya, Beni Amart, Beni Iteft, Beni Bufrah, Targuist, Beni Amart, Beni Bechir, Beni Bu Chibet, Senhaya Srir (a Confederation including seven tiny kabyles), Beni Gmil, Mestasa, Beni Erzin, Ketama, Beni Smih, Beni Guerir, Beni Mansur, Beni Kalid, Beni Yahmed, Beni Zerwal, Gezawa, Al Ajmás, Beni Sakkar, Beni Selman, Beni

Buzra, Beni Ziat, Beni Zeyel, Beni Hassan, Beni Said de Gomara, Beni Lait, Beni Hosmar, Beni Ider, Beni Arós, and Sumata. The four partially subdued kabyles would be Beni Goffet, Beni Mosuar, Geznaya, and M'Talsa. With 750,000 inhabitants in the Rif for the 70 existing kabyles (64 Kabyles if we count the Senhaya Confederation as just one Kabyle), and assuming a mobilisation of 7 percent of the population, even higher than that of the French Revolution and that of Frederick the Great of Prussia, we would get about 750 warriors per kabyle on average. Thus, for the 37 Kabyles and four half kabyles uncontrolled by Spain, it would be about 29,250 warriors in total under Abd el-Krim. Another way to deduce this calculation is by the number of heavy weapons that the Rifeños had: 150 pieces and 250 machine guns, which, taking into account the custom of having about two pieces and three or four machine guns for every 300 warriors, gives us about 80 groups of Rifeños, or about 24–32,000 warriors, which coincide more or less with the magnitudes expressed here. Obviously, such 'groupings' did not exist, at least in that number, since the Riffian army was not standardised, and except for 1,500 men, it was not organised in tabors, but these figures also give us an idea of the real magnitude that their army could have had. Finally, between May and October 1926, when Abd el-Krim's army disappeared, the allies recovered precisely 28,000 rifles from the Riffians, another definitive piece of information that points in the direction of a smaller number of troops than generally mentioned.

31   Up to the end of May, when Abd el-Krim surrendered, 14,500 rifles had been collected from among his kabyle. Regarding the Riffians on the French front, we know that about 6,000 started the invasion in 1925, and although they were later reinforced, the bulk of them later departed for Alhucemas, so we have kept the initial figure at about 3,000 in each French sector. Regarding the western zone, we know that 3,000 warriors from Gomara and Yebala attacked Kudia Tahar in 1925, and that 3,000 rifles were later collected from the 9 or 10 kabyles that surrendered in the area of Yebala and Luccus in 1926, so we can assign them about 4 or 5,000. The rest up to 29,000, about 4,000, could be left looking to the east, to the Melilla District. These figures are consistent with the scant resistance put up by the kabyle in the French and eastern sectors, while to the north, in Alhucemas, where the bulk of them were, the resistance was fierce.

32   Muñoz Bolaños, DFC nº 11, pp. 41. Map by De La Rocha, DFC nº 11, pp. 39.

33   Villalobos, pp. 267–269. SHM, sketches no. 7 and 8. For the material captured in Marín Ferrer. Muñoz Bolaños, pp. 41–42. Sánchez & Kindelán, p. 104. For the Do Wal attack, Velarde Silió, p. 75–76.

Chapter 8

1   Villalobos, pp. 269–272. Capaz's actions have been interpreted according to SHM, sketch no. 9. For the order of battler and deployment of columns against El Jeriro, see SHM, pp. 150–151.

2   This is another indicator of Beni Urriaguel's true military potential of some 3–4,000 warriors.

3   Villalobos, p. 272.

4   Villalobos, pp. 273–274.

5   Villalobos, pp. 274–275. For the order of battle and details of operations see SHM, pp. 154–156, and sketch no. 13.

6   Villalobos, pp. 276. See the Order of battle, and operations for Beni Khaled, Ahmed and east of Ajmás, in SHM, pp. 163–169. Curiously, the few African commanders who remained with the Republic, such as Riquelme or Asensio, had also served together, which leads us to wonder to what extent the camaraderie between comrades was not one of the factors that conditioned belonging to one side or the other.

7   Sánchez & Kindelán, pp. 104–105 and 93. For the Loring aircraft, see Velarde Silió, pp. 91–92.

8   Sánchez & Kindelán, pp. 105 and 94. For the AME VI and the Loring, see Velarde Silió, pp. 83–84 and 91–92.

About the Author

Javier Garcia de Gabiola is a corporate lawyer from Spain with a degree from Universidad Autónoma de Madrid, and has worked in the profession since 1998. He has published numerous articles and books on legal issues. Always interested in military history, he has contributed more than 50 articles to Spanish magazines and has published multiple pieces with the Universidad Autónoma de México, Medieval Warfare, Aviation History, Desperta Ferro, and Aventura de la Historia. Javier is the author of Helion´s Paulista War and Rif War, Volume 1. His other interests include boardgames, arts, architecture, politics and astronomy.